Don Quixote an
Subversive Tradition or
Golden Age Spain

This study offers a reading of *Don Quixote*, with comparative material from Golden Age history and Cervantes' life, to argue that his greatest work was not just the hilariously comic entertainment that most of his contemporaries took it to be. Rather, it belongs to a "subversive tradition" of writing that grew up in sixteenth-century Spain and which constantly questioned the aims and standards of the imperial nation state that Counter-reformation Spain had become from the point of view of Renaissance humanism.

Prime consideration needs to be given to the system of Spanish censorship at the time, run largely by the Inquisition albeit officially an institution of the crown, and its effect on the cultural life of the country. In response, writers of poetry and prose fiction – strenuously attacked on moral grounds by sections of the clergy and the laity – became adept at camouflaging heterodox ideas through rhetoric and imaginative invention. Ironically, Cervantes' success in avoiding the attention of the censor by concealing his criticisms beneath irony and humour was so effective that even some twentieth-century scholars have maintained *Don Quixote* is a brilliantly funny book but no more. Bob Britton draws on recent critical and historical scholarship – including ideas on cultural authority and studies on the way Cervantes addresses history, truth, writing, law and gender in *Don Quixote* – and engages with the intellectual and moral issues that this much-loved writer engaged with. The summation and appraisal of these elements within the context of Golden Age censorship and the literary politics of the time make it essential reading for all those who are interested in or study the Spanish language and its literature.

R. K. Britton is an honorary research fellow in the Department of Hispanic Studies, Sheffield University, where he is also a part-time tutor in Spanish in The Institute of Lifelong Learning. His research interests are modern Latin American literature, the literature and culture of Golden Age Spain and literary translation. His *The Poetic and Real Worlds of César Vallejo (1892–1938)* was widely reviewed: "Bob Britton's book brings César Vallejo fascinatingly to life", Adam Feinstein, author of *Pablo Neruda: A Passion for Life.*

Don Quixote and the Subversive Tradition of Golden Age Spain

R. K. BRITTON

sussex
ACADEMIC
PRESS
Brighton • Chicago • Toronto

2 4 6 8 10 9 7 5 3 1

First published in 2019 by
SUSSEX ACADEMIC PRESS
PO Box 139
Eastbourne BN24 9BP

Distributed in North America by
SUSSEX ACADEMIC PRESS
Independent Publishers Group
814 N. Franklin Street
Chicago, IL 60610

British Library Cataloguing in Publication Data
A CIP catalogue record for this book is available from the British Library.

Library of Congress Cataloging-in-Publication Data
Names: Britton, R. K., author.
Title: Don Quixote and the subversive tradition of Golden Age Spain / R.K. Britton.
Description: Brighton ; Chicago : Sussex Academic Press, 2019. | Includes bibliographical references and index.
Identifiers: LCCN 2018035923| ISBN 9781845198619 (hbk : alk. paper) | ISBN 9781845198626 (pbk : alk. paper)
Subjects: LCSH: Cervantes Saavedra, Miguel de, 1547–1616. Don Quixote. | Spanish literature—Classical period, 1500–1700—History and criticism. | Opposition (Political science) in literature.
Classification: LCC PQ6352 .B77 2019 | DDC 863/.3—dc23
LC record available at https://lccn.loc.gov/2018035923

Typeset and designed by Sussex Academic Press, Brighton & Eastbourne.
Printed by TJ International, Padstow, Cornwall.

Contents

Preface and Acknowledgements

Not long ago, I made an informal enquiry to a well-respected British university press in a city, whose name, at this moment, I choose not to recall, about whether it would be interested in a proposal for a book on Cervantes and *Don Quixote* that I was writing. The voice of the editor at the other end of the telephone hesitated before she replied: "Cervantes? ... mmmmm, ... *Don Quixote*? ... There is *rather* a lot out there already you know." I pursued the matter no further.

In this respect, she was quite right. There *is* a lot out there. More than on any other single text probably, except for the Bible and the Koran. And *Don Quixote* is still only four hundred years old! Nevertheless, why should any sensible twenty-first century reader bother to plough through nearly a thousand pages of a story written four centuries ago? One answer may lie in the astounding amount of critical and academic "baggage" that this book, now hailed as the world's first modern novel, brings with it. This intimidating body of work reveals the very considerable changes in approach and interpretation that different generations of scholars and critics have brought to the task of interpreting this amazing text, which seems to offer to each one a different key facet of itself that has previously been overlooked or underestimated. It is, perhaps, the nature of great art that it can be reconstructed, or reconstruct itself, so as to speak directly to each new and changing audience, but *Don Quixote* seems to have served not only as a mirror that reflected the face of sixteenth and seventeenth century Spain, but also one in which succeeding generations recognised themselves.

To briefly illustrate this point, there is a great deal of evidence that in seventeenth and eighteenth century Europe, notably in Spain, France and England, *Don Quixote* was regarded simply as a funny, entertaining book in which the reader did not seek for human and moral complexities or historical judgements. Later critics saw things differently however. For the Romantics the mad knight of La Mancha became a tragic symbol of the failure of heroic idealism in a material and corrupt world; for the Generation of 1898, he became an allegory of Spain's loss of national vision which led to its decline from an imperial world power to a national backwater stifled by tradition. By the 1920's, this view began to be rejected (along with symbolism and modern allegory) in favour of one that saw

Don Quixote as essentially a product of its own age and circumstances, which could only be understood from a historicist standpoint. New biographical studies of Cervantes, based on fresh documentary evidence, also began to appear so that the figure of the historical Cervantes, as distinct from the writer who hid behind a variety of literary masks, began to emerge. Furthermore, it did so against a more detailed and certain backdrop of the social history of Spain under Hapsburg rule.

The picture was further influenced by changing intellectual tastes and fashions derived from recent disciplines, such as psychology, sociology and linguistics, together with the evolution of traditional ones such as history, politics and economics. The twentieth century also saw the emergence of Critical Theory and a varied current of sophisticated, forensic literary scholarship that has become an integral part of university education in the arts and humanities in Western Europe and the USA. Indeed, if we now ask who the twenty-first century readers of Cervantes' masterpiece are likely to be, the answer is – certainly in the so-called developed countries – that they will mostly be people who have passed through a system of mass higher education, extending to some 40 percent of the national population. This, I suggest, marks the emergence of a new kind of reader for all kinds of literature, but for old books it is especially important. The educated reader of today – the precise equivalent of what Cervantes referred to as the *lector discreto* (the reader of good judgement) of his own time – is likely to bring to the task, and to a degree that would have been rare in the past, a new sense of history, a keen awareness of the cultural diversity of the world, and at least some of the specialist tools of critical appreciation honed in today's universities degree courses.

Another significant point regarding the contemporary *lectores discretos* is that the greater part of them will almost certainly be reading Cervantes' masterpiece in translation. In England, France and the USA, Cervantes has been excellently served in this area and, if the publishing industry in these countries is a reliable indication, it is worth noting that since John Ormsby's highly respected London translation of 1885 (it had been preceded by over twenty others, beginning with Shelton's 1610 version of *Don Quixote* Part I) British and American translators have produced four new English versions in the twentieth century and a further three in the first decade of the twenty-first.[1] All have been praised for their respective strengths despite the challenging nature of their task, and we can conclude that the apparent continuing market for new English translations of *Don Quixote* marks an ongoing public demand on both sides of the Atlantic, rather than simply the limited need for a set text in university departments of Spanish or Comparative Literature.

The present study therefore seeks to explore two themes, both of which have begun to claim increasing attention from Cervantists. The first of these – one which until recently would not have been entertained by most scholars and commentators – is a re-examination of the underlying purpose of *Don Quixote*, in which I argue that it is essentially a work that employs fiction as a means of social, artistic and political criticism of Hapsburgh Spain and its spiritual values, which, were it not for the artistry and skill with which this message is masked, would almost certainly have aroused the wrath of the censors. In making this claim, I place *Don Quixote* within the humanistic tradition of reforming ideas which had been increasingly suppressed in Spain since the works of Erasmus were placed on the *Spanish Index of Forbidden Books* in 1550. It is to this often satirical and subversive current that such works as *Lazarillo de Tormes, El crotalón, Viaje de Turquía* and the *Dialogues* of Alfonso de Valdés belong.

The second but related theme is that of the nature of the "modernity" which scholars are beginning to explore seriously in *Don Quixote*. Here, making reference to the recorded responses of a small number of mature undergraduate students who studied the novel as part of a degree course, I suggest that what twenty-first century readers identify as the modern aspects of this four hundred year old text can largely be attributed to the presence of the subversive elements just mentioned, which develop and are modified as the story moves over time between the composition of Part I and that Part II. Though no longer in tune with the conventions of the fictional genres that Cervantes quotes and questions in this purposely ageneric masterpiece, present-day readers focus instead upon the familiar sense of "realism" with which Cervantes describes his fictional world, the acute social observation that he shows with its mixture slapstick and surreal, self-reflexive humour.

Four centuries of critical comment have witnessed some remarkable changes of understanding and interpretation of the book. To ask what *Don Quixote* might hold for contemporary and future generations of readers, therefore, is surely a valid question. Indeed, topics such as its "influence," reception and dissemination have already been examined in books which began to appear in the 1990s and continue to do so.[2] Evidence strongly suggests, however, that readers and critics alike will continue to search this many-layered text for those aspects most relevant to their historical concerns, and that when they have been identified they will present them as the book's "real" meaning. It is the matter of **what** they are most likely to find that will constitute a new reading of *Don Quixote*. It will probably be something that was intentional on the part of the author, but sufficiently well disguised to have escaped seventeenth-century censorship, the book's earlier critics, and to have been of only passing interest to scholars of the nineteenth and twentieth centuries.

One of the great improbabilities that sooner or later occurs to most of today's readers is that, despite his impecunious state, Cervantes should have devoted so much time and effort over a space of seventeen years, from 1597 to 1614, to writing *Don Quixote* if his sole aim was to produce two large volumes of comic entertainment. Furthermore, the hard, precarious life he was forced to lead, despite his outstanding qualities and courage, and the frustrating difficulties with which he frequently struggled, indicate a man whose acute perception, humour and integrity would demand something original and special from his talent. We have also to bear in mind the truism that great books – indeed works of art of any kind – become the property of future generations largely because they are also completely and authoritatively the product of their own times and circumstances. *Don Quixote*, most evidently in Part I, is a satirical work that employs humour to attack bad writing, naïve and injudicious reading, and the popular genre of the chivalresque novel. The ironical vision that is almost a prerequisite of satire pervades both parts of the novel, but the satirical targets are much more diverse, subtle and evasive in Part II. If the state of literature, the role of writing within society and the accompanying literary politics, are the main focus of Part I, it has changed in the ten years between it and the second part. Indeed, despite cleverly contrived appearances, *Don Quixote* Part II is a darker, more complex sequel to Part I rather than a continuation of it.

To return to the idea that great books are essentially the product of their own times and circumstances, in which the life experience of the author plays a major part, it is important to enquire what evidence history gives us about the nature of those circumstances in Golden Age Spain, and how they might have affected the literature of the times. There are a number of facts, well-known to historians, that literary scholars who specialise in this period have traditionally underplayed in their judgements. The first is the effect of censorship; the sensitivity of the Church (backed by the Inquisition) to anything that might question matters of religious dogma or suggest heresy, and almost equally strong objection, on the part of the monarch and the state, to writings that directly criticised royal policy. The system of censorship was controlled by the state, but the censors who examined texts for publication were mainly churchmen. Church and state therefore worked closely together to control the intellectual and artistic life of imperial Spain, and to channel it along the desired lines. The system was not always consistent but it was effective, and writers who had things to say that were critical of the *status quo* had to be very careful how they said them, unless their criticisms echoed and reinforced those which the authorities levelled against what they saw as being morally and politically dangerous. Debate – often fierce – therefore existed, but only one side was able to express itself freely, if at all.

The second important set of circumstances that historians have clearly identified is the social and economic situation of Spain, whose huge empire and European wars placed immense pressures on its people and economy which progressively weakened and impoverished them. The burden of the taxation which supported Spain's international role and imperial ambitions fell squarely upon the peasants and ordinary towns-folk, with an increasingly idle landed aristocracy and an equally rich and well-endowed Church virtually exempted from the system. The impoverishment of the countryside led to major migrations to the cities and towns, where the new economic refugees formed a floating, under-employed proletariat that existed on the fringes of society and frequently turned to crime for a living. The third divisive factor in Golden Age society was the combination of officially sanctioned racism and religious intolerance which saw institutionalised discrimination meted out against the *conversos* (people of Jewish origin who had converted to Christianity) and the *moriscos,* the descendants of the Moors of medieval Spain who had been allowed to remain in the country (unlike the Jews) after 1492. The *moriscos* were officially regarded as having converted to Christianity, but the majority probably continued to follow the Muslim religion in secret, and were themselves expelled from Spain in 1609, with considerable suffering, and economic disruption to Spain's already failing agriculture. These factors made up the social, cultural and spiritual context within which Cervantes lived and wrote, and it is hard to imagine that a man who had suffered the injustices, frustrations and disappointments that Cervantes experienced, despite his abilities, integrity and courage, would not have something to say about them, despite his unswerving service to his king, first as a soldier, then as a prisoner of the Moors in Algiers, as a commissioner of supplies for the Armada and lastly as a tax collector.

An additional purpose of this study is therefore to explore Cervantes' masterpiece for evidence of his response to the historical and political circumstances of his time, and to deploy the findings to help form a reading of *Don Quixote* that reflects the concerns of the twenty-first century reader. To accomplish this requires us to penetrate beneath the author's carefully constructed satirical and humorous surface, with its extravagant literary subterfuges and diversions, to reach the cleverly shielded thread of critical observation on seventeenth-century Spain that lies beneath. In *Don Quixote* this is often made to seem little more than passing comment, or else is conveyed through an ironical or shrewdly manipulated point of view which raises questions in the reader's mind without imposing answers that the censor might have regarded, if plainly stated, as undesirable or dangerous. Cervantes was no revolutionary, but his criticism is all the more humane, tolerant and heartfelt because of it.

Instinctively given to open-minded discussion, he thus hit upon a narrative strategy which used social gatherings and private conversations as a vehicle for philosophical and moral debate, which left conclusions open for the reader to decide for him or herself. But it would be misguided to suppose that Cervantes himself had no firm opinions on these topics. In the interests of truth, nevertheless, which, as a writer of fiction, weighed heavily with him, he also seems to have recognised that his opinions were just that – personal stances which were always open to rational questioning. Not only had Cervantes received, as a schoolboy, the kind of humanist education and moral formation which placed him among the ranks of those given to questioning the *status quo,* but he had a plentiful tradition of critical and subversive writing in sixteenth-century Spain on which to draw.

The central theme of this book, however, rather like the main plot of a Spanish *comedia* or Shakespearean comedy, is accompanied by a minor one. This is the already mentioned question of what understanding the twenty-first century reader is likely to seek, and hopefully find, in *Don Quixote.* This "sub plot" probably requires a brief explanation which begins with a personal reminiscence. I first read *Don Quixote* at the age of nineteen as a first year undergraduate in Spanish and French at the University of Nottingham. I had virtually no prior knowledge of the book, but had bought a copy of Martín de Riquer's Spanish edition, and I set about ploughing through thirty pages a day until I had finished it. It was one of the few achievements of my "term abroad" in Spain, which included attending classes at the University of Seville. In those years, before the Spanish tourist industry had taken off, and nearly every bridge and post office was watched by two armed *guardias civiles* on bicycles, foreigners were still a fairly rare occurrence in Franco's Spain. Mule-drawn carts vied for road space in city streets with new cars, exhaust-spewing lorries, dilapidated buses and archaic trams, while the rural roads, villages and countryside had probably been unchanged for centuries. Indeed, it was still possible to imagine that the mad knight and his squire might suddenly ride over the crest of a hill on their unending journey.

To this day, I cannot be certain of what I gained from my efforts, other than a series of vivid impressions and a sense of the rambling immensity of the book with its quaint chapter headings. Some months later, I galloped through J. M. Cohen's robust Penguin translation, and only then began to realise how deficient my first attempt at understanding the book had been, despite the number of times I had laughed out loud at some humorous episode or other. With the characteristic arrogance of the young and largely inexperienced, and feeling secure in my personal capabilities to come to terms with this great work, I avoided a third year optional course at University on Cervantes in favour of other things. Yet the impact of these two reading experiences was to stay with me permanently.

Fast forward fifty years or so, and I found myself working as a part-time tutor in Spanish in the Institute of Lifelong Learning at Sheffield University. One evening a week I taught modules in Modern Latin American literature and Golden Age prose and drama to mature students from all walks of life, who were studying for the part-time B.A. in Spanish and Latin American Studies, which was run as one of a number of part-time degree courses by the Institute. The cohorts of students made up small, but reasonably representative, groups of mature students, whose ages ranged from 25 to 72, and whose occupations varied from a bus driver to a dentist. At that time, courses in Golden Age Studies were getting thin on the ground in British universities. Whether it was ageing bravado or my innate enjoyment of sailing against any prevailing wind, I decided to canvass opinion among the students on whether they would be interested in a new third year module on Cervantes and *Don Quixote*. To my surprise, and that of the course director, the answer was a very positive "yes." So the research was done and the course written as a twelve-week, ten-credit module, with two class contact hours a week and the usual quota of essays and private study. The enthusiastic response of the students, whose discussions, questions, arguments and ideas were released in what felt like a torrent, provided much of the raw material on which I have subsequently worked in writing this book. Virtually all of them read the novel in Spanish before the teaching began. We even ended one of the courses with a special Cervantes Evening, held in a local pub, at which still more ideas flowed, and the students present completed a brief reader response survey that recorded their individual reactions to the book.

From this I have drawn two rather tentative conclusions. The first is that the response of the various cohorts of Sheffield students to the course on *Don Quixote* was typical of the traditions of part-time, adult education in industrial Yorkshire, where debate, argument, discussion and constant questioning drew upon the greater store of experience and enthusiasm that older students tend to bring to the challenge of learning. In this case my tiny sample readership might well be dismissed as untypical. The second is that, like youth itself, some books – *Don Quixote* included – may be wasted on young people. Today's full-time undergraduates between the ages of 18 and 21 are no more likely to derive any deep benefit from reading *Don Quixote* than I did as a nineteen year old, wandering around Franco's Seville. Given the guidance of a good course of university or school study this difficulty may be resolved, but there are still occasions when university students (and even sixth form pupils) are asked to read classic works which prove to be simply the wrong books at the wrong time.

Over the years, I had frequently wondered what Cervantes' intentions were in labouring over this book which has been hailed as the first modern novel. The answer is almost certainly that however the book might have started out, by the end of the knight's brief first sally, any single intention that might initially have existed had multiplied into a number of aims as the author began to realise the potential scope of the narrative that was growing under his pen. A fascination for artistic experimentation, the urge to prove himself as a writer, the wish for recognition and the need for money, which dogged him for most of his life, all added to the mix. But what decided all important questions was his search for originality, his penchant for literary and intellectual polemics, the deeply-felt humanity which he continually hid behind a mask of detached irony, his stubborn pursuit of truth and a sense of humour that must often have saved him from despair. In what follows, therefore, I have tried to set out how the story that Cervantes created – its episodes, characters, events and digressions – has been constructed to explore nearly every facet of life in sixteenth- and seventeenth-century Spain, not through the medium of history but through literature which reveals truths while disguising facts. In doing so, I have been privileged to be able to draw on the insights gained from the work of the students mentioned to suggest how twenty-first century readers might respond to the author's intentions (such as we can ascertain them) across the space of four centuries.

Like so many books of its kind, this study is really a joint venture to which numerous contributions have been made. For many of these I am especially grateful to the following former students John Airton, David Bell, Josephine Blewitt, Daniel Burgess, Neil Dunk, John Foster, Rubi Foulstone, Joanna Gorecka, Robert Hope, Joanna Iwanowicz, Margaret Morlan, Lizzie Mussell, Sara Narayan, Sandra Rossi, Jane Steeples, Dennis Walsh, Pat Battams and the late, sadly missed Sidney Kenny-Levick. The ideas and comments they provided have been my constant source of encouragement and a salutary guide.

Other and different debts are owed which were incurred over the period of research and writing. In this connection, I would like to thank Toni Ibarz and Luisa Carneiro for reading and commenting upon this Preface and the two succeeding chapters. I have also had valuable assistance and encouragement from friends and colleagues in Hispanic Studies at the University of Sheffield, and would particularly like to thank Professor Philip Swanson, Dr Carmen Ramos Villar, Dr Paul Quinn and Dr Louise Johnson for their interest and suggestions, not to mention the enjoyable conversations in which numerous ideas were exchanged.

To
the memory of
Robert Brian Tate
Magister exigendis sed causas aptior

1

Don Quixote
The Author, Readers and Critics

[La historia de Don Quixote de La Mancha] es tan clara, que no hay cosa que dificultar en ella: los niños la manosean, los mozos la leen, los hombres la entienden y los viejos la celebran ... la tal historia es del más gustoso y menos perjudicial entretenimiento que hasta ahora se haya visto, porque en toda ella no se descubre ni por semejas una palabra deshonesta ni un pensamiento menos que católico.

> Sansón Carrasco in conversation with Don Quixote and Sancho Panza in *Don Quixote*, Part II, Chapter 3. Edited and with notes by Francisco Rico (Punto de Lectura, Madrid, 2009), p. 572.

Four hundred years after its publication, Miguel de Cervantes' imperishable masterpiece *Don Quixote* is still being read, translated and re-translated into virtually all the world's main languages, studied in universities and argued over by scholars. Even more surprising, however, are the differences in critical interpretation that have, at various times, marked its progress since the early seventeenth century. Given that the succeeding generations of scholars concerned have all been ruminating upon the same text, it must follow that part of *Don Quixote's* enduring attraction is that it is a sufficiently multifaceted work to lend itself to each change of approach and understanding that has been brought to it across the centuries. Indeed, even one of the most ardent historicists among contemporary Cervantes specialists, Anthony J. Close, has remarked:

> Every age tends to cast the literary classics in its own image. Scholarly criticism, with its aim of recovering the original sense and circumstances of creation sets out to secure a historically authentic point of view. Yet it too is inevitably influenced by the interests of its own age, and this affects the sort of questions it asks about old books, its methods of analysing them and, to a greater or lesser extent, its image of them.[1]

There are, of course, major question marks over Close's statement of the aims of scholarly criticism. The first is how far the recovery of the original "sense and circumstances of creation" is possible. Though a very necessary benchmark for the better understanding of a work, even the most exhaustive historical and biographical research cannot reach into the areas of the writer's personal experience and feelings which have made a book what it is. An empathetic estimation, by means of our own reading, is the best we can usually hope for.

On the other hand, few would nowadays reject the principle of Marxist criticism that, as a literary form, the novel is very much the product of the social and economic forces of its time; to which should also be added the cultural and aesthetic models that have preceded it and the extent to which it questions or accepts them. In the particular case of *Don Quixote* this has been a recurring critical admonition since the 1920s, but historians were slow to define precisely what, in Golden Age Spain, those social, cultural and economic forces were. The work in the second half of the century of outstanding figures like Raymond Carr, John Lynch and Henry Kamen has, however, largely altered our understanding of everyday life in Spain's age of empire, with corresponding benefits for literary and cultural research.

In 1605, at the age of fifty-eight, Miguel de Cervantes y Saavedra saw the publication of the first part of *Don Quixote;* it was to be a decade before the second part appeared in 1615. By which time the first book of the mad knight's adventures had acquired fame and popularity throughout Europe. Cervantes' reputation was especially high in France, England and the Americas, but he did not live to judge the success of Part II of his master work, dying just over a year after its publication. He left behind him a surprisingly large and varied body of writing, given the demands of a difficult, sometimes dangerous and permanently precarious, life. He was over fifty before he was able to devote himself to writing full-time, but he had been a committed student of literature from his early years. He attended the Jesuit school in Seville, where he was fortunate enough to have as his teacher the well-known humanist Lopez de Hoyos, and though he was unable to go to university these beginnings seem to have given him an early passion for writing. Indeed, three things impress the reader of any of his numerous biographies. These are his literary versatility, his willingness to experiment and his sheer determination to succeed as a writer.

In his own day, and indeed up to the end of the eighteenth century, the evidence indicates that in Spain and abroad *Don Quixote* was mainly appreciated as a wonderfully inventive comic book, whose style set new narrative standards. A frequent critical view of the work, which survived into the twentieth century, was that the reader should not search within it for philosophical or critical depth, controversy or heterodoxy. Even modern Spanish scholars of the eminence of Milá y Fontanals, Menéndez y Pelayo and Rodríguez Marín subscribed to the view that Cervantes was a "natural" talent, with a remarkable imagination, a happily orthodox turn of mind and a gift for putting well-chosen words in the right place, but little more. It was a view echoed also by the Anglo-Irish hispanist James Fitzmaurice-Kelly, in his *A History of Spanish Literature* (1898):

> Tomémosle como fue: como un artista mayor en la práctica que en la teoría, grande por sus facultades naturales más bien que por las adquiridas. . . . Tiene a menudo la hermosura sencilla y la fresca lozanía de la Naturaleza. . . . de aquí el carácter humano y universal de su obra.[2]

> (Let us take him as he was: as an artist greater in the practice of his art than in the theory of it, as a result of natural faculties rather than acquired ones. . . . He often shows the simple beauty and the fresh luxuriance of Nature . . . from which comes the human and universal nature of his work.)

Nevertheless, as Anthony Close points out in *The Romantic Approach to "Don Quixote"*, his important and scholarly study of the history of *Quixote* criticism,[3] the "neo-classical" view of the book was largely overturned after 1800 by the ideas of the German Romantics which, with the exception of Spain itself, where the Romantic Movement was relatively weak, were widely influential across Europe.

The Romantic approach was based on the view that *Don Quixote* should be seen as a symbolic work, and that its symbolism expressed ideas about the human spirit's relation with reality. (For the Generation of '98, this reality became the history of Spain.) The symbolic interpretation not only made the hero-protagonist into a metaphor for the idealist whose vision of the world brings him into direct confrontation with the materialism and self-seeking of the society in which he finds himself, but also largely disregarded the novel's satiric intention and burlesque tone. The result is an interpretation of the work's spirit, style and purpose which reflects the ideology, aesthetics and sensibilities of the modern (i.e. post-romantic) era. As Close remarks:

> The Romantic tradition – serious, sentimental, patriotic, philosophical and subjective – has pulled criticism away from the questions that the novel most obviously and naturally prompts.[4]

In 1925, Américo Castro had opposed the limited, neo-classical view-point of Menéndez y Pelayo, the doyen of Spanish literary historians, when he published his groundbreaking study *El pensamiento de Cervantes*. In this book, he drew upon the writings on the theme of Don Quixote (all of them philosophical meditations rather than scholarly works) of Azorín, Miguel de Unamuno and José Ortega y Gasset, the dominant intellectual figures of the Generation of '98. Taking their lead from the Romantic interpretation of the book, these writers had seen in the fictional Don Quixote a symbol of the Spanish character, in which idealism, aspiration and nobility of purpose are eventually broken on the wheel of materialism and Spanish conservatism. Castro did not support this view, though the Romantic vision that had inspired them touched him also. A historian by early training, Castro maintained that *Don Quixote* could be understood only as the product of the book's time and circumstances, and in doing so he set out a framework for analysis and understanding that has continued to be influential to this day.

Close's differences with Américo Castro are not those of opposition to this central tenet so much as the conviction that much of what Castro saw as comprising the social, intellectual and spiritual realities of Golden Age Spain was, in fact, wrong. But Close's position within later twentieth century Anglo-American Cervantes criticism is not an isolated one. Other eminent scholars have stood outside the wide circle of the Romantic approach. For example, Catholic critics like Helmut Hatzfeld and A. A. Parker have aligned Cervantes – following Castro's historical principle – with the ideology of the Spanish Counter-Reformation. Hatzfeld sees the novel as a satire against Erasmianism and Illuminism, while Parker argues that it is an ingenious fable that warns against the sins of Deception and Self-Deception, as conceived by moralists and theologians of Spain's Baroque period. Peter Russell's now famous article "Don Quixote as a Funny Book"[5] was, however, possibly the critical intervention that turned Cervantes scholars back to a consideration of the importance of the novel's humour and satirical invention. He also addressed the complex issue of what it was that actually made Cervantes' Spanish contemporaries *laugh*. This is a topic to which Close returns in his last book, *Cervantes and the Comic Mind of his Age*. The humour of *Don Quixote*, and its narrative importance, has been reappraised in a number of studies since the 1980s,[6] and will form the subject of a later chapter in this work also.

Writing in 2001, James Iffland, the distinguished American Golden Age scholar and Cervantist, claimed that most of those then involved in the subject were well aware that, for the past two centuries, debate on *Don Quixote* had revolved around the issue of whether the book was in any way socially or politically "dissident" in its focus, and whether it was perceived as such by the readers of Cervantes' time. Certainly in the second half of the twentieth century, the big divide in Cervantes studies had been between the so-called "hard school," which insisted that *Don Quixote* is "primarily a 'funny book,' with little or no contestatory pretensions whatsoever," and the so-called 'soft school,' which suggested that there might in fact be something at least mildly heterodox about it."[7] The former group attacked the latter for being ahistorical in projecting the "isms" of twentieth-century culture wars back onto a seventeenth-century literary parody which burlesqued the sixteenth-century novel of chivalry. The latter group maintained that each generation had the right to interpret a work of art according to the extent to which it spoke directly to their time and concerns, though it recognised that it was not always possible to attribute such an interpretation to authorial intention.

These tensions and groupings were neither as simple nor as clearly defined as Iffland's snapshot picture suggests. The "hard line" did not prevent the emergence other lines of enquiry, which were pursued to good effect by "non-aligned" researchers. Edward Riley in 1962 and 1968, and Stephen Gilman in 1989, turned their attention to Cervantes' ideas on what comprised the kind of narrative fiction he was writing, how it related to notions of poetry and history propounded by classical authorities, the extent to which it should resemble real life (which Cervantes and many of his contemporaries equated with the "truth"), how far it should be mediated by "invención," or the writer's imagination, and the style in which it should be expressed.[8] This approach examined Cervantes' prose fiction in relation to what was a crucial intellectual and literary argument in his day, as well as his own artistic practice and formation.

It is now well recognised that Hispanic scholarship was slow to respond to the challenge of the diverse body of literary theory that grew up in the second half of the twentieth century. Nevertheless, postmodernism, structuralism, post-structuralism, feminism, Marxism, psychoanalytic criticism and new historicism all added new dimensions to the study of literature and language, and despite the tensions among hispanists in general, and *cervantistas* in particular, fresh approaches were introduced which left important imprints upon the discipline as a whole. In this respect, possibly the most significant of the new critical departures have been psychoanalytic criticism, feminism and gender issues, the influence on writing of "cultural authority," and the relationship between *Don Quixote* and modernity. In all these, the movement has tended to be towards the more layered, heterodox elements of the novel, and all have been marked by the publication of key works, often edited collections of essays by a range of specialists, that also map out the theoretical ground on which they are based.

Perhaps in sturdy opposition to the historicists who decried tendencies to interpret past works of literature in the light of contemporary –

and therefore anachronistic – ideas and theories, Ruth El Saffar published, in 1984, *Beyond Fiction: The Recovery of the Feminine in the Novels of Cervantes.*[9] In his review of the book, Salvador Fajardo wrote:

> One of the major achievements of *Beyond Fiction*, in itself sufficient to make it a critical contribution of the first order to Cervantes studies, is to trace the overall development of his narrative art in the four longer fictions: *La Galatea* (1585), *Don Quijote* 1 (1605), *Don Quijote* 2 (1615), and *Los trabajos de Persiles y Segismunda* (1617). . . . But beyond this, in the course of her investigation, Professor El Saffar offers the most cogent interpretation to date of Cervantes' manipulation of interpolated tales, gives a persuasive psychological profile of the main characters, establishes the gradual emergence and ultimately conciliatory role of the 'feminine' and works out a convincing analysis of the *Persiles* as a *terminus ad quem* for Cervantes.[10]

Until then, the importance in Cervantes's full length fiction, as well as in his *Novelas ejemplares*, of female characters whose energies, desires and ingenuity drive the narrative had received only sporadic attention, and El Saffar herself came under some fire for being a feminist in a niche of modern academe that had previously thought itself free of the contagion.

Undeterred, and in any case with powerful allies, El Saffar and Diana de Armas Wilson edited, in 1993, a further collection of essays entitled Quixotic Desire: Psychoanalytical Perspectives on Cervantes.[11] It no doubt provided further irritation for the historicists and "hardliners." The basic assumption behind this book is, indeed, a strongly implied rejection of the neo-classical and romantic or symbolic interpretations of Don Quixote. As the editors explain in their Introduction, what they call "Cervantes' maddeningly elusive and insistently heteroglossic" works constantly induce in the reader's mind doubts about the writer's reliability, intentions, authorship, referentiality, the nature and status of fiction and, ultimately, identity itself.

> Whether structuralist or Marxist, New Historicist or psychoanalytic, the theory that insists on preconceived formulations and seeks with nets and traps. . . . to master its quarry becomes ultimately the object of its own hunt. Were the contributors to this volume to stay wedded to such issues as penis envy, breast deprivation, castration anxiety, or any of the other stalwarts of classic Freudian theory, the tools of psychoanalysis would surely have become traps. . . . The prime psychoanalytic question addressed through this volume has to do not with meaning or intention or characterisation *per se*, but rather what drives material generally analysed according to categories such as plot, character, narrator, sequence, closure or levels of discourse. Psychoanalysis challenges the identification of any symbolic

system with its manifest content, displacing attention from what is presented to what remains hidden. . . . Desire, together with the signifiers in which it appears and through which it hides, becomes, therefore, the object of psychoanalytic enquiry. The text becomes a complex web of intersecting forces designed to tell an *Other* story, a story of that which cannot be told.[12]

From the 1980s on, a fresh approach to the available biographical evidence was also apparent. As Daniel Eisenberg has observed, the biographer of Cervantes has no easy task. There is no shortage of source material, but it is difficult to deal with. The interpretation of the numerous documents requires detailed knowledge of contemporary commercial, legal and administrative practice, and even then the light these sources shine upon the personality of Cervantes himself is at best indirect. Furthermore, though the testimony of Cervantes' writing is of central importance, it is literature not autobiography.

> His prologues and dedications are full of indispensable facts, but are often slanted and self-serving. Once he [the biographer] has used these materials, there remain great gaps and unanswered questions. Finally one must master an immense secondary literature, including, of course, the mammoth, unbalanced and poorly organised documentary biography of Astrana Marín. In the process, the biographer must take positions on many controversial issues, such as Cervantes' religious background and views.[13]

Eisenberg's last observation is, of course, particularly pertinent. As Michael McGaha pointed out in 2004,[14] the argument that Cervantes' family was of *converso* origin has attracted increasing support during the last half of the twentieth century. It derives partly from the unsubstantiated claim that Miguel was born in the village of Cervantes in the Sanabria region of León, which, after 1492, acquired an influx of Jewish families on their way to exile in Portugal. The refugees were welcomed by the local people, settled there and continued to live as crypto-jews thereafter. Several Jewish families with the name Saavedra can be traced to Sanabria at this time, though Cervantes' baptismal certificate, which has not been questioned by historians, records his place and date of birth as being Alcalá de Henares in 1547. To circumstantial evidence of this kind has been added the kind of symbolic and allegorical reading of *Don Quixote* first proposed by Dominique Aubier in 1966 in her study *Don Quichotte, prophète d'Israel*[15] Aubier's conclusions depend upon arcane decodings of names and references found in the thirteenth-century masterpiece of Jewish mysticism written in Castile and entitled *Sefer ha-Zohar* (The Book of Splendours).[16] But if, as Aubier maintains, only a

reader steeped in Jewish religion and history would possess the intellec-
tual tools and conditioning to understand the hidden meaning of *Don
Quixote*, then, as McGaha observes, she offers no evidence of how or when
Cervantes himself would have come by such knowledge.

On the contrary, the copious documentary evidence which charts the
fortunes of the Cervantes family from Juan de Cervantes, the writer's
grandfather, a well-known lawyer and magistrate, to his father Rodrigo
and to Miguel himself, reveals nothing that could be regarded as firm
evidence of *converso* origins or connections. However, both Miguel and
his brother Rodrigo made use, at different points in their lives, of
notarised documents bearing attestations to the fact that the family was
Christian and without suspicion of Jewish ancestry. This was a standard
ploy, of course, used both by *cristiano viejo* and *converso* families, in the
first case to prove their ancestry and in the second to conceal it.
Nevertheless, as Américo Castro pointed out, and McGaha reminds us, it
is hard to explain the marginalisation Cervantes suffered following his
release from Algiers in 1580 unless the suspicion of Jewish blood hung
over him. He was not rewarded for his courageous military service to the
crown, or for his exemplary conduct as a Moorish prisoner, and two
applications he later made for official appointments in the American
colonies were rejected. Even his patron, the Count of Lemos, turned down
his request for an appointment in the cultural entourage of the
Viceroyalty of Naples.

For McGaha and many others, the most convincing evidence of
Cervantes' *converso* origins can be found in the attitudes he displays in
his writings. As McGaha says:

> I think it is beyond question that Cervantes held heterodox views, and that
> in *Don Quixote* he created an amazingly ingenious way of planting seeds of
> doubt in the minds of thoughtful readers without arousing the suspicion
> of the censors. As for the question of whether any of those heterodox views
> were specifically Jewish in nature, I must at this point remain agnostic.[17]

There are, of course, a number of good reasons for McGaha's caution. It
is true that many *conversos* of the early sixteenth century found themselves attracted to Humanism and Church reform, and the revitalised
classical learning that it represented. They were often open admirers of
Erasmus, whose reputation in Spain was at its height during the first three
decades of the century. But the Reformation brought Erasmus' teachings
under suspicion of being too close in spirit to the Lutheran heresy. His
writings were forbidden in Spain and in 1559 were placed on the
Inquisition's list of prohibited books. Humanism was either driven
underground or disguised under a number of literary masks. Not all

conversos were humanists, however, any more than all humanists were *conversos*. Cervantes certainly received a humanist education from the Jesuits in Seville. During his years as a soldier in Italy he also had the opportunity to experience Italian humanism at first hand and to read books that would have been unavailable in his native country. Indeed, the intellectual and reforming roots of humanism can be seen to run deep in Cervantes' character, at least on the evidence of his writings.

McGaha's reference to writing under censorship is a consideration that should not be overlooked in Golden Age studies, but is rarely taken into full account in modern academic criticism. If the authors of all but the most uncontroversial and orthodox texts had to exercise care to avoid the wrath of the censor, the position of the book sellers and publishers was equally precarious. They risked fines, imprisonment and the confiscation of their goods and equipment if they were found guilty of printing or disseminating works which were considered "dangerous" because they questioned Church dogma, undermined public morality, spread heterodox and heretical ideas, or criticised the actions and policies of the Monarch. Furthermore, religious and political censorship reinforced the notion of cultural authority, which present-day scholars are beginning to explore.[18] This is based on the proposition that, in each age, social, moral, religious, political and cultural ideas combine to form a "hegemonic discourse," fashioned by the dominant classes and institutions of a country, which determine how society thinks and functions. This discourse recognises historical models which serve as examples that artists and thinkers observe and imitate, but it also reinforces the position and values of the dominant classes and institutions. Inevitably, however, a parallel and opposing counter-current which, either directly or covertly, questions and subverts the prevailing orthodoxies, is also present. Often this is built upon alternative sources of authority which, in modern democracies, is often seen as a kind of pluralism to be tolerated and even encouraged. In totalitarian regimes, this pluralism, or heterodoxy, is usually opposed or even suppressed. Yet it invariably continues to exist under the surface – for example the *samisdat* writers of Soviet Russia – forming a dialectical continuum with the dominant discourse.

Spanish Golden Age literature is particularly apt for study as an example of artistic output mediated by cultural authority. When one takes into consideration the nature of early modern Spain under the Hapsburg monarchs, its imperial absolutism supported by a landed aristocracy and the spiritual authority of the Catholic Church, behind which lurked the threatening shadow of the Inquisition, we see the perfect recipe for a climate of cultural authority reinforced by the institutions of the state. By the second half of the sixteenth century, Spaniards were forbidden to study abroad except in named universities in Portugal and Italy, the content of books printed in Spain, and the importation of books from abroad, were strictly (though not always consistently) controlled, ostensibly to protect the purity of the Catholic faith and the moral standards of the populace. Even so, the profusion and variety of Spain's literary output, notably between 1550 and 1660, was remarkable. Discussion was not stifled so much as guided along certain acceptable lines. Moral and religious writing of all kinds abounded. Furthermore, treatises and handbooks on moral behaviour, religion, government and the conduct of princes, history, law, economics, philosophy, medicine and aesthetics continued to be produced, alongside popular fiction, collections of plays and poetry.

But the impression so often given of Spain in the Golden Age as a country which exhibited a monolithic, internal unity under the combined aegis of monarch, aristocracy and Church is a mistaken one. Historical understanding of the century and a half of social, economic, religious and cultural pressures that created what Henry Kamen has called "a society of conflict" has recently sharpened.[19] Divisions in Spanish society, which began with the fall of Granada to the army of the Catholic Monarchs, after which the victorious Christians refused to accept the Jews, or give fair treatment to the Muslim subjects of the newly unified kingdom, sowed bitter seeds. These actions resulted in permanent discrimination against the *conversos* and *moriscos* on racial grounds. The preoccupation of the *cristianos viejos* with the notion of "pureza de sangre," the proven guarantee that they were untainted by Jewish blood, was one factor. The two uprisings against Spanish treatment by the *moriscos* in the Alpujarras of Eastern Spain, from 1499 to 1500 and again from 1568 to 1571, both conflicts which assumed the scale of civil wars, was another. Between them the Comuneros Revolt of 1520–1521, saw towns in Castile, which feared the loss of their traditional rights and freedoms under the crown, rebelling against the rule of Charles V.

Other strains became apparent by the 1550s. By the beginning of the reign of Philip II, the intellectual and religious climate of the country had become much more strict in response to the Reformation and the Protestant heresy in Northern Europe. By the 1570s, with Spain at the forefront of the Counter-reformation, it had hardened further still. Charles V's foreign wars had drained the country's resources, the importation of silver from the New World had caused inflation across Europe, while Spain balanced its books by means of huge loans from Genoese bankers. Spain's tax system, which largely exempted the higher and lower aristocracy and the Church, meant that the financing of the whole national and imperial enterprise was carried on the broad but resentful backs of the Castilian peasantry and the towns. The resulting impoverishment of rural Spain meant an influx of people to the growing towns and cities, which rapidly became a floating underclass that scraped a marginal living or turned to criminal activity. Despite the famous victory over the Turkish fleet at the Battle of Lepanto in 1571, and the annexation of Portugal in 1580, the failure of the Armada in 1588 had catastrophic effects on the country and the reputation of the ageing Philip II. Suddenly Spain's inherent economic and military weakness was exposed, together with the failings of its ambitious but idle aristocracy which no longer provided the kind of military and civil leadership on which Charles V had been able to count. The continued burden of the wars in the Lowlands against the Protestant Dutch, who were trying to rid themselves of Spanish rule, and Spain's reluctant involvement in the Thirty Years War from 1618 to 1648, weakened the country still further, to which could be added the relative incapacities of Philip III and IV as rulers.

If the ups and downs of an individual life closely followed the path of Spain's fall from greatness, it was that of Miguel de Cervantes. Born in 1547, when Spain's political and military power was still at its height, he lived through the long reign of Philip II, and for most of that of the pious, but indolent and pleasure-loving Philip III. He served his king as a soldier in Italy, showing great courage at the Battle of Lepanto, the national triumph in which he was wounded, and set off to return to Spain in 1575 with the commendations of both the Duke of Sessa, his commanding officer, and Don John of Austria, the King's half-brother and commander of the Spanish army. His eventual return in 1580, after capture by Moorish pirates, and five years of captivity in Algiers, which he endured no less heroically than his military service, came in the year that Spain annexed the Kingdom of Portugal. But Cervantes' achievements were not rewarded. He did not obtain the office under the crown that he hoped for, and with Don John and the Duke of Sessa now dead, he had no powerful patron at court.

His family had been impoverished by raising the ransoms to free Miguel and his younger brother Rodrigo, also a soldier, who was captured and imprisoned with him. So to try to restore the family's fortunes Cervantes set out to become a writer and playwright. By 1585 he had produced his first book, a pastoral novel called *La Galatea*. He had also gained some reputation as a poet and had written numerous plays and interludes for the theatre. His career as a playwright ended abruptly however. The new *comedias* that the prolific young Lope de Vega and his followers began to turn out proved so popular with the audiences of the time that theatre managers no longer showed any interest in the classical style tragedies and comedies that Cervantes had, up to then, been writing with some success. Cervantes put aside his theatrical aspirations, and married Catalina de Palacios Salazar Vozmediano, barely a month after the birth of his illegitimate daughter Isabel following an affair with Ana Franca, a former actress and wife of an innkeeper. Catalina was half Cervantes' age, a country girl of respectable but impoverished family. Both probably thought that the other was better off than they actually were, but Cervantes found himself in the Manchegan village of Esquivias, managing a tiny estate laden with debts inherited by his mother-in-law from her dead husband. Despite her youth, Catalina bore him no children, and after two precarious years, Cervantes left Esquivias to become a government officer, a commissioner charged with collecting oil and corn from villages in Andalusia to supply the Armada, with which Philip II was preparing to invade England.

The work was arduous and difficult, requiring constant travelling from inn to inn along the roads of his extended "territory." Bad harvests, church tithes and heavy taxation made the peasants reluctant to contribute further to the royal exchequer. Cervantes' wages, and the funds to purchase the supplies were often delayed, and he was constantly obliged to argue with his masters in the Treasury to justify his accounts and returns. Yet in an area of work where bribery and dishonesty were frequent, and commissioners unpopular and often corrupt, Cervantes earned himself the reputation of an honest dealer, and grudging admiration from his clients. He thus soldiered on at his thankless task. But his time as a commissioner made huge demands upon him. As Donald P. McCrory observes:

> Long winter journeys followed by the scorching heat of summer, the seemingly incessant squabbling of farmers and labourers, the unchristian behaviour of the clergy, the delays in salary payments, a life on the back of a mule or in a cart and, to cap it all, aspersions cast on his honesty had conspired to sap Cervantes' morale. The demands of his job occupied him day and night, and he had then to write up every transaction in an atmosphere which, at best, was tense on account of the frauds, thefts, percentage cuts and bribes which hunger or greed create.[20]

But the failure of the Armada, and the inefficiency that had characterised its preparation, caused an outcry that dented even the position of the King. In 1590, clearly ill at ease, Cervantes made an application for a post in the Indies, stressing his distinguished military service and his scrupulous and honest labours as a commissioner. His petition was returned with the words: "Look for something here" scrawled laconically across it. In August 1590 an enquiry was launched into the irregularities in the dealings of a number of commissioners working, like Cervantes, under Antonio de Guevara, who was in overall charge of commissioning food for the Armada. In the witch hunt that followed, a number of

Guevara's commissioners were imprisoned and four were hanged. Cervantes' accounts showed a shortfall at this time, which he was able to explain as a fault in his calculations. He was summoned to Madrid to explain himself, but lacking the money for the journey, persuaded Guevara's secretary, Juan Serón, to appear for him. No charges were brought against Cervantes as a result, but commissioning was suspended while the enquiry continued and his contract was, in any case, due for renewal. To make some money, Cervantes agreed to write six plays for the actor manager Rodrigo de Osorio, but they were never finished because Guevara was replaced as Chief Commissioner by Pedro de Isunza, who immediately renewed Cervantes' commission and sent him to collect wheat and oil in Granada and Baeza.

Isunza, whose job was also to weed out fraud within the Commission, proved a staunch supporter of Cervantes. But he was soon in trouble himself, falsely accused of illegally selling wheat for his own profit. The case dragged on, and Isunza demanded that Cervantes go to Madrid to support his refutation of the charges. But at the same time, Cervantes was charged, with equal unfairness, with a similar crime by Francisco Moscoso, a magistrate from Écija, and imprisoned. Isunza intervened and secured his release. The authorities dismissed all charges against both Isunza and Cervantes, but Isunza, already a sick man, died in 1593. He was replaced by Miguel de Oviedo, who immediately dispatched Cervantes to gather wheat for the Spanish navy because he was, in Oviedo's words, "competent, experienced and trustworthy."

But 1593 was a bad year for Cervantes. Poor harvests forced up the cost of wheat far above what the War Council was prepared to pay for commissioned supplies, making the commissioners' positions almost untenable, and Cervantes heard of the death of both his mother Doña Leonor de Cortinas and his uncle Andrés, the mayor of Cabra, while he was on the road, pursuing the King's business. But the next year, Philip II decided that, after the Guevara scandal, the Commission would be wound up, and the government would deal with the landowners, farmers, townships and constabulary directly. In 1594, Cervantes' final set of accounts was approved; he was a free man but once more unemployed. He left the service with his reputation intact, and shortly after, still in need of money, became a government tax collector for the same area in which he had worked as an army supplies commissioner. His task was to collect 2.5 million *maravedís* in tax arrears. The government demanded that each tax collector appoint guarantors, so that in the event of fraud or theft, the Treasury would not lose out. Cervantes secured one, Francisco Suarez Gasco, who guaranteed 4,000 ducats, but failing to find a second, he had to pledge the modest personal fortune of himself and his wife.

Cervantes' new choice of profession was made at a very unpropitious moment of history. Spain was, at the time, facing financial ruin. The collection of taxes was a measure that was judged crucial to the stabilisation of the regime, and the fiscal obligations to the Crown of Castile and other regions of the kingdom became an argument that plagued the last years of Philip II's reign. Cervantes' work would have been mostly concerned with the *alcabala,* a sales tax levied at the rate of ten per cent of all purchases, but with numerous complex exemptions from it. In practice, however, as little as a half to a fifth of this amount was collected as a result of agreements reached between the Treasury and tax payers. The allocation of the tax was also something of a bureaucratic nightmare. Once an overall sum had been fixed, it was divided between the forty districts of the eighteen provinces of Castile, then reapportioned by the district councils to their various trading sectors and ultimately down to individual merchants and traders. Discussion and dispute accompanied each stage of the process, even down to the actual collection of the tax by the government's commissaries.

Cervantes would, however, have been as keenly aware as the government of the economic depression that had hung over Castile since the late 1580s. An increasing number of subsistence crises due to bad harvests had resulted in a malnourished population – especially in Andalusia – that was highly susceptible to outbreaks of plague, drought and invasions of locusts. Though plague, especially between 1598 and 1602, was Cervantes' worst enemy as a tax collector, almost equally disruptive were violent swings in agricultural production due to bad weather and resultant fluctuations in prices. Indeed, it has been estimated that by the end of the sixteenth century, the burden of dues, taxes and rents absorbed over half the average peasant's harvest. Over the same period, the value of Spain's imperial trade, particularly with the Americas, had also dropped markedly.

In this unprepossessing climate, Cervantes was authorised to collect from various townships within his allocated area of Granada the sum of 2,557,029 maravedís. But when the amounts finally reached Madrid, he was charged with a deficit of 79,000 maravedís, though a careful re-scrutiny revealed that the error was the responsibility of the government auditors not Cervantes. Unaware of this, Cervantes decided to go to Madrid to present his accounts personally, taking with him further moneys collected. This he did by giving 7,500 reales to a merchant banker, Simón Freire de Lima in return for a letter of credit for this amount to be redeemed in Madrid. (Travelling from Granada to Madrid through bandit-ridden countryside carrying a small fortune in currency would have been exceedingly unwise.) Arriving in Madrid in May 1595, Cervantes waited for the money from Freire only to discover that, amid claims of bankruptcy, Freire de Lima had absconded with 60,000 ducats. Cervantes thus found himself in the middle of what was potentially another financial scandal, and passed a fraught few months while the matter was investigated. He also won a national prize for poetry, organised by the Dominican friars of Saragossa, for which he was awarded three silver spoons.

Cervantes returned quickly to Seville to hunt down Freire de Lima, only to find that other creditors had beaten him to it, and impounded the banker's possessions. His case that money owed to the Royal Treasury must take precedence over other debts required him to return to Madrid to obtain written authorisation from the King. This was finally granted on 7 August 1595, and for the next two years, the case seems to have dragged on, though Cervantes' whereabouts are not recorded during this period. Inexplicably though, even by 1597 Cervantes had still not submitted his accounts to the Treasury. Determined to get to the bottom of the alleged 79,000 maravedís shortfall, the Treasury officials again summoned him to Madrid. The Treasury also informed Suarez Gasco his guarantor, who requested a delay of twenty days and sent notice of Cervantes' summons to Gaspar de Vallejo a presiding judge in Seville. Unbelievably, Gaspar de Vallejo fixed Cervantes's bond at 2.5 million maravedís – the entire sum he had been authorised to collect – instead of the 79,000 maravedís of the alleged shortfall. Unable to raise such a vast sum, Cervantes, quite unjustly, found himself in prison in Seville instead of clearing his name in Madrid.

It is to this period of imprisonment that the beginnings of *Don Quixote* are attributed, primarily by the author himself in the Prologue to Part I of the novel, though whether this means that the writing itself was embarked upon in Seville prison, or whether it was more a question of producing notes and ideas for what was written later is not clear. Cervantes refused to try to gain his release by bribing de Vallejo, and appealed to the King. Philip II replied in December 1597 requesting his presence in Madrid within thirty days. Gaspar de Vallejo found grounds not to release him however, and Gasco and Cervantes' wife Catalina, whose small possessions had also been made the subject of a guarantee, refused to part with a penny until he had appeared in Madrid. The matter dragged on until the early months of 1598, when Cervantes was finally released. Donald P. McCrory observes:

Few can doubt that the psychological blow of his incarceration. After all, he was now in his fiftieth year of a life that had been both restless and precarious. It is no real surprise that the concept of justice and the relationship between crime and punishment should become a recurrent theme in *Don Quixote*.[21]

Not much is known of Cervantes' life between the years 1598 and 1602. He is thought to have ended his appointment as a tax collector by mutual consent. His accounts were finally accepted by the Treasury, whose own auditors had been in error over the original 79,000 maravedís shortfall. The impulse to write had never deserted him, although his years as a civil servant had seriously disrupted any consistent efforts to do so. He had clearly tried his hand, sporadically, at short works of prose fiction and poetry between the late 1580s and 1597, and turned back again to writing and literary politics as soon as he ceased working for the Treasury. A resumption of writing for the stage, however, was not possible. The theatres had been closed in 1597 as a mark of respect for the death of Philip II's daughter, the Infanta Catherine Michelle, Duchess of Savoy, and with the death of Philip himself a year later, they remained closed until 1600.

Amid the mourning that accompanied the death of the King in 1598, Cervantes suffered a personal loss. Ana Franca, his former mistress and mother of his only child Isabel, died in May that year, leaving their daughter homeless. Cervantes, then living in Seville, acted quickly, and persuaded his sister Magdalena, who was single and worked as a seamstress, to give Isabel a home and protection. At around this time, the City Council of Seville decided to honour the dead monarch by constructing an extravagant honorary tomb in his memory. Cervantes wrote a funeral sonnet for the occasion, which although it is often read as a celebratory poem, contains a large element of satirical burlesque which criticises Hapsburg Spain's concept of Catholic royalty, while ironically reflecting that the splendour of the catafalque cannot hide the reality of the death it conceals. Almost immediately after this, Castile suffered a new outbreak of plague which continued unabated until 1601. It is estimated that a tenth of Castile's population died during this period, including eight thousand from Seville alone. This probably persuaded Cervantes to leave the city and go north, either to his wife's small landholding in Esquivias or to Madrid. Freed from his duties as a tax collector at the age of fifty-two, Cervantes seems to have used his financial knowledge to dabble in business as a broker of letters of credit and other monetary transfers, for which a commission was charged. He is also thought to have resumed his literary interests.

Meanwhile, the transition from one monarch to the next proceeded seamlessly, and Philip III, his father's youngest and only surviving son, became King of Spain. Described as "docile and obedient," Philip had from his childhood shown a strong religious fervour and piety, but little interest in affairs of state. His father's reluctant conclusion that, should the boy become King, someone else would have to rule for him quickly proved to be the case. His *valido*, or favourite, Don Francisco Gómez de

Sandoval y Rojas, better known as the Duke of Lerma, successfully took on the task of the day-to-day running of the country and its empire. Nevertheless, Philip was careful to keep all the powers of final decision on major matters in his own hands, and his rule saw the progress towards absolute monarchy, begun by Philip II, continued and reinforced. In 1601, Philip III recognised that Madrid was too overcrowded, noisy and dysfunctional to be a serviceable capital city, and following consultation, by means of a specially created royal committee, he decided that the Court should transfer to Valladolid, the former capital of the Kingdom of Castile.

In 1603, Miguel de Cervantes reappears upon the page of history, following thousands of others who chose, for various economic or political reasons, to relocate themselves in the environs of the new Royal Court. His two sisters Andrea and Magdalena, Andrea's daughter Constanza de Ovando y Figueroa, and Isabel de Cervantes, now seventeen, set up a household in a new building in Valladolid, and were joined both by Cervantes and his wife Catalina in 1604. We know virtually nothing about the actual relationship between Miguel de Cervantes and Catalina Salazar. Having lived apart for eighteen years, its seems strange that they should resume domestic relations as part of an extended family, comprised, with the exception of Cervantes himself, entirely of women. Perhaps the separation had been less total than it appeared. Cervantes was by that time fifty seven years old. Catalina, forty and childless, had carried on the day-today management the family's debt-laden property in Esquivias well enough not to have been obliged to rejoin Cervantes out of necessity. In Valladolid, she became a lay member of a religious order – a not uncommon step for older married people in seventeenth-century Spain – and the two seem to have passed their later years together in a celibate partnership. The family had already been saddened by the death of Cervantes' younger brother Rodrigo in 1600, killed at the Battle of the Dunes in Flanders. He had joined the army at the same time as Miguel and had been a prisoner with him in Algiers, being ransomed after three years in captivity. On his release, Rodrigo had decided to pursue his military career but, like his older brother, gained little from it, having risen only to the rank of a junior officer when he was killed on active service.

Whatever the beginnings of *Don Quixote,* it is clear that once he had settled his accounts to the satisfaction of the Treasury in 1598, Cervantes straight away got down to writing the story, which may account for his virtual disappearance for four years, though he was haunted by a fresh demand from the Treasury for the unpaid sum of 79,000 maravedís which the auditors claimed was still owing from his last returns as a tax collector. This had been accepted as a Treasury mistake in 1598, but the matter was renewed in 1601 and was not settled until 1603, when the error was finally recognised for a second time. When his new domestic arrangements in Valladolid began in 1604, the first part of the book was complete. Cervantes made contact with the publisher Francisco de Robles, whose father, then plying the family business in Madrid, had published Cervantes' first novel, *La Galatea*, in 1585. The manuscript of the first part of *Don Quixote* received the license allowing it to be printed. This was undertaken by Juan de la Cueva in Madrid, and appeared the following year in 1605 dedicated to the Duke of Béjar.

Don Quixote was an immediate success, though Mateo Alemán's two-part picaresque novel *Guzmán de Alfarache* (1599–1604) outsold it at the time. Robles made a first edition of 1,750 copies, somewhat higher than the average first print numbers. Much was clearly expected of it. This was followed by a second edition of 1,800 copies, and both were sold out by 1607. The waters were muddied, however, by two pirate editions which appeared one in Portugal and one in Barcelona. Francisco de Robles apparently had no trouble in securing a further license for the book to be exported to the American colonies. (Ironically, the importation and sale of chivalresque novels in the Americas was forbidden on the grounds that they would have a deleterious moral effect on native Indians.) His first license having been limited to Castile, he also immediately obtained licenses to publish in Portugal, Aragon, Catalonia and Valencia. Cervantes had by now established himself in the literary circles of the capital, which revolved around the Royal Court and the literary salons presided over by noble families.[22] Furthermore, he was now able to do so as a famous writer, whose latest work was on everybody's lips, and whose financial position was – temporarily at least – relatively solvent.

Though he persevered with writing his second best known work, the collection of short fiction known as the *Novelas ejemplares* (The Exemplary Novels), Cervantes' life was not destined to be a peaceful one even now. Five months after the publication of *Don Quixote*, a well-known nobleman, Don Gaspar de Espeleta, was found in the street outside the building where the Cervantes family rented the second floor. He was dying from wounds received in a brawl, almost certainly the result of a revenge attack by a jealous husband, Melchor Galván, a notary who lived close by and who suspected Espeleta of having an affair with his wife, Iñes Hernández. The local mayor, however, no doubt prompted by gossip, was convinced that those responsible lived inside the building, which Espeleta was known to visit on regular occasions. In particular, he seems to have suspected the women of the Cervantes household – with the exception of Catalina, who was in Esquivias at the time – of immoral conduct which might have involved the dead man. At no time, despite the insistence of Espeleta's servant that Galván had been the assailant, did the mayor question Galván or his wife, but instead arrested Cervantes, his sister Andrea, her daughter Constanza and Isabel de Cervantes, and imprisoned them for forty-eight hours until they were released for lack of evidence. The family reputation was undoubtedly stained by these arrests and the flawed judicial process that led to them.

It is worth pointing out here that Cervantes' household was neither conventional nor uncontroversial. The determination, enterprise and independence of his mother, Doña Leonor Cortinas, and his sisters Andrea and Magdalena,[23] had, on several occasions, saved the family financially. As Donald McCrory points out:

> What should not be forgotten is that in their actions the Cervantes women were driven by economic necessity, and their liaisons – mostly unhappy ones – solved the family's money problems.[24]

Cervantes therefore needed to look no further than the examples of his mother and sisters to appreciate the limitations on women's position in Spanish society, where virtually the only possibilities open to them were marriage or life in a convent. Those forced by circumstances to earn their own living had very few options if they had no land or property of their own.

Isabel de Cervantes was a major family concern. She appears to have fallen out with Magdalena, and to have become increasingly estranged from her father. (Catalina, who probably always resented her, had no time for her whatsoever.) Around 1605 she began an affair with Juan de Urbina, having been openly associated with a Portuguese financier Simón Mendez. Urbina, secretary to the Duke of Savoy was rich, fashionable and moved in court circles. He was also married with a wife and family in Italy. The family's stay in Valladolid ended abruptly however. In 1606, the King and the Duke of Lerma decided to return the court to Madrid, on the pretext that Valladolid was unable to create the kind of infrastructure needed to maintain the King and the Court in the lavish style to which it had become accustomed. Like many others, Cervantes decided that his best interests would be served by following the Court. In December 1606, Isabel, now in Madrid, was married to a man named Diego Sanz, gave birth to a daughter (also called Isabel) whose father was almost certainly Urbina, and was a widow by 1608. At this point Cervantes decided his unruly daughter's life must be put in some kind of order. He confronted Urbina, with whom there was no marriage possibility for Isabel, and obliged him to break off the relationship and to give her a settlement of 2,000 ducats and a house for her use. Within three months she had remarried, to a man named Luis de Molina y Castillo, an acquaintance of Urbina who later worked for him. Sadly for Cervantes, the infant Isabel died at the age of two in 1609, and this prompted Urbina to try to back-track on the settlement made to her mother. The matter ended in a flurry of reciprocal law suits which lasted until the 1620s. However, the fruits of Isabel's dubious conduct kept her and her second husband in far more prosperous circumstances than her father ever achieved.

The year 1609 saw events occur in the world outside the family which clearly troubled Cervantes. Philip III expelled the *Moriscos* from Spain, causing serious social and economic disruption. The decision had been taken in principle by Philip II after the second Alpujarras revolt was put down in 1570, but it was suspended in 1571 after the Spanish victory at Lepanto ended the Turkish naval threat in the Mediterranean. In theory the *Moriscos* had been converted to Christianity, but in the main they retained their traditional customs and dress, and many continued to practice the Muslim religion in secret, a fact to which many of their Christian neighbours turned a blind eye. The expulsion was opposed by many Spaniards, principally the aristocratic land-owners of Granada, Valencia and Aragon, who foresaw the damage that would be done to the economy of their rural estates without their skilled *Morisco* tenants, who provided many of the best artisans and craftsmen, as well as farmers who were expert in the complex system of irrigated agriculture that traditionally flourished in these mountainous areas. The *Moriscos* were given three weeks to leave their land and homes, and were forbidden to take gold, silver and other valuables with them.

Cervantes had been critical of the conduct of those *Moriscos* who had plotted with the Suleiman the Magnificent, the Emperor of Turkey, before and during the second uprising. They were still regarded as a potential fifth column in the eventuality of a Turkish incursion into Spanish territory. Over a quarter of a million *Moriscos* were affected by the expulsion order, people whose ancestors had lived in Spain since the eighth century, spoke Spanish, and many of whom were Christians. Cervantes the humanitarian was horrified by the suffering undergone by many innocent people as a result of the royal decision, on which he expanded at length with the stories of Ricote and Ana Felix in Part II of *Don Quixote*.

Having completed their move to Madrid, and with the turbulent events surrounding the life of Isabel de Cervantes to some extent settled, Cervantes' existence entered a more peaceful phase after 1609. This allowed him a final late flowering as a writer at the age of sixty-two. But in addition to the death of his infant granddaughter Isabel Sanz, in that year, his elder sister Andrea also died, four months after receiving the habit of the Trinitarian Order of St Francis, which Catalina and Magdalena had also joined. This double loss seems to have persuaded Cervantes himself to seek closer links with the Church, which he did by joining the Society for the Holy Sacrament.

In the literary academies he now frequented in Madrid, he rubbed shoulders with the nobility and great writers of the period, literary figures such as the young Francisco de Quevedo, Vicente Espinel, Luis de Góngora, the Argensola brothers and Lope de Vega, with whom he was by no means reconciled. It was here also that he met his future patron, the Count of Lemos, to whom the second part of *Don Quixote* was dedicated. Despite the urging of Francisco de Robles, however, Cervantes did not get down to writing the promised second part of the book immediately. Instead he collected his still extant works for the theatre, and prepared the *Novelas ejemplares* for publication. He suffered bereavement again in 1611, when his favourite younger sister, Magdalena, died after a protracted illness. The *Novelas* were finally published in 1613, to be followed in 1614 by his long, mock epic poem on writing and writers, *Viaje de Parnaso* (Journey to Parnassus). His collected theatrical works, eight full-length plays and eight one-act *entremeses* (interludes) followed in 1615.[25]

Cervantes had probably begun to work seriously on the second part of *Don Quixote* at some point shortly after Magdalena's death. Circumstances had by this time made him a different man from the one who began the story in 1597. He had aged and suffered personal loss, his financial position was as precarious as ever, but at least he had achieved international fame as the writer of the first part of the knight's adventures. Even so, he had clearly set himself a punishing schedule. At the time of beginning the continuation of his novel, he was also completing the *Novelas ejemplares,* published in 1613, and had almost certainly begun to write his final work, the romance entitled *Los trabajos de Persiles y Segismunda*[26] (The Labours of Persiles and Segismunda) published a year after his death. Indeed, in the prologue to *Las novelas ejemplares* he informs his readers that this forthcoming tale is now almost complete.

But Cervantes' relatively untroubled progress with Part II received a serious jolt. In October 1614, when he had reached chapter 59, he received the news that an illicit rival version of *Don Quixote* had been published in Tarragona. The name of its previously unheard of author, Alonso Fernández de Avellaneda, was undoubtedly a pseudonym, and his identity is still unknown, though the theory that Avellaneda was in fact a group of Lope de Vega's friends and followers, who were doing their best to sabotage Cervantes' efforts to finish the second part of the now famous book, has a number of supporters. Cervantes was, however, clever enough to write the appearance of this spurious version of the knight's adventures into his own story, and to hold it up as a completely false account by making the knight and his squire alter their plans to go to the jousts at Zaragoza, where Avellaneda's version takes them, and to head off instead to Barcelona. From chapter 59, Cervantes takes only just over 100 pages to reach the story's end at chapter 74, with the death of the now sane Don Quixote and his dying testimony. Just before the final pages, in chapter 72 in fact, he makes Don Quixote encounter Don Álvaro Tarfe, a character out of Avellaneda's book. This gentleman, on encountering the defeated Don Quixote who is now returning home, is quickly persuaded to sign a notarised declaration to the effect that he had never before seen the Don Quixote or Sancho whom he now confronts, and that the "Don Quixote" and "Sancho" with whom he had previously associated (in the history recorded by Avellaneda) were entirely different people.

There can be no doubt that the appearance of Avellaneda's spurious sequel also spurred on Cervantes' determination to finish and publish the genuine Part II as quickly as possible. By having his protagonist regain his sanity and die repenting the deeds done under the influence of his madness, Cervantes made it virtually impossible for any fraudulent future versions to appear. Whether this was the ending he had originally intended is hard to say. Nor can we guess where the story might have gone had the knight and his squire reached Zaragoza and taken part in the jousts there. But Cervantes' last hundred pages are a helter skelter passage of adventures – which include the encounter with the bandit Roque Guinart, the affair of Doña Claudia Jerónima, the story of Ana Félix, and Don Quijote's defeat by the Knight of the White Moon (the ever-determined Sansón Carrasco, masquerading as a rival knight-errant) and the end of the pretended passion for Don Quixote by Altisidora, the Duchess' maid.

It is possible that these adventures were all new, thereby involving the author in a good deal of fresh work. But the speed with which the book was then completed – by the end of 1614 – indicates that only chapters 59 and 72 were in fact new additions made necessary by Avellaneda's version, and that the rest may well have been the story as planned, with only the place names altered. Thus the long-awaited Part II of *Don Quixote* by its original author, was published in 1615, leaving Cervantes, who was now seriously ill with diabetes, to finish writing his Byzantine novel, *Los trabajos de Persiles y Segismunda,* This was finished shortly before his death on 22nd April 1616, and appeared in print the following year.

It is difficult to believe that a writer whose life even remotely resembled that of Miguel de Cervantes should have excluded autobiography and even personal statements – with the exception of the clues and brief pen portraits contained in his prologues – almost completely from his fiction. This is however the case, though in his play *El trato de Argel* (Life in Algiers)[27] and the novella entitled *La historia del cautivo* (The Captive's

Tale) probably written in the late 1580s or early 1590s but later inserted into Part I of *Don Quixote*, his first-hand knowledge of the life led by Christian prisoners of the Moors in Algiers is clearly evident. Yet if he eschews personal and biographical information, Cervantes reveals in considerable detail his preoccupation with the social, philosophical and political questions of his time, and constantly enters into a carefully calculated, and often well disguised, debate on these intellectual issues with his contemporary readers.

These topics and debates are introduced into the narrative of *Don Quixote* in a number of ways. For example, we have in Part I Don Quixote's impromptu disquisitions on "The Age of Gold" and "Arms versus Letters" to two surprised and rather inappropriate audiences. There are also the dialogues between characters which pursue a key theme. In Part I again, we find the three-way conversation between the Priest, the Barber and the knight's housekeeper on the contents of Don Quixote's library. This is the beginning of a long-running debate on literature and its moral effect upon readers, which recurs throughout the book and is rejoined in chapters 49 and 50 in the discussion on writing and authorship between Don Quixote and the Canon of Toledo.

As the story progresses, Cervantes adopts in Part II more informal ways to air ideas and to debate them, by exploiting the opportunities offered by private conversations, increasingly between the knight and his squire, and chance meetings with others. For example, as a result of the knight's experience in the Cave of Montesinos, the theme of what constitutes reality and how it is to be distinguished from dreams and illusions, is introduced and subsequently argued over between the two. The question is added to by the fact that Don Quixote and Sancho are the victims of elaborately organised deceptions and charades devised for their amusement by the Duke and the Duchess, with the aid of their numerous servants. The incidents include the "voyage" through the heavens on the wooden horse Clavileño, which cleverly reverses the positions of Sancho and his master following their disagreement over the Montesinos Cave experience, and further blurs distinctions and distorts judgements. The deceptions of the ducal pair are the context for the centrally important debate which surrounds Sancho's governorship of the "island" of Barataria, his master's advice to him on the proper conduct of a ruler, and his own down-to-earth, practical solutions to the pretended cases and questions that are brought before him during the brief tenure of his rule.

A good deal of distance has been travelled by scholars and critics since Américo Castro's game-changing work *El pensamiento de Cervantes* (1925), though it must be admitted that progress was initially slow. After the Second World War, however, investigation into the theoretical perspectives of Cervantes' masterpiece began in earnest. Probably the first major contribution was Edward Riley's *Cervantes' Theory of the Novel* (1962), which examined his literary ideas as based on classical precept and the contemporary work of humanist scholar El Pinciano (Alonso López Pinciano) *Filosofía antigua poética* (1596). Stephen Gilman's *The Novel According to Cervantes* (1989) took Riley's work a step further, reflecting upon how Cervantes adapted his theoretical sources (Aristotle, Horace, Boccaccio, Bandello and El Pinciano) to create a new, experimental narrative formula. The timely reminders of the "hard line" historicists that for two centuries after its publication, *Don Quixote* had been viewed as a funny, entertaining book, and that Romantic and post-romantic symbolic readings had pulled the text away from its satirical and burlesque intentions, were largely recognised by scholars, mainly in the USA, where a number of new approaches to Golden Age Studies generally have been developed over the past three decades. These have seen new questions arise – gender and sexuality, the self and the other, the political and social contexts of literary production and reception, historiography and its relationship to writing and poetry – which have been addressed in a variety of original ways. Inevitably Cervantine studies have benefited from this wider vision, which has opened new avenues of investigation across Cervantes' complete *oeuvre*.

The emergence of the notion of "cultural authority" as a body of theory around which these new approaches to Golden Age literature could be organised is a further important advance. The overarching theory can be applied to virtually any historical period and to the culture of any identifiable people or nation state. It posits that in all national cultures the combined forces of their history, language, institutions and power structures blend to form a dominant, or hegemonic, discourse[28] which establishes the parameters within which mainstream spiritual, moral, political and social ideas are developed and expressed. Inevitably, this dominant cultural voice reflects the interests and priorities of the governing classes and institutions of the national or ethnic group to which it belongs, constituting a source of authority which shapes the intellectual, spiritual and social life of the people and the artistic expression of it.

The theory of cultural authority is a very appropriate one to apply to writing in the Spanish Golden Age. As Marina Brownlee points out,[29] cultural authority in sixteenth- and seventeenth-century Spain can be clearly seen to be the product of an increasingly absolute monarchy, supported by a centralised bureaucracy and the power of a landed aristocracy whose interests were mainly aligned with those of the monarchy. The third contributing force was the spiritual and moral authority of the Catholic Church of Spain, behind which stood the shadow of the Inquisition. After the 1560s the Church of Spain became the spearhead of the Counter-reformation against the Protestant heresy of Northern Europe. All three of these institutions were able to call upon the country's founding myths of origin, legitimising chronicles, historiography and genealogy which were allied to the legacy of Ancient Greece, Rome and the Italian Renaissance to form a dominant mainstream that Brownlee calls the "positive" face of cultural authority, which marked the intellectual and artistic life of early modern Spain.

In the written culture of the Golden Age, particularly in poetry and the growing demand for narrative fiction that fed the rapidly expanding book trade, the overwhelming sign of this authority was what Brownlee refers to as "continuation," or the imitation[30] of classical forms and themes. In such a climate, wit and originality were judged mainly by the ways in which an author appropriated and adapted these models for the entertainment and instruction of his readers. Humanist scholarship, and the early sixteenth-century Church reform that it inspired in Spain, also had a radical effect on education, with new universities – the foremost being at Alcalá de Henares, Cervantes' birthplace – creating, by the later sixteenth century, a professional class in which women, as well as men, became avid readers. But Brownlee also reminds us of the parallel existence of a "negative" cultural authority; that is to say, "responses to the official culture which themselves both require a cultural authority of their own and problematise that authority, as it were by definition." In Golden Age Spain, these negative responses took on two distinct but complimentary aspects. On the one hand we see the self-questioning tendencies built into the dominant discourse; such as the self-reflexive, distorting vision and philosophical scepticism of the Baroque. On the other are the subversive counter-tendencies, or alternative discourses, that challenge mainstream assumptions in areas such as class, gender, race, imperialism and political power. These two elements functioned as a kind of moral and political dialectic which often reflected or advocated the ideas and attitudes of discriminated against minorities, whose critique of established authority was often disguised and "unofficial." By the second half of the sixteenth century the two most significant of these were probably the *conversos* and the humanists. As we have already seen, Cervantes had been given an early Humanist formation through his Jesuit schooling in Seville, and may also have been suspected of having *converso* roots, which would explain his failure to obtain any official post under the Crown, despite his record of military and administrative service to the state.

A further supremely important factor influencing the position of any group with heterodox or contestatory ideas and opinions was the system of state censorship. Scholars have, in the past, been reluctant to recognise its centrality in the formation of a critical response to the cultural authority of the time. It is now, however, recognised that, in literature in particular, the role of the censor was a vital formative factor. Writers, publishers and printers, if found guilty of producing and disseminating material that was considered to be religiously, morally or politically deviant in any way could incur severe punishment, including imprisonment and the confiscation of goods. All books published in Spain had to secure the legally required licences and privileges, including the censor's approval of the manuscript before publication, and books imported from abroad for sale were tightly controlled. However, matters did not end there. Books approved for publication were often re-reviewed at a later date and either expurgated or banned altogether, if the official view of their content had changed over a period of time. Similarly banned books could subsequently be reconsidered and the ban be lifted, so that they could be republished in full or redacted form. For these reasons, the search for the expression of heterodox or critical ideas became a game of literary cat and mouse between authors, publishers and the censor, or else the author opted for the underground dissemination of "unofficial" and anonymous manuscript texts. But his also could prove dangerous for those found in possession of them by the authorities. The frequent use of satirical modes, including parody, irony and hyperbolic fantasy, to mask subversive messages therefore becomes a feature of heterodox works for which publication in official, printed form was sought.

One aim of this study is to explore the extent to which Cervantes' masterpiece *Don Quixote* belongs to this subversive Golden Age literary tradition, as opposed to the critical view which placed the work – as did his contemporaries – wholeheartedly within the mainstream of orthodox literature; that is to say morally sound and unquestioning entertainment which hilariously debunked the novel of chivalry. The latter was already a dying genre. Only one new chivalresque novel was written in early seventeenth-century Spain, and though the existing ones continued to be read and were occasionally reprinted, the public was losing interest in the adventures of Amadís of Gaul, Belianis of Greece and the enchanted worlds of their numerous brethren. The genre was also under continuous attack from Platonists and moralists, who condemned its lack of truth and bad moral influence on gullible readers. Cervantes' ingenious parody knocked the nails securely into the chivalresque coffin, but this was only part of the book's intention, and its importance as a defining theme soon began to diminish, until in Part II, though the framework has to be maintained for the sake of the main protagonists, it has virtually ceased to have any significance. The fact is that *Don Quixote* was never a one-idea book, and if it had been it would, despite its brilliant humour, have long ago become dated and no longer read.

Over the past thirty years, Cervantes specialists, beginning with James Parr's *"Don Quixote." An Anatomy of Subversive Discourse* (1988), have begun to accept the existence of this deeper level of debate beneath an easily acceptable and largely uncontroversial parodic disguise. Increasingly their attention has been devoted to identifying the ways in which Cervantes has broached other moral and philosophical debates of his time, and the implications of these discussions for his readers. This interest is shown in near contemporary works such as Diana Armas Wilson's *Cervantes, the Novel and the New World* (2005), Roberto González Echevarría's *Love and the Law in Cervantes* (2005), Anthony Cascardi's *Cervantes, Literature and the Discourse of Politics* (2012) and Susan Byrne's *Law and History in Cervantes' "Don Quixote"* (2012).

It is, perhaps, the case that *Don Quixote's* many readers have, over the centuries, been more alive to the potential of this novel than its specialist commentators and critics. Certainly the mad knight and his gullible squire seem to have led generations of the book's audience through a vivid and credible historical landscape, showing the lives of all classes of people in early seventeenth-century Spain, the nature of their relationships with one another, the law and representatives of the state and Church, which were mediated through their reactions to Cervantes' two chief protagonists. Those readers, it is true, seldom pause in their eager page-turning to reflect on the contents of the innumerable conversations, lectures, arguments and discussions which intersperse the disparate, episodic adventures of the mad knight and his squire, nor do they tend to question the elaborate charade of Cervantes' narrative device, or the frequent switches of literary genre that blur the lines between the naturalistic observation of the picaresque, the idealistic conventions of the pastoral, and the palpably unreal intrigues of the Italian *novelle*.

Our tentative conclusion therefore has to be that Cervantes' skill in hiding his critical and moral judgements from the censor beneath a light-hearted façade of entertaining humour has been largely self-defeating. Left to themselves, the majority of his readers have devoured the novel – as he probably assumed they would – without digesting its philosophical riches, yet managing to catch glimpses of them that have contributed to the book's long-lasting attraction. Literary scholarship now appears to be on the brink of digging beneath the attractions of the finely-worded fun and entertainment to mine the ore that Sansón Carrasco claimed was so valued by those readers who had reached a certain age.

2

Cervantes' Library of Literary Ideas

Since Américo Castro's ground-breaking work *El pensamiento de Cervantes* (1925), attitudes towards Cervantes, and particularly *Don Quixote*, have undergone a gradual but radical change. To a large extent this has been shaped by the new departures in Golden Age studies taken by social and cultural historians, or literary scholars using similar historical methods. The academic study of the culture of the Spanish Renaissance and the Baroque was slow to recognise the effect on Spanish artists – especially writers – of the intellectual and religious climate of the times. The combined forces of the State and Church created a system of censorship (behind which lurked the regressive menace of the Inquisition) which not only sought to preserve the purity of the Catholic faith but also to reinforce the attempts of the monarchy to forge a unified, bureaucratised nation state out of a feudal aristocracy. The Golden Age nevertheless gave rise to an artistic and literary outpouring of astonishing quality and diversity. The ideas that shaped the intellectual climate of Spain in the first half of the sixteenth century derived from the classical legacy of Greece and Rome, mediated through Italian Renaissance humanism, which had been introduced to Spain at the end of the fifteenth century. From the beginning of the reign of Charles V, with his Burgundian upbringing, the tone was set by the great Renaissance scholars Desiderius Erasmus (1466–1536) and Juan Luis Vives (1493–1540), both of whom spent most of their lives in the Netherlands. Their work, and that of other humanists, was locked in a struggle with the declining traditions of medieval scholasticism that were so mercilessly satirised by Rabelais in *Gargantua* (1534).[1] But at the beginning of the sixteenth century, and again towards its end, two generations of Spanish scholars at the University of Salamanca also made important contributions to the new thinking.

The first generation of the "School of Salamanca" was mainly active between 1520 and 1560. One of its most prominent members, Francisco de Vitoria, died in 1546, but two of its number, Diego de Covarrubias y Leyva (1512–1577) the churchman and jurist, and Martín de Azpilcueta (1493–1586), a philosopher and moralist who formed the basic principles on which modern economics was founded, continued to teach for many more years. These men were all in holy orders, but their philosophical interests covered politics and government, morals, theology, law and economics. The second generation of the School flourished between 1565 and 1600, with which Fray Luis de Leon had close contacts in the 1570s. It numbered in its ranks the Jesuits Francisco Suárez (1548–1617), Luis de Molina (153–1600), Padre Juan de Mariana (1536–1624), the outstanding intellectual figure of the time, and the Dominican priest Tomás de Mercado (1525–1575) a theologian and economist who further developed the theories of the older Azpilcueta. The work of the Salamanca scholars, however, written in Latin and intended more for discussion by students and other scholars than for popular consumption, was less well known than it should have been, and attracted the constant attention of the Inquisition.

Political matters such as the practical education and upbringing of a Christian prince, statecraft and what constituted the *polis* and *res publica*, had, on the other hand, become part of public debate in Golden Age Spain. Their origins were Aristotle's *Politics*, Plato's *Republic* and Cicero's *De Re Publica*, though, in Cicero's thinking, politics and rhetoric – the language in which political ideas were expressed and argued – were virtually inseparable. Politics was also a practical extension of the virtuous life outlined in Aristotle's *Nicomachean Ethics*, which examined the role that the political "classes" should follow in order to enable the citizenry to lead a virtuous and moral existence. These ideas were influenced by Humanist teachings through books like Erasmus's *Institutio principis chistiani* (The Education of a Christian Prince) published in 1532 but written in 1515 for the young Charles I, Antonio Guevara's *El reloj de príncipes* (The Dial of Princes), Alfonso de Valdés' *Diálogo de Mercurio y Carón* (A Conversation Between Mercury and Charon) and his *Diálogo de las cosas ocurridas en Roma* (A Discussion on What Happened in Rome).[2] These became well-known works that were translated into French, English and German, thus earning serious recognition abroad for new Spanish culture and ideas.

Thus political thought was, at that time, a body of theory which sought to establish patterns and principles of governance that allowed the largest possible number of citizens or subjects to live according to Christian principles. It generated a debate throughout Western Europe during the Renaissance. For Spain it was particularly significant. The country had to negotiate the transition from feudalism to a centralised, early modern monarchy, while coming to terms with the totally new demands posed by an immense and far-distant empire that could barely be comprehended, and facing up to the long-standing racial and religious problems at home. Despite the challenges caused by these circumstances, the idea of a Christian people living under the just rule of a Christian monarch remained the guiding principle of political philosophy. Political ideas in Spain were also at moral odds with the cold-eyed, cynical reductionism of Machiavelli, for whom politics became the "science" by which a ruler achieved and, above all, maintained power. For Machiavelli, "reasons of state" overrode all other considerations of morals and justice. Written in 1513, *Il Principe* (The Prince) was not published until 1532, but then immediately became a subject for argument and condemnation on the part of the majority of moral and political thinkers, writers and even play-wrights across Europe.

Linked to this growing political discourse was a keenly contested debate on the nature of history and the role of the historian. It signalled a movement away from the tradition of the medieval chroniclers, with their combination of history, hearsay, folklore, legend and myth, to a more focused and neutral style of historiography, one which enjoined the historian to record *what actually happened*, and to avoid the adornments, additions and fictions that characterised the old chronicles. But what *did* actually happen was another matter, as was the point of view from which it was written down. Whose testimony was the reliable one? Usually, the history of any encounter was the version of the victors, but how was that of the vanquished different? How many valid points of view were there, and did they all constitute the record of what actually took place? Was López de Gomara's official version of the conquest of the New World, which justified imperial conquest, the true story? Or did the truth belong to Bartolomé de las Casas, whose account recorded the destruction of the native people not the triumph of imperial glory? Which evidence could therefore be trusted, which facts were relevant and which not? Whether, in the final analysis, historians are, through their discipline, any better guardians of "truth" than poets and writers of novels is a question which Cervantes constantly asks and tests in the course of *Don Quixote*.

The relationship between history and literature was thus a challenging and contentious subject. Historical events and episodes were integral to the subject matter of literature, as, for example, in the case of epic poetry, which was regarded as the highest form of literary expression and authority. The Renaissance epic, together with most other lyrical poetry in Golden Age Spain, also leant heavily upon the resources of classical myth for its rhetorical expression and imaginative power. Indeed, classical imitation, in form as well as content, was the basis for the sixteenth and seventeenth Spanish lyric, blended with the moral and spiritual imagery of Christianity. But many Neo-Platonists, among them numerous humanists, opposed the reading of "fiction" of any kind, whether imaginative prose or verse. They saw it as harmful to the moral development of people generally, but particularly dangerous for young women. Many of these attackers were churchmen, like the theologian and Platonist, Fr Pedro Malón de Chaide and the Jesuit, Gaspar de Astete, but their number also included outstanding humanist scholars like Juan Luís Vives and Juan de Valdés. Many of them, along with Saint Teresa of Ávila and Saint Ignatius Loyola, freely admitted to having read fiction for enjoyment in their misguided youth, but stated that they had come to regret this misspent time. Indeed, Fr Pedro Malón de Chaide claimed that the influence of poetry, such as that of Garcilaso de la Vega, the greatest Spanish lyricist of the sixteenth century, was just as obnoxious and inflammatory to the passions as the tales of chivalry. As Barry Ife observes:[3]

> Attacks [on imaginative literature] of undiminished virulence continued well into the second half of the following century [the seventeenth], when the vogue for the chivalresque was all but dead, showing that novels of chivalry bore the brunt of opposition which was directed, through them, at imaginative literature in general. Indeed, it is rare for a complainant to restrict himself to the novels of chivalry without making clear his wider reference by use of some catch-all formula embracing other equally vain and fictitious books of profanity and falsehood.

The language in which these denunciations were couched was often intemperate and extreme, the complaint being that books of fiction and poetry were trivial, and that since what they recounted had not happened – and probably could not – they were also lies; furthermore, they were falsehoods which inflamed the passions and undermined the reader's moral fibre.

The invention of printing and the consequent rapid expansion of the book trade in sixteenth-century Spain, created new forms of behaviour. The availability of cheap, printed books provided the numerous *hidalgo* class, together with an expanding urban bourgeoisie of commercial and professional people, with a new interest. As Barry Ife has also pointed out, the reader who, in 1508 (or thereabouts) read a printed copy of the chivalresque romance *Amadís de Gaula,* or *Carcél de amor,* would have been doing three previously unheard of things: he or she would be reading a printed book which they owned, they would be reading silently to themselves and they would be reading in the vernacular. Book production was a capital intensive process however, and like present-day publishers, Golden Age printers and booksellers had try to ensure sales by printing books for which they could anticipate a demand. This conservative tendency was the reason that so much matter was printed reflecting medieval tastes and interests in the Age of Humanism. A large trade in printed books written in Latin and imported from France, Italy and the Low Countries, also grew up to cater for Spanish scholars, clergy, doctors, lawyers and state officials.

For the majority of readers, the process was a necessary professional tool. But by the second half of the sixteenth century, a new and potentially troubling increase in diversionary reading had taken place. This new readership was as likely to be female as male. Reading was a sedentary occupation, and aristocratic and middle class women now had time to devote to it. As Ife observes, much of the material that writers of prose fiction offered the market was not particularly new, but the ways in which chivalresque romances and pastoral novels were being absorbed certainly was:

> In an atmosphere of silence and solitude [readers] recreated for themselves the thoughts and fantasies of others in a language which resembled their own, and which they culled from what they were used to thinking of *as the ultimate source of learning, the book.* [My italics]

Cervantes' preoccupation with the differences between history and literature, as well as with their similarities, is evident from the first chapter of *Don Quixote,* but is not fully apparent until the Moorish chronicler, Cide Hamete Benengelí, is revealed as the author of the account of the knight's adventures. His manuscript version is written in Arabic and translated into Spanish by a cooperative *morisco* for a small fee advanced by the Spanish bibliophile and antiquarian who, realising its probable content, has purchased it in the Toledo market place. He it is who Cervantes now makes into his main narrator, an assiduous if sometimes naïve editor, who frequently questions the veracity of the text from which he is working. This piece of narrative invention is made to serve a number of purposes which will be explored later on. But the first of them is the question it raises in the mind of the "discrete reader" concerning the reliability of actual historical sources and the point of view of the historian. The subversive, underlying question that Cervantes poses is that if history cannot always be regarded as a record that is reliable in every detail, the writing of historiography may be no more likely to reveal the "truth" than the composition of a poem or prose fiction. The comparative value of literal and figurative versions of what is true thereby becomes an unavoidable question.

The problematic nature of history also had direct and intimate connections with other matters, for example the law. A major debate was in progress across Europe on how far Roman Law, designed for a totally different age and society, could be made to apply to early modern Europe, as the mainly Italian jurists who advocated the *mos italicus* maintained. Or was it necessary to adapt historical legal codes before they could be used in the sixteenth century, as French jurists argued on behalf of the *mos gallicus*. This was an argument in which history and law became virtually inseparable. Indeed some juridical scholars maintained that to pronounce on the law, required the speaker to be first and foremost a historian. Susan Byrne argues very convincingly that the synergy between the two disciplines was not only a subject of broad intellectual debate in Italy, France and Spain in the sixteenth century, but that:

> History, as a preceptive commentary, and justice, as a thematic content, are two key elements of Miguel de Cervantes' *Don Quixote*, as evidenced in the author's multiple references to the contentious literary debates of his day, his use of formal and thematic aspects of contemporary historiographical questions and his protagonist's exploration of the meaning of justice.[4]

The gulf between justice and the administration of the law was clearly a question on which Cervantes was well qualified to reflect. Although he himself had no legal training, his paternal grandfather had been a well-known practitioner of the law and a magistrate, and the family as a whole had frequently found itself embroiled in legal cases over matters of money, or had fallen foul of badly administered legal measures. Furthermore, with numbers of ambitious young lawyers emerging from the universities in sixteenth-century Spain, Spanish society became increasingly given to litigation, particularly over rights to land and property.

The picture that is starting to take shape is one in which Cervantes' novel – far from being simply the funny and entertaining work it has so often been taken to be, in which we should search for little by way of background thought or deeper intentions – is beginning to seem like a work which takes on board all the main questions of its day. Not only are history, how it should be written, the reliability (or otherwise) of historians, and the nature of law and justice examined within it, but political ideas are also explored. The exact nature of Cervantes' political discourse in *Don Quixote* and its relation to literature has been studied by Anthony Cascardi with the same assiduity and detailed scholarship as that shown by Susan Byrne. As Professor Cascardi immediately points out, thinkers such as Hobbes, Locke, Montesquieu and Rousseau have been largely responsible for shaping our ideas of what politics is in the modern world, thus fashioning the kind of discourse which surrounds it. He, on the other hand, says he wishes

To explore the specific ways in which *Don Quixote*. . . . is itself involved in thinking about what the polis and political discourse might be. At stake is both a new understanding of one of the pillars of modern European literature and an alternative to "scientific" views of politics, an alternative that bears directly on how we ourselves might grasp the place of literature within the political sphere.[5]

This is, of course, no small undertaking! What Professor Cascardi might call "the interrelated places of literature and politics within the human sphere" is a question which the tormented history of the twentieth century strives continually to address, particularly in the inter-war years with the rise of Fascism and Communism in Europe. How poets and novelists were to speak about the overwhelming political circumstances of those times, and still maintain the aesthetic qualities which were necessary for serious literature, was a question many struggled with and few resolved. Cascardi goes on to say:

Taking *Don Quixote* as my pivotal exhibit, I hope to show that literature in the early modern age was regarded as having the potential to think both speculatively and, with critical scepticism, about the important political concerns of the day. . . . What is the nature of justice, and how can it be brought to bear on the historical world? Who ought to govern the state and how? What are the sources of authority that can legitimately underpin the force of law? What are the roots of political virtue? Where does the private world end and the public sphere begin?[6]

In his book *Cervantes and Modernity: Four Essays on "Don Quijote,"* E. C. Graf produces a similar list of intellectual discourses with which Cervantes has concerned himself in his novel, and which, he argues, account for its "modernity." Graf states that his intentions are:

[To trace] the novel's anticipations, even its projections, of modern discursive arguments for racial diversity, feminism, secularisation and materialism. These, it seems to me, are the principal axes on which to plot any evaluation of the novel's modernity.[7]

In his first chapter, Professor Graf examines Cervantes' treatment of Moors and Islam in *Don Quixote*. The second chapter appraises his attitude towards women, sexuality and marriage, while the third looks at the social and political implications of Cervantes' religious beliefs. The fourth and last chapter explores the implications of what today's readers would identify as Cervantes' "realism;" that is to say his attention to material detail regarding the people and happenings he describes, which is free of generic convention (except for the purposes of parody) and religiosity. Leaving aside – for the moment – consideration of how the themes he discusses contribute to his notion of *Don Quixote's* modernity, Graf"'s chapters add reinforcement to the work of a number of critics, including Byrne, Cascardi, El Saffar and González Echevarria who have examined the place of law, history, gender and sexuality, politics and ethics within the novel's pages.

On the other hand, the examination of Cervantes's ideas on literature, its purpose, and how it should be written and read have recently received a good deal of critical attention, particularly since the appearance of Edward Riley's *Cervantes's Theory of the Novel* in 1962.[8] Given that its humorous and satirical attack on the chivalresque romance and its readership gives Cervantes's novel its apparent *raison d'être,* the literary debates that the novel sets up can hardly be overlooked. Yet even this self-evident area of discussion is not without its puzzling aspects. Certainly the chivalresque romance had been the whipping boy of the anti-literature forces in sixteenth-century Spain. Its pseudo-fantasy medieval world, replete with knights, ladies, castles, giants, enchanters and magic in which the Amadises, Palmerins, Lisuartes and a host of other knight errant "superheroes" rampaged through the landscape in the service of their ladies, slaying enemies, righting wrongs and creating mayhem with impunity, were an all too easy target for Spain's moral crusaders who used them as the stalking horse for their attacks on literary art in general. Yet by the time Cervantes began to write Part I of *Don Quixote,* the chivalresque romance was on its last legs after a century of popularity. Only one more new novel of chivalry was written in Spain after 1600, and though the most famous were occasionally reprinted thereafter, its days – like those of the pastoral novel – were strictly numbered.

Why, then, should Cervantes take so much time and trouble to deliver a largely unnecessary *coup de grâce* to an already moribund genre of popular fiction? In some respects, he was doing precisely what the neo-platonist, would-be abolishers of literature were doing but for the opposite reason. His attack on the bad writing of the novels of chivalry, and misguided kind of reader that Don Quixote himself represented was, in fact. a well-concealed defence of literature in an increasingly intolerant society. So well-concealed in fact, that it slid easily under the moral radar of the censor who apparently saw nothing controversial or subversive in it. Additional gains, furthermore, could be derived from a protagonist who suffered from the kind of madness that convinced him he was a knight errant from the romances he had so obsessively devoured, yet remained, in all respects other than his obsession with knight errantry, a cultured, well-read man capable of conversing or debating with all-comers on equal terms. Cervantes' deluded knight was, indeed, a figure of fun. But the heroic code, sense of mission and courtly ideals of service and justice that his madness induced were nevertheless a challenge to the world of counterreformation Spain, with its rigid hierarchies, economic and social injustices, its privileged, self-seeking aristocracy, its corrupt and inefficient bureaucracy and an increasingly intolerant Church. Cervantes' humorous assault on the chivalresque romance, though genuine enough, was thus able to serve also as a mask for a much more fundamental critique of contemporary Spain, and the ideology which, in the name of imperial greatness and religious and racial purity, it imposed upon its people.

Cervantes was among the first generation of authors who became professional writers. Like the publishers, printers and booksellers who had harnessed the invention of the printing press to the needs of a commercial book trade, he was anxious to exploit the potential it offered him as a writer, and became a serious student of public tastes, literary themes, genres, style and the practice of writing. Cervantes's ideas on writing, like those of most educated people of the time, had a classical foundation. Their basis was Aristotle's *Poetics*, and *Rhetoric*, Plato's dialogues and Horace's *Ars poetica*. But Edward Riley's study of Cervantes' approach to the novel (1962) was notable for the fact that it called attention to the influence upon the author's literary ideas of El Pinciano's *Filosofía antigua poética* (1596).[9] Riley observes that Cervantes's theoretical notions of poetry, theatre and prose fiction – inasmuch as his early work reveals them to us – undergo a process of change and development from Part I of *Don Quixote* in 1605, through to the second part, the later *Novelas ejemplares* and the posthumously published *Persiles* (1617). Over this period we see a new and consistent focus upon key questions, such as the nature of "truth" in narrative fiction and poetry. This, Riley argues, comes from Cervantes having read and absorbed the lessons of the *Filosofía antigua poética,* and he observes:

> His [Cervantes'] concern with the nature of truth in literary fiction, which impinged on every major aspect of his theory [of the novel] evidently increases. So do his scruples, which are part of that concern, about the use of rhetorical language. At the same time, in the *Coloquio de los perros* (The Dialogue of the Dogs) and the *Persiles*, he shows an inclination to push experimentally towards the limits of what he considers novelistically permissable. . . . to explore the main domain of verisimilitude and to see to what extent the exceptional and the marvellous could be included in it.[10]

However, the precise directions in which Cervantes followed El Pinciano's theoretical lead are often far from obvious. The latter's aim, as a humanist scholar, was clearly to advocate that contemporary writers and poets return to classical principles, which he clarifies and expounds in *Filosofía antigua poética* by means of a fictional dialogue[11] between himself and two friends, named as Don Fadrique and Hugo. In this interchange, the author gives himself the role of the eager enquirer searching for enlightenment on matters literary and poetic from his better-informed interlocutors. A verbatim account of the three-way discussion is then sent to a fourth but absent friend, Don Gabriel, in a series of thirteen letters or *epístolas,* to each of which he responds with further observations, thus presenting arguments which can be seen to represent all sides of any question.

In typical aristotelean and horatian terms, El Piciano's characters stress that the basic function of poetry is to delight while providing instruction through *imitación* (imitation), whether this be of classical literary models or of nature in the broadest sense. Indeed, Hugo is made to assert:

> Poesía no es otra cosa que arte que enseña a imitar con la lengua o lenguaje. Y porque este vocablo 'imitar' podría poner alguna oscuridad, digo que imitar, remedar y contrahacer es una misma cosa, y con dicha imitación, remedamiento y contrahechura es derramada en las obras de naturaleza y de arte.[12]

> (Poetry is nothing other than an art that teaches imitation, either through speech or written language. And since the term "imitate" may cause confusion, I should add that to imitate, mimic or copy all amount to the same thing, and it is by successful imitation, mimicry or copying, that the process is spread throughout works of art and nature.)

Having identified imitation and verisimilitude as the necessary ingredients of poetry, El Pinciano places all imaginative writing in this category, claiming that metre is not a necessary element of the poetic mode. Nevertheless, where fictional narrative is concerned, whether in verse of prose, it consists of *fábula* (fable or story) which is the poem's "soul" and *lenguaje* (language), which is its "body." Fable is then conflated to include the narrative elements of both poetry – particularly the epic – and prose fiction, and is claimed to be of three kinds: *historias mentirosas* (lying stories) which make no attempt to embrace either imitation or verisimilitude. (Into this category he places the chivalresque novels, one of his very few direct references to contemporary writing.) The second category of fable is that which demonstrates a universal truth by means of the narration of a fiction. Into this category he places works such as Aesop's *Fables.* Lastly, there are the types of *fábula* which, on the basis of an element of historical truth, spin out numerous fictitious adventures and incidents; a category which could be said to apply to all realist narrative, particularly the modern historical novel. These clarifications are offered with the strict proviso that: "Las ficciones que no tienen imitación y verisimilitud no son fábulas sino disparates." (Fictions which display neither imitation nor verisimilitude are not stories but nonsense.)

There is good evidence that *Filosofía antigua poética,* the first major exercise in literary theory by a native Spaniard in the sixteenth century, directly influenced Cervantes' ideas on poetry and drama, but how far it also had a bearing upon his prose fiction is a more complex question. Certainly El Pinciano's book presented the writing of fiction – i.e., narrative which concerned imaginary characters, events and situations – in a positive light, much to the likely chagrin of its neo-platonist enemies. He also argues, through his characters, that the same event can be considered either *fábula* (a fictional story) or *historia* (history) according to whether it is written by an eye-witness or by an author who was not present and who has had to use his or her imagination to piece together second-hand information. Cervantes, on the contrary, was aware, as the debate about the truth of events in the Cave of Montesinos shows (*Don Quixote,* II, Ch. 23) that eye-witnesses are not always reliable; indeed, there can be as many versions of a happening as there are witnesses to behold it. How, then, is the evidence of a single witness to be treated in the absence of any corroborating versions? As Susan Byrne points out:

> López Pinciano's "fiction," or the detail of invention in creative writing is, for Cervantes, "lies." Whereas López Pinciano has the physical proximity of the writer a key to a determination of "fable" or "history," Cervantes makes the physical context of the written work key to its truthfulness.... To write 'fiction,' Cervantes joined dissonant yet pleasing 'lies' to legal conundrums and so made literary history."[13]

Cervantes persistently and ironically asserts that *Don Quixote* is a history. He creates a host of fictitious eye-witnesses who are party to its various episodes, and bases its innumerable fictions on the historical facts, laws, politics and social classes of his time. Cervantes makes no attempt, in fact, to maintain El Pinciano's careful distinction between history and poetry, or the three types of *fábula* on which he stipulates that imaginative literature turns. Instead he liberally mixes pure imagination with verisimilitude, and fuses fact with fiction in an inseparable combination which he nevertheless insists on calling a "true history." Indeed, his continual assertion that the story being told *is* a "history," together with his elaborate games with narrators, translators, editors and the ever-present Arab chronicler of the tale, Cide Hamete Benengeli, is arguably the longest running literary joke of all time. For some nine hundred pages it fuels the narrative energy of the book with its dizzying amalgam of genres and literary conventions, yet does so without adopting any of them as its own identifiable form.

So far, this chapter has focused upon the broader, formal currents of the cultural and intellectual environments in which Cervantes lived, and has reflected upon how they may have been drawn together by the writer in shaping *Don Quixote* and his other works. However, a substantial number of quite different factors – personal, informal, contemporary and experiential – undoubtedly played an equally important part in the book's formation, though they are more difficult to identify with certainty, especially at a distance of five centuries. Nevertheless some, which can be supported by biographical and historical evidence, announce themselves within the novel with some clarity. Thus while it can be argued that Cervantes' thoughts on justice and the law (no doubt coloured by his personal brushes with Spain's legal system, and those of other family members) straddle both the formal and informal streams of experience which have a bearing upon the novel, other very marked aspects of his work and ideas do not. For example, despite the tact and nuanced care with which his tolerant, balanced and humane attitude towards the *moriscos* and Islamic culture are expressed, and his skilful depiction of women and the role they occupy in seventeenth-century Spain, his views on both clearly run counter to the mainstream attitudes of his time and to official policy. These differences can be partly ascribed to his highly individual reaction to the five years he spent as a prisoner in Algiers, and the difficulties he witnessed the women of his own family – his mother, his sisters and his illegitimate daughter – having to undergo.

A similar kind of questioning ambivalence on Cervantes' part can be seen in his attitude to literature itself. His own preferences and instincts naturally allied him with the classically derived views of El Pinciano concerning the basic theory, aims and practice of literary art, and the defence that *Filosofía antigua poética* offered against neo-platonist attack. On the other hand, the Aristotelean distance from the world of literary and publishing activity that Cervantes inhabited solved very few of the writer's practical problems and challenges. Cervantes was, formed by his humanist education, a classicist and a probable supporter of the early sixteenth-century religious reform in Spain inspired by Erasmus. On the other hand, this humanist formation may also have accounted for his tendency towards scepticism, and his command of a humane but some-times devastating sense of irony. This led him also to a position where he consistently questioned the cultural authority that confronted him, seeking answers to his questions through literary experimentation. Furthermore, while possessing a marked gift for successful appropriation and imitation, he was also a clever and critical manipulator of established literary genres. It is for this reason that Cervantes' parodies of the situations and styles of the chivalresque novels are so funny and unflinchingly accurate in *Don Quixote*, making the object of their humour seem far more ridiculous than any amount of vehement moral condemnation could possibly have done. By reason of a similar familiarity and skilful process of reapplication, he interweaves pastoral episodes with the realistic detail of the unfolding narrative in the same way that he brings the conventions and personal relationships that characterise the Italian *novelle* into his experimental and ageneric novel.

The reality of the market for popular fiction when Cervantes began what would become Part I of *Don Quixote*, was that the chivalresque novel, which had for nearly a century been a mainstay of recreational reading, was virtually dead. Furthermore, interest in the pastoral romance, which had enjoyed a high point between the 1550s and 1580s in Spain, was rapidly declining. Indeed, Cervantes' own contribution to this genre, *La Galatea* (1585), was one of the last to be written. At the end of the 1590s, however, a new type of fiction, the picaresque novel, burst upon the scene with the publication of the two parts of Mateo Alemán's *Guzmán de Alfarache* (1599 and 1604). The book was a major commercial success, and the next thirty years saw the publication of nearly forty other picaresque narratives, including Francisco de Quevedo's *El Buscón*, Vicente Espinel's *Marcos de Obregón*, and *La pícara Justina*, attributed to Francisco López de Úbeda.

The picaresque genre seems to have been uniquely Spanish in origin, and its popularity – some three decades – was relatively short, but its influence was still apparent in France, England and Germany in the early eighteenth century. Its roots have been traced back to Fernando Rojas's realistic portrayal of low life in *La Celestina* (1499–1502), while the title of the first picaresque novel has rested happily upon the shoulders of the intriguing and anonymous *Lazarillo de Tormes* (1553–4). There are, nevertheless, some key differences between *Lazarillo* and the avalanche of picaresque novels that followed it forty-five years later. *Lazarillo de Tormes* is an Erasmian satire that takes the form of a highly selective and self-justifying account of his life given by Lázaro, the first-person narrator and protagonist of the story, to a person in authority referred to simply as "Vuesa Merced." In it he defends his life of dubious morality and petty crime, pleading a deprived childhood, irresponsible parentage and the necessity to live on his wits from the age of six in order to survive the bad treatment he received from a succession of exploitative masters. The majority of these are churchmen of different kinds, and the criticisms, direct and implied, of the conduct of the clergy are pointed. At the end of Lázaro's testimony it is finally disclosed that it has been drawn up in answer to the charge that he has connived in his wife's conduct as the mistress of the Archpriest of San Salvador, Toledo, his erstwhile patron in securing the lowly public appointment of town crier. The book was very popular and went through a number of editions, but its criticisms of the clergy resulted in its being banned in 1559 and placed on the Index of Prohibited Books. In 1574, the ban was partially rescinded, and a heavily censored edition was published from which chapters 4 and 5 had been removed altogether.

Common to *Lazarillo de Tormes, Guzmán de Alfarache,* and virtually all other picaresque works, is the use of a first person narrator who has become a rogue and trickster and leads a life of petty crime on the edges of Spanish society. Born on the wrong side of the tracks, picaresque anti-heroes (and occasional anti-heroines) inevitably find that their subsequent attempts to cross over lead to failure, either through personal weakness or misfortune, and are set about by the bad examples of those who should know better. Some *pícaros* are defiant and unrepentant, like Lázaro and Ginés de Pasamonte, the galley slave released by the mad knight in *Don Quixote*, Part I, Chapter 22, who claims he is writing his autobiography, beside which all other picaresque adventures will pale to insignificance. Others, like Guzmán de Alfarache, are – or at least seem – repentant, and take every opportunity to give the reader a moral lecture after every misdeed or deception they admit to. In Lázaro we are shown a picaresque protagonist who, when his testimony ends, claims he has reached the high point of his life and has, by "arrimándose a los buenos" (snuggling up to the virtuous) established himself as a respectable citizen. The lot of the later *pícaros* was completely different. The moral lesson that all these novels preached was that crime does not pay and cheats do not prosper. The life stories of virtually all of their protagonists are told at a time when they are facing punishment, sentenced to the galleys, a term in gaol or making a hasty getaway to the Americas to escape justice.

Cervantes was not attracted by this kind of narrative fiction. The first person narrator greatly reduces the breadth of vision and multiple perspectives that he developed with such success in *Don Quixote*. However, the way in which the first person protagonist thrusts the reader into the role of judge seems to have impressed him. Barry Ife observes that the picaresque marks the way in which "the author as creator" hands over his narrative responsibilities to the "protagonist as narrator," thereby changing the reader from a passive consumer to an active participant in the story.[14] "This is my story," the *pícaro* seems to be saying, "and it is up to you, reader, to decide the rights and wrongs of my situation, my culpability or otherwise!" In this, the picaresque differs from many of the other literary genres which spoke to a largely passive reader, whose role was simply to listen and marvel. But the reader of a picaresque adventure is drawn into it willy-nilly, not least by having to decide on the trustworthiness of the narrator as the sole witness to the events of his life. It is precisely questions of this kind that Cervantes asks of the reader of *Don Quixote*. It is quite clear from the Prologue to Part I of the novel that he had decided to demand a degree of active participation and judgement from his *lector discreto*, and we witness his narrator and editor at times questioning the evidence of Cide Hamete's history, and even passing over the responsibility for a decision to the reader, while he proceeds with the story.

Numerous other instances can be taken into account where the author's perceptions can be seen to respond to historical circumstances. From what we can deduce from biographical evidence, the strain of Cervantes' exhausting labours as a Government official, first as a commissioner for military supplies and then as a tax collector, meant that whether or not *Don Quixote* was begun while its author was in prison in Seville, the book grew out of a gathering sense of disappointment, frustration, disillusionment and hardship, to which the continually impecunious state of the Cervantes family added. But Cervantes probably suffered most from the erosion of the ideal of service to his king and country which had inspired his years as a soldier in Italy and a prisoner in Algiers. This had won him neither reward nor recognition however, and even his two applications for a government post in the administration of the American colonies had been refused. Furthermore, the nationally humiliating failure of the Armada, which he had worked so hard to help provision and prepare, had laid bare the level of inefficiency, corruption, greed and personal ambition with which Spain's bureaucracy was riddled. This revelation had led to a wave of anger and bad feeling throughout the country – a sense of betrayal from within – which affected even the reputation of the ageing Philip II until his death in 1598. The swift decline of Spain's national fortunes led inevitably to questioning and pessimism. The fear that God had deserted the Spanish cause fuelled both the scepticism and mystic passion of the Counterreformation, turning the country's gaze inward.

Cervantes' outlook and education had been formed by the open-minded, optimistic and reforming ideas of late Renaissance humanism. But even as he was growing up the Inquisition had moved to suppress Protestant adherents in Seville and Valladolid, whose leaders were arrested and executed for heresy in 1559. The Catholic mystic sect, the *alumbrados*[15] (enlightened ones) were denounced for the first time as early as 1525, and continued to be harassed by the Inquisition until the mid seventeenth century. The final response of the Vatican to Protestantism, inscribed in the edicts of the Council of Trent in 1565, had been shaped by the militancy of the Spanish Church, and saw the creation in Spain of a still stricter regulation of the religious, intellectual and artistic life of the country, whose moral climate became more intolerant, inflexible and repressive.

The views of modern scholars are divided on the precise nature and extent of the influence the Inquisition exercised upon Spanish artists, writers and intellectuals in the sixteenth and seventeenth centuries. Despite the documented account of the history of the Holy Office written by Fr. Juan Antonio Llorente (1756–1823), and the later ground-breaking account by the American scholar, historian and publisher Henry Charles Lea (1823–1909),[16] *A History of the Inquisition in Spain* (Macmillan & Company, London, 1906–7, 4 vols.) modern scholars have been reluctant to attribute to the Inquisition any specific impact upon the intellectual and cultural life of Spain. Like Llorente and William H. Prescott before him, Lea saw the Inquisition as: "An engine of immense power, constantly applied to the furtherance of obscurantism, the repression of thought, the exclusion of foreign ideas and the obstruction of progress," which at its worst amounted to "an example of theocratic absolutism" which hastened Spain's decline from the mid-seventeenth century on.

The present-day scholarly reservation is, perhaps, understandable in view of the apologist arguments put forward by no less a figure than Marcelino Menéndez Pelayo, who has questioned Lea's findings as part of the "black legend" of the Inquisition, and who points out that it is diffi-cult to regard a literary culture that has produced a Cervantes, a Lope, a Góngora and a Quevedo as backward or repressed.[17] A revisionary view of the Inquisition was later put forward in 1965 by Henry Kamen, who argued that the Holy Office had never wielded the power that critics had claimed it to have, and that its judgements and punishments were remarkable for their infrequency and relative leniency after 1550.[18] Indeed, after an initial outburst of activity against the *conversos*, protes-tant sympathisers and the *alumbrados* in the first half of the sixteenth century, the Inquisition had little direct influence – or so it was argued – on the intellectual and artistic life of Spain.

As a major representative of the new post-1975 approach to the study of the Holy Office, Angel Alcalá has pleaded for an end to the adversarial critical and revisionist views of the past, and a balanced, "scientific" process of research which depends not only on documentation (despite its secrecy, the Inquisition kept excellent records) but also on the effect of the institution on the lives of ordinary Spaniards. These enquiries must also take into account not only the records of the various Tribunals and *autos de fe* of the Inquisition, but also the fear and suspicion that they spread in a world where people could be secretly denounced and impris-oned without being told of the charge against them, and subjected to interrogation and even torture. The "familiars," or informers and agents, employed by the Inquisition were hated and feared by many people.

Furthermore, the public shaming of anyone found guilty of transgressing the Inquisition's rules – for example being forced to wear the *san benito* – almost certainly spelt the ruin of a guilty individual and his or her family. The resulting climate of fear was, apparently, one that the Holy Office created and maintained as a matter of policy. A position of scholarly distance is not easy to maintain, therefore, when investigating the social and personal effects of involvement with the Inquisition. Alcalá is, however, no apologist. The Inquisition, he states, was: "The Spanish form of social control by the state . . . which may be recognised as a deplorable and shameful historical constant, embodied in multiple versions of the inquisitorial mind in the present day."[19] Spanish culture, spirituality and politics have all been diverted from their probable natural paths by the Inquisition, which nevertheless allowed many of the positive elements of Spain's Golden Age to flourish.

Humanism suffered a setback at the hands of the Inquisition in the early sixteenth century, but did not die out. Its early supporters, like Antonio de Nebrija (1440–1522), Antonio Guevara (1481–1545), Juan de Valdés (1500–1541), his twin brother Alfonso de Valdés (1500–1532) and Diego Hurtado de Mendoza[20](1503–1575) were eminent men, aristocrats and scholars, some of whom also held important political, diplomatic or ecclesiastical posts under Charles V. Others, such as the classical scholars and philologists Hernán Núñez de Toledo y Guzmán (1475–1553) and Francisco Sánchez de la Brozas (El Brocense) (1523–1600) occupied a succession of university chairs, while Alonso López (El Pinciano), whose influence on Cervantes' literary ideas we have already discussed, was an eminent physician. Thus beneath the surface of Spanish society, the broad principles of humanism – good classical scholarship, tolerance and open-mindedness, and a strong Christian moral code – lived on in Spain's universities and among its educated and professional classes, and continued to underpin moral philosophy in Spain throughout the seventeenth century.

Even so, individual humanists were often targeted and denounced for heterodox ideas. The *Diálogos* of the brothers Valdés suffered a speedy prohibition, and trials occurred of humanists from the University of Alcalá, including the Chancellor, Pedro de Lerma, Juan de Castillo, a Greek scholar burnt at the stake in 1537, while Juan de Vergara, another Hellenist and friend of Erasmus, was imprisoned for four years. A generation later, Humanists like Fray Luis de Leon, Arias Montano, Gaspar de Grajal, Martín Martínez de Cantalapiedra and Alonso Gudiel – all with Jewish ancestry incidentally – were jailed. (Grajal and Gudiel died in prison, while the celebrated El Brocense, died under house arrest while being investigated by the Inquisition. One strand of humanism however, the Erasmian tradition of satirical social and religious criticism, which was opposed to war and conquest, and argued for greater justice and religious reform, virtually went "underground." The authors of *Lazarillo de Tormes*, the satire *El Crotalón* (1553?), now attributed to Cristobal de Villalón, and of *Viaje de Turquía* (who may or may not be one of Cristobal de Villalón, Andrés de Laguna or even Juan Ulloa de Pereira) all resorted to anonymity, pseudonyms and the circulation of their works in manuscript to avoid the wrath of the Church and the censor for what were then regarded as dangerously heterodox and subversive ideas and criticisms.[21]

The Inquisition was introduced into Castile in 1478, as a result of a petition to Pope Sixtus IV by the Catholic Monarchs, and held its first *auto de fe* in 1481 in Seville. The Holy Office thus came into being as much for political and economic reasons of state as those of religious and spiritual orthodoxy, and its aims and interests remained almost indivisible from those of the monarchy thereafter. Its chief characteristics were the dogmatic nature of its normative principles, the secrecy of its actions and coercive structure, a judicial system which placed the assumption of guilt upon the accused, requiring him or her to prove their innocence, and the defamatory nature of its sanctions. The state-sanctioned system of censorship, which was dominated and controlled by the Inquisition by the mid sixteenth century, was an automatic response to criticism by a centralised monarchy intent on exercising social and religious control over a society heavily affected by social, racial and religious conflict. It was also a reaction to the diffusion and democratisation of knowledge, which suddenly became possible as a result of the printing press and the book trade based upon it. As Virgilio Pinto points out: "Censorship expresses the conflict between established power and its dissidents over this basic instrument for the diffusion of ideas."[22]

With the fight against dissidence, secular and religious, as a shared aim of both the state and the Inquisition at the beginning of the sixteenth century, the book became an object of suspicion and a target for those who saw it as a means of disseminating heterodoxy – particularly the ideas of Luther and Calvin. The Inquisitors took the position that a suspected book was a "mute heretic," and could be tried in much the same way as an individual person.[23] If a tribunal of the Holy Office found a book contained culpable error, it was publicly denounced and placed on the *Index of Prohibited Books*. Before 1559, this might entail a book being banned completely, and therefore lost. The introduction of expurgation half way through the sixteenth century saved many works from disappearance, since they could be republished with their offending passages deleted. (This happened to *Lazarillo de Tormes*, which was banned in its entirety in 1559, but reprinted in 1574 in an expurgated edition.)

As we have noted, the years between 1570 and the 1590s saw the Inquisition begin a second phase in its battle with humanism. In the course of it, a number of scholars of national standing were put on trial on various pretexts. As Angel Alcalá shows, this attack was aimed largely at philosophers, theologians, writers of medical treatises and philologists, and the effect that the trials had on scholars is recorded in a number of extant documents. In a letter to the great Spanish Humanist Luis Vives, enjoying the comparative freedom of the Low Countries, Rodrigo Manrique, nephew of the famous poet and son of the Inquisitor General observes:

> It is increasingly evident that no-one will be able to cultivate *belles lettres* in Spain without there immediately being found in him a multitude of heresies, errors and Judaic defects. In this way silence has been imposed upon the learned and a tremendous terror has been inspired in those who would have called themselves scholars.

Thirty years later, López Pinciano wrote to the historian Jerónimo Zurita in similar terms:

> Worst of all is that [the inquisitors] would have no-one develop an interest in these human letters because of the dangers, they say, that are in them: just as a humanist would alter a text by Cicero, he might alter the Holy Scriptures. . . . These and other similar stupidities upset me and take away my desire to continue.[24]

In Spain, the Holy Office, which recognised scholasticism as the only acceptable philosophical system, was particularly energetic in its opposition to new ideas such as scepticism and natural philosophy. Consequently, Montaigne's *Essays*, Charron's *De la sagesse* (On the Subject of Wisdom) and Bacon's *Novum Organon* were all placed on the *Index Expurgatorius*, though only the *Novum Organum* was actually expurgated. The other two remain technically banned. More significantly, the most influential work of Spanish scientific thought of the sixteenth century, Juan Huarte de San Juan's *Examen de ingenios para las ciencias* (1575) (The Scientific Examination of Human Minds) was prohibited by the Holy Office, despite its Europe-wide reputation which saw it translated into six languages, The Jesuit theologian, historian and political thinker Padre Juan de Mariana (1536–1624) was kept under house arrest by the Inquisition, and two of his works, *De morte et immortalitate* (On Death and Immortality) and *De mutatione monetiae* (On Change in Money) were placed on the *Index Expurgatorius*.[25]

Cervantes himself, whilst imbibing a core of humanistic ideas and moral principles, was born at the crucial mid-point of the sixteenth century that saw the beginning of the changes which the

Counterreformation ushered in as part of its fight against Protestantism, and the reassertion of the purity of the dogma of the Church of Rome. These coincided with the decline in Spain's political and military fortunes which followed almost on the heels of the high points of the victory over the Turks at Lepanto in 1571 and the annexation of Portugal in 1580. As a soldier and veteran of Lepanto, Cervantes had been a patriotic idealist, who hoped that his courage and loyalty would be recognised and rewarded. His five-year incarceration in Algiers effectively prevented this outcome. Yet it seems to have been an invaluable, formative experience, in which Cervantes learned a good deal about his fellow Christians, and a good deal more about his Moorish captors. He returned to Spain in 1585 with a marked understanding of and respect for Muslim culture, which was unusual in Golden Age Spain. His subsequent struggles as an official in two of the more unpopular and difficult areas of government service – military provisioning and tax collection – not only saw the gradual erosion of his ideals, but coincided with the growing scepticism and spiritual unease which marked the changing intellectual climate of what we now call the Baroque.

In his study of the Spanish Baroque entitled *Arts of Perception,* Jeremy Robbins observes that:

> A preoccupation with knowledge and perception is the defining feature of the Spanish Baroque ... what all Spaniards share during the early modern period is a view of human perceptual fallibility and a concomitant belief in the need for sustained rational enquiry and perceptual scrutiny prior to any commitment to the external world, whether in word or deed.[26]

The influences of scepticism and stoicism, which, despite the efforts of the Inquisition and the censorship, fed these attitudes and perceptions, turned upon the contrasting polarities of *ser/parecer* (being and appearance) and *engaño/desengaño* (deception and clear-sightedness), which are mirrored in much of the art of the period. These antinomies shaped the terms of virtually every discourse, exercising a strong influence over questions of agency, which Robbins defines as morality, reasons of state, trust and honour. Spain was thus well aware of the challenge that scepticism posed to the moral and religious certainties of the time and the largely Aristotelean intellectual *status quo* of the Spanish Renaissance, and its thinkers engaged in the process of embracing and exploring its boundaries and accommodating to them. By comparison, one of the contentions of this study is that in *Don Quixote,* and notably in Part II, the reader is offered a work of fiction that stands as an experimental "space" in which the discourses that constituted the key intellectual issues of the time – truth, falsehood and perception, morality, justice, history, politics, gender relations and artistic freedom – are discussed and tested in a parallel world mirroring our own, but in which fact and fiction have been deliberately and inseparably mixed.

This is a considerable claim to make on behalf of both the book and its author. It immediately gives rise to the question of why it has taken until the end of the twentieth century for scholars to begin to arrive at this kind of assessment of the novel's intentions. The answer is a complex combination of suppositions. Of course, different ages see texts in different lights, according to their respective historical and social circumstances. But the lights also change according to the ways in which critical tools develop, and the guidance that scholarly activity can sometimes give to readers. What the reader expects from him or herself is also a factor. Some literary texts are written for a largely passive audience simply to absorb and enjoy unquestioningly. Others demand a much more active, critical and questioning role from the reader, and it is this kind of reading that modern authors and present-day education systems tend to encourage. All this adds up to the rather unsatisfactory answer that better critical standards, and a growing body of better informed and educated readers, have combined to question the established view of *Don Quixote* as solely a brilliantly funny and imaginative piece of entertainment. A student once commented to me: "I can't believe that a man would take so much time and effort to write a thousand pages of a story over a period of twenty years, if it was just intended to be commercial entertainment." It is a view I completely agree with. But how was it that the long-held view of *Don Quixote* as simply a brilliantly funny, imaginative *tour de force*, which delighted rather than informing the reader, gained such a lengthy acceptance?

The answer to this second question is as speculative as that of the first, and consists of a similar combination of probable factors. Not the least of these was the ten-year gap between the publication of Part I of the book in 1605 and Part II in 1615. A critical response to Part I had therefore been formed and celebrated, both in Spain and abroad, some years before the second part appeared. The first part of the story is notable for its humorous and at times light-hearted tone. It presents the reader with generous helpings of parody of the style, characters and events of the chivalresque romances, and dwells in detail on the slapstick but rueful comedy of the knight's beatings and misadventures and the gullibility of his squire. But beneath this, there lies from the outset a veiled debate on writing, artistic freedom and responsibility and literary politics, whose most evident expressions are the examination and destruction of Don Quixote's library in Chapter VI, his lengthy debate on writing and literature with the Canon of Toledo near the book's end in Chapters XLIX and L, and the novel's continual process of ironical subversion – itself at times hilarious – of the very processes on which it exists as a piece of fictional narrative. In his book *"Don Quixote": An Anatomy of Subversive Literature*, James Parr goes as far as to question the accuracy of the label "novel" for the book, preferring instead to classify it as a Menippean satire. He goes on to say:

> *Don Quixote* is a potentially subversive document because it calls into question not only the authority of books of chivalry, but also of translations and . . . of history itself as a reliable medium for truth.[27]

and points out that this level of questioning of the text can even be made to apply to the Bible, which Don Quixote claims "cannot err a jot from the truth." The Bible offers one of the greatest examples in the world of faith in translation, one that *Don Quixote* shares by purporting to be history.

Yet up until very recently, scholars have been reluctant to explore the possibility that Cervantes sought not only to entertain, but use the humour and novelty of his story as a vehicle through which he could engage with the main intellectual and cultural debates of his time, and do so in a way that camouflaged any heterodoxy of thought that might attract the scrutiny of the censors. The whole topic of censorship in early modern Spain, and its impact upon cultural production, has tended to be overlooked or oversimplified. It is without doubt a mistake to regard literary censorship as a means whereby privileged classes and dominant institutions limit peoples' freedom of expression, and consequently their intellectual and cultural potential, solely in order to maintain themselves in a position of power. As Julian Weiss points out, definitions of censorship should be "historically specific and epistemological." In early modern Spain he suggests: "Literary censorship was less a matter of denying liberty of speech than a legitimation or delegitimation of specific discursive practices."[28] In practical terms, however, the difference is somewhat academic! This carefully distanced, historically specific approach to censorship may be necessary for a literary or cultural historian, but the living author will inevitably take a different view of the blocking or prohibition of his or her ideas by a system of censorship. He or she is therefore often involved in a risky game, where strategies of concealment, such as ambiguity, irony and even obfuscation, are needed to avoid intervention by the censor, and play a major part in what Professor Weiss calls "fashioning the discourses." In this respect, he says of *Don Quixote*:

> Cervantes' novel provides at once the most adequate expression of, and challenge to, the ideological role not of the state, but of *the subject of the state*

[my italics]. . . when confronted by a "classic", in particular the recently constituted vernacular classic.[29]

The degree to which a text sets in motion the dialogue between the past and the present is almost certainly the key characteristic of the vernacular classic as Professor Weiss describes it. As far as present-day readers are concerned, it is precisely this aspect of *Don Quixote* that impresses them most, since it appears to account for the book's "modernity"; namely, how far the dialogues and situations it contains succeed in raising comparisons with, and questions about, today's post-industrial world.

If, as many modern scholars suspect (and some even assert) Cervantes was descended from a *converso* family, and possessed a well-established humanist education and outlook, it would have been natural for him to be particularly careful about writing anything that might have resulted in even a minor brush with the censors. Proof of Jewish ancestry would have been necessary before any direct discriminatory action could have been taken against him, but even unproven suspicion could be enough to damage a man's professional or social prospects, and we have a certain amount of circumstantial evidence that he might have suffered in this way. A brief glance, furthermore, at Cervantes' prose *oeuvre*, particularly *Don Quixote* and the *Novelas ejemplares*, is sufficient to show that the prohibitions, pressures and restrictions of Spain's system of censorship were seldom far from the author's mind. Indeed, they probably contributed to what he wrote and how he wrote it, almost as much as the personal experiences and educational and moral formation that have until recently been the preferred focus of scholarly attention.

The following chapters will explore different aspects of *Don Quixote* in detail, and will examine, as part of that study, specific instances of calculated censorship evasion on Cervantes' part. Nevertheless, an interesting clue to the author's intentions and literary strategy in this respect can be found in the ambiguous and satirical Prologue to Part I of the novel, in which the author receives the heavily tongue-in-cheek advice of a fictitious friend which he claims he has followed in writing the book. In the Prologue, the author laments to his friend that his plain and unvarnished "history" of Don Quixote de la Mancha lacks all the trappings that contemporary books seem to require; namely introductory poems by famous people, marginal notations and footnotes, and plentiful references to classical and other learned authors. How, he asks, can his work give the reader confidence in the writer's seriousness and knowledge? His friend's response is that this is all authorial vanity, which can easily be added by a number of simple ploys and deceptions, which he will undertake on Cervantes' behalf. These, however, he observes are completely unnecessary, not least because readers never bother to check the accuracy of what they read. He goes on:

> Solo tiene que aprovecharse de la imitación en lo que fuere escribiendo, que, cuanto ella fuere más perfecta, tanto mejor será lo que se escribiere.[30]

> (All that is necessary is to make use of imitation in what you write, because the more perfect the imitation, the better what you write will be.)

The classical principle of imitation having been established, the anonymous friend continues with some further stylistic advice:

> Y pues que vuestra escritura no mira a más que a deshacer la autoridad y cabida que en el mundo y en el vulgo tienen los libros de caballerías, no hay para qué andéis mendigando sentencias de filósofos, consejos de la Divina Escritura, fábula de poetas, oraciones de retóricos, milagros de santos sino procurar que a la llana, con palabras significantes, honestas y bien colocadas, salga vuestra oración y período sonoro y festivo, pintando en todo lo que alcanzádes y fuere posible vuestra intención, dando a entender vuestros concetos sin intricarlos y escurecerlos.

> (And since what you are writing seeks only to undo the authority and influence that books of chivalry exercise in this world and among the uneducated, there is no need to go begging maxims from philosophers, counsel from the Holy Scriptures, poets' fantasies, orators' speeches or saints' miracles, but to attempt to proceed in a straightforward, plain way, using words that are meaningful, honest and well-placed, so that what you say emerges harmoniously and enjoyably, and is depicted to the best of your ability and intention, so that your ideas are understood without making them complex or obscure.)

This is a cleverly conceived piece of special pleading designed to pacify even the most suspicious of censors. A uniquely experimental piece of imaginative fiction is presented as a plain, unadorned history of a famous Manchegan knight, which nevertheless has as its aim the destruction of the chivalresque romance, a genre which had no classical antecedents or models, and was a sitting target that had already been shot to pieces by the country's literary and moral critics. It was a very safe disguise for other things that Cervantes was also seeking to achieve with the book. The plainness and honesty of expression, the "right words in the right places" in fact, to which Cervantes also lays claim, may be true enough at face value of the text. But one that can be read in so many ways by different types of reader – a claim Cervantes also makes for it in the Prologue – is likely to contain more than its author claims on its behalf.

Indeed, many puzzling aspects of *Don Quixote* may be attributable, at least in part, to the strategy he devised to divert or mislead the judgement of the censors. This is certainly one of the purposes that the book's consistently ironic tone, its ambiguity and endlessly inventive experimentation might be seen to fulfil. The narrative complexities so carefully studied by El Saffar and Parr, themselves a major part of the experimental and subversive nature of the book, are now generally understood to raise three questions. The first is to place a general doubt in the reader's mind about the reliability of the historical record and the nature of historiography. The reader is constantly reminded that he or she is perusing a "history" whose sources are simultaneously revealed as being questionable – both the accuracy of the Arabic original and the translation of it into Spanish. The second question arises from the way the book blurs the borderline between history and imaginative literature, creating a hinterland in which fiction may be seen to reveal more about the truth of human existence than history. As James Parr remarks:

> Don Quixote is a potentially subversive document because it calls into question not only the authority of books of chivalry, but also of translations and. . . . of history itself as a reliable medium for truth . . . [but] the potential for subversion extends further still.[31]

Indeed, Parr goes on to suggest that it extends as far as the text of the Bible, whose New Testament passed into modern vernacular knowledge through versions in Aramaic, Greek and Latin, and is a monument to trust in translation. Thirdly, through a process of self-reflexive irony (which at times plays outrageously with the dignity of the reader) Cervantes calls into question the status of imaginative writing and how it should be read, at the same time undermining the validity of the very text he is writing.

A book that so humorously and ironically subverts itself in this way is hard to pin down, both for the censor and the reader; particularly so when it lays claim to an easy target for parody and satire recognised by all, and does so in a style that is engaging and harmonious. Furthermore, its two main protagonists are a cultivated but insane hidalgo and an illiterate, gullible peasant, who are both portrayed as figures of fun, and whose attempts to understand one another across their cultural gulf, despite their innumerable shared conversations and adventures, never quite succeed. Any injudicious remarks or questionable events that might have set alarm bells ringing in the censor's mind could therefore be explained as the ramblings of the mad or the ignorant in circumstances their shortcomings had led them to misjudge. Thus, though both knight and squire change as their adventure progresses from Part I to Part II, the fiction of

Don Quixote's selective madness is maintained throughout. Part I sees him largely trapped in his own unsuccessful attempts to impose a defunct, chivalresque code upon the reality of an emerging nation state, while Part II sees the society he is flouting take its revenge by playing along with his delusions for its own amusement, setting up for the purpose a world of coarse make-believe in which he and Sancho are deceived into living out their fantasies.

Yet there had to be closure at some point. Cervantes was clearly not considering a third part to his story. Indeed, in *Los Trabajos de Persiles y Segismunda*, he was writing the book he thought would prove his finest work, even as he brought Part II of *Don Quixote* to an end. Neither was he willing to risk the appearance of a second spurious sequel by another would-be Avellaneda. He had very little alternative therefore but to kill off his famous protagonist. But significantly he turned this artistic necessity to a very practical end. Don Quixote might have been given a "heroic" death, still fighting to restore the code of chivalry to an unheeding world. Instead, defeated by the Knight of the Mirrors, Don Quixote returns home brooding on his failure, falls ill, recovers his sanity and on his death bed repudiates all he has done under the influence of his madness. He dies as Alonso Quijano, reconciled to the world he has challenged, to God and the Catholic Church, having forsworn Don Quixote and all his deeds as vanity and deception. As Ryan Prendergast points out, this return to social and moral order, which was also a feature of the endings of the *comedias*, can also be read as a final concession to the censor. After all, what better way to rebut any objection by the authorities than to point to the mad knight's final repudiation of everything he has up till then represented?[32]

Two additional points are worth making at this juncture. The first concerns Angel Alcalá's comments on the relatively tiny number of proceedings taken by the censors against works of creative writing and their authors after 1570.[33] Neither the *Index of Prohibited Books,* nor the edicts that were issued in between its various editions after 1559, give details of the criteria that governed the decisions of the tribunals, from outright prohibition to minor expurgations, or their interpretation. The rules were sometimes precise – for example, Rule 7 ordered the prohibition of any book that dealt with lascivious or erotic subject matter – but they were often of a general kind that allowed considerable latitude for interpretation. A handful of documents exist containing unofficial suggestions for how the Inquisition should treat creative literature, the most complete being Zurita's *Dictamen acerca de la prohibición de obras literarias por el Santo Oficio,* (Report on the Prohibition of Literary Works by the Holy Office) which is thought to have pre-dated the *Index* of 1583. This document reflects a tolerant perspective towards literature at precisely the time when the Inquisition was renewing its onslaught against scientific thought and scepticism. Whatever the attitude of the Holy Office at that time, it was lenient enough to enable the outburst of poetry, novels, plays, short fiction and essays that characterised the Spanish Baroque to take place. Nevertheless, Alcalá suggests, the fact that the vast majority of the literature of the time was "barely grazed" by the censor was probably also due to "self-censorship" by writers, and their cleverness in concealing beneath a veil of irony, satire, comedy, metaphor and allegory any subversive or heterodox opinions.

The elements and ideas that contributed to the writing of *Don Quixote* are therefore varied and complex. As scholars like Edward Riley and Stephen Gilman have pointed out, the intellectual and cultural impetus behind Cervantes' writing was his education in the classics, his humanism and his predominantly Aristotelean view of the role and value of imaginative literature, mediated by his familiarity with Italian Renaissance authors and the theories of Horace and El Pinciano. With the exception of the late influence of the *Filosofía antigua poética,* these fundamental elements were, nevertheless, the basis of all his works, not just *Don Quixote.* Cervantes' prose fiction contained a pastoral romance (*La Galatea*), *Los Trabajos de Persiles y Segismunda,* an appropriated reworking of the *Aethiopica,* an early Byzantine novel by Heliodorus, and the short moral stories that made up the *Novelas ejemplares,* with their origins in the Italian *novella.* Cervantes acknowledged all of these generic antecedents. But the fictional genre to which *Don Quixote* might be said to belong did not exist in early seventeenth-century Europe. It was both a kind of "metafiction," in which elements of many of the main genres of the age could be traced, and the progenitor of most kinds of the realistic fiction that was to follow, despite Cervantes' own ironical insistence from first to last that it is a "plain, unvarnished history."[34]

But as *Don Quixote* develops, we see a work of startling originality and humour beginning to emerge that also seeks to accommodate within it an exploration of the more urgent intellectual and moral questions of the time – such as what constitutes good literature, how should history be written and how is it different from imaginative fiction, does the administration of the law necessarily lead to justice, how should a country be governed and how should a monarch prepare for the task, and what are the tensions between love, the law and individual freedom? This was, perhaps, the greatest challenge of all. Even if Cervantes proved able to invent a story that was not aesthetically disadvantaged by taking up these issues, it constituted a high-risk strategy in view of the likelihood that it might touch upon "errant subjects" and heterodoxies that the censor would suppress. Furthermore, if the whisper that *converso* blood might be found in his family had any substance, Cervantes would have needed to be doubly careful.

Cervantes was destined to overcome all these obstacles. His dedication to a particular notion of what constituted good writing – a style that was harmonious, clear and accurately reflected the details of the world around him – no doubt helped to set him upon his way. Nowhere is this more graphically illustrated, together with his formidable talent for parody, than in Don Quixote's musings upon what words the wise chronicler who sets down the record of his deeds might use to describe his first setting out upon his knightly adventures:

> Apenas había el rubicundo Apolo tendido por la faz de la ancha y espaciosa tierra las doradas hebras de su hermosos cabellos, y apenas los pequeños y pintados pajarillos con sus harpardas lenguas habían saludado con dulce y meliflua armonía la venida de la rosada aurora, que, dejando la blanda cama del celoso marido, por las puertas y balcones del manchego horizonte a los mortales se mostraba, cuando el famoso caballero. Don Quixote de la Mancha, dejando las ociosas plumas, subió sobre su famoso caballo Rocinante y comenzó a caminar por el antiguo y conocido campo de Montiel.[35]

> (Scarcely had the rubicund Apollo shaken the golden locks of his beautiful hair over the face of the wide and spacious land, and the little, painted birds had saluted with the sweet, mellifluous harmony of their harp-like tongues the rosy coming of Aurora from the soft bed of her jealous husband to show herself on the Manchegan horizon before the doorways and balconies inhabited by mortals, than the famous knight, Don Quixote of la Mancha, left the idle comfort of his feather mattress, mounted his equally famous steed Rocinante and began to cross the ancient and familiar countryside of Montiel.)

In imagining the beginning of his own story in the overblown, artificial style of a typical romance of chivalry, Don Quixote condemns his own literary taste and holds up the idiom of the genre as a whole to ridicule. At the same time, this parody is an implicit statement of Cervantes' own standards, which reject ornate invention and classical allusion as a technique for portraying everyday reality. If, as Cervantes pretends, his book is to be seen as a history, then the language of historiography is called for in recording the deeds and events that comprise the narrative, further eroding the boundaries between history and imaginative fiction.

The calculated and ironically funny conflation of reality and fantasy that this produces not only asks a question about how far what is imagined becomes part of what *is* – and vice versa – but also subverts the received wisdom about the Aristotelean division between poetry and history, thus forming a first line of defence against the censor's ability to distinguish the truly deviant from what is satirical or parodic. The "self-censorship" of Golden Age writers which Alcalá discusses is therefore not so much the deliberate omission of anything the censor might object to as a means of devising ways of making critical comments and challenging cultural authority, in indirect or metaphorical terms, that the censor would either not notice or regard as acceptable. In this respect, the imaginative writer has many more rhetorical resources at his or her disposal than a philosopher, scientist or even a historian, and can call upon irony, satire, symbolism, allegory and metaphor, all of which could, in early modern Europe, be used with classical allusion and example, to disguise his or her intentions. In Cervantes' case, the disguise he created proved virtually total. Only two or three lines in Part II were expurgated in the entire work, those where the Duchess reminds Sancho that the self-flagellation he has reluctantly agreed to perform to break the spell on Dulcinea, should be undertaken wholeheartedly.

Y advierta Sancho que las obras de caridad que se hacen tibia y flojamente no tienen mérito ni valen nada.[36]

(And take note, Sancho, that charitable acts done feebly and half-heartedly are valueless and worth nothing.)

Furthermore, for three hundred years critical opinion of the book proved to have been just as much misled as the censor.

The calibre of the readers employed to censor books in sixteenth-century Spain was not uniformly high. Some were men of scholarship and ability, whose appreciation of what they were reading was sound. Others were men of theological training but limited to this field. The chief concern of both categories was, however, to detect and remove expressions of doctrinal irregularity or error, rather than to conduct an analytical "reading between the lines" to detect political or moral criticism. This accounts for what often appear as inconsistencies in the application and interpretation of the rules of censorship. Bartolomé Bennassar, in recognising the impact of the Inquisition as an instrument of Church and State observes:

It is worth the trouble to consider for a moment the nature of the creations of the Golden Age . . . These creations are of an aesthetic nature: they concentrate on formal . . . or a plastic beauty. They often exult the ideals of the Counter-Reformation . . . The most profound works, those by Cervantes and Calderón, though they may express a "tragic sense of life," do not discuss, at least not explicitly, the order of the world ... To think had become dangerous and thousands of Spaniards learned this at some cost.[37]

While few would nowadays question the second half of this statement, some eyebrows might be raised by the assumption – all too prevalent in literary scholarship even in the nineteen-eighties – that Baroque ornamentation in Spanish literature existed for its own sake, particularly in poetry, but carried within it nothing – either indirect or covert – that could be understood to reflect on "the order of the world." Certainly whatever might be argued on behalf of the poetry of Góngora, would be difficult to maintain in 2016 in the case of Calderón, and virtually untenable with respect to Cervantes and *Don Quixote*,

Between 1480 and 1550, the early work of the inquisition had resulted in the persecution of racial and religious minorities, an attack waged against new scholarship and independent thought, and the innovative, intellectual current of humanism driven underground. Although the later practice of expurgation resulted in relatively lenient treatment for literary works, the Inquisition did not relax its efforts suppress new ideas in areas such as theology, biblical interpretation, politics, science or philosophy, and to punish those who sought to introduce them. The opposition to the cultural and spiritual authority of the Church and state therefore manifested itself in imaginative writing of the Golden Age, which although subject to severe criticism at times for its lack of truth, and bad influence upon the emotions and moral standards of its readers, offered writers a greater opportunity to disguise dissent by rhetorical means. This tendency is now being increasingly recognised by present-day scholars as a "subversive tradition" and is being studied as such. It is difficult to argue that the "subversive" or "heterodox" writings of sixteenth and seventeenth-century Spain took on a coherent character with its own distinct values that we have come to associate with the term "tradition," except in as much as the authors were frequently *conversos*, or humanists, and often both.

In recent years, since the publication in 1978 of the monumental *Historia social de la literatura Española* by Carlos Blanco Aguinaga, Julio Rodríguez Puertolas and Iris M. Zavala,[38] the social context of Spanish Medieval and Renaissance literature has been afforded greater attention by Medieval and Early Modern specialists. It is now permissible to speak of a "subversive tradition" in Golden Age literature, as Antonio Pérez-Romero has done in his study *The Subversive Tradition in Spanish Renaissance Writing*.[39] Pérez-Romero enlists the evidence of numerous Spanish historians to demonstrate that what he terms "a subversive tradition" in Spanish thought and literature existed with its roots in the fourteenth and fifteenth centuries, reflecting tensions between the highly stratified social elites of the Middle Ages, the growing bourgeoisie and the peasantry. Royalty, which under the Catholic Monarchs became increasingly centralised and autocratic, sided with the Church, an increasingly pliant and subservient aristocracy and the military orders, to impose a model of imperial orthodoxy on Spain and its vast overseas possessions. This pattern, continued by the Hapsburg dynasty, was consistently questioned on matters of social justice, government and the conduct of the clergy by a dissenting and reforming minority among the privileged classes whose position often led them to reflect the complaints of ordinary people. A further area of heterodox thought surrounded the social position of women (derived from the French *Querelle des femmes*), which, whether arguing for their supremacy or their suppression, challenged a patriarchal society and the moral teaching of the Church.

In prose fiction, however, moral and social comment was refashioned in the new form of the picaresque novel, beginning with the publication between 1598 and 1604 of the two parts of Alemán's *Guzmán de Alfarache*. The argument put forward by Ryan Prendergast that the line from the picaresque novel, through the satires and *conceptismo* of Francisco de Quevedo to Baltasar Gracián's *El Criticón* (1651–57) is not the only perceptible continuation of the subversive tradition, and that it derives a whole new impetus from Cervantes' *Don Quixote*, suggests a broader and more profound picture. Prendergast states:

> *Don Quixote* ... though innocuous at one level represent[s] a serious, albeit at times veiled critique of early modern Spain's orthodox environment. Don Quixote resists the control that various characters representing religious and secular orthodoxy seek to impose. In a parallel fashion, Spanish subjects, including authors and readers, found ways to challenge the limits set for them and to confront the spectre of inquisitorial control.[40]

Far from seeing the mad knight as a figure of fun within a work of comic literary entertainment, Prendergast starts from the premise that both the novel *Don Quixote* and its eponymous protagonist are actively engaged in an intellectual critique of the society and culture of Counter-Reformation Spain. While therefore fulfilling one of the two classical duties of literature to entertain, the novel responds to the other – namely to instruct – by questioning the imposition of orthodoxy from above and the truth of that orthodoxy.

It therefore seems increasingly clear that *Don Quixote* is now to be considered as a book of ideas that are presented by means of an entirely new and experimental kind of fiction. This is a mode which examines literature itself, history, politics, law and the place of women in contemporary Spanish society alongside essential notions of truth, justice and equality. Cervantes' personal viewpoint was not only fashioned by his education, reading and moral formation, but also by his hard-earned experience as a frequently impecunious soldier, playwright and civil servant. In later life he saw the erosion of his youthful ideal of service to king and country by the victory of privilege, materialism, ambition, exploitation and corruption over the Christian principles to which Spain still laid claim. In the chapters that follow, therefore, this study will examine and seek to interpret *Don Quixote* taking as a guideline the theory of cultural authority, and the dissidence which its imposition from above inevitably generates if it inhibits freedom of thought and expression. The gradual process of re-evaluation to which it therefore hopes to contribute is one which takes into account not only Cervantes' probable aims and intentions, but the technical dexterity he showed in disguising them.

Indeed, an increasing number of present-day scholars now feel able to argue that not only did a coherent, heterodox and subversive literary current exist in Goldcn Age Spain that ran counter to the orthodox mainstream, but that the interests of State and Church in creating political and spiritual unity made it increasingly necessary for those who sought to express a contrary viewpoint to do so under a heavily-veiled façade to escape punishment. *Don Quixote*, therefore, represents a many-sided and critical national debate, but does so as one of the best-disguised examples of heterodox literature which carried the tradition from the Renaissance (arguably 1480–1570) through the Counter-Reformation and into the Age of the Baroque.

3

Don Quixote

A Book in Two Halves

[handwritten note in top margin:] i think quite a lot would agree there is more refs to problems in Spain in part 2.

The reputation that *Don Quixote* has acquired over the last four hundred years as a "funny book" is due almost entirely to the mood, contents and reception of Part I. The book had a decade in which to establish itself in the minds of the public before the publication of Part II, and had by that time created an impression that Part II did little to alter. Nevertheless, as has frequently been observed, the mood of Part II is noticeably darker, more pessimistic and less ebulliently comic than Part I, and seems to have provided the reason for the Romantics to find a tragic element in the story and in the figure of Don Quixote himself. Most scholars now seem content to attribute the differences between the books to the effect on the author of the years in between them. Nearly eighteen years passed from the beginning of Part I in 1597 to the completion of Part II in 1614. During this period Cervantes suffered the deaths of his sisters, Andrea (1609) and Magdalena (1611), a rancorous feud with Lope de Vega, the ravages of old age and failing health, and the rejection by his patron, the Duke of Lemos, Viceroy of Naples, of his application for a post as a cultural attaché there. Disillusionment at the decline of Spain and its government under Phillip III also seems to have settled upon his resilient spirit. The author who, between 1611 and 1615 laboured over the writing of Part II of his great work was not the same man who had put pen to paper in 1597, to set the mad knight wandering across the Manchegan plain. Then he had been a beleaguered civil servant, known as something of a poet and playwright, and author of *La Galatea* (1585) a well-regarded pastoral novel. By 1610 he was a writer with an international name whose creations, Don Quixote and Sancho Panza, were paraded as figures of popular merriment at festivals up and down Spain. But literary fame brought problems of its own, including professional jealousy and rivalry, and the challenge of producing a sequel to Part I which matched that book's achievement and the expectations of its immense readership in Europe and the New World.

But ultimately, two other factors account for the dissimilarities between the two books. The first was the changing spiritual and philosophical mood of the age that marked Spain's intellectual transition from the optimistic, reforming drive of Renaissance humanism to the questioning doubt that characterised Spanish Baroque thought in the early sixteen hundreds. The second factor was the impact upon Cervantes' narrative of Avellaneda's false second part to the novel, which was published in the summer of 1614. The extent of its effect is difficult to assess. Although some aspects of Cervantes' response to Avellaneda's criticism and personal insults can be clearly seen, the full extent of their effect may have been a good deal greater than appears. Some reflection on the likely revisions and rewritings that Avellaneda's book probably occasioned is, therefore, necessary, given that Cervantes decided to respond to this literary attack in like terms, and to rebuff Avellaneda's assault by holding it up to ridicule as part of the narrative of his own Part II.

The rediscovery and adaptation of the classical philosophies of Stoicism and Scepticism in the second half of the previous century provided the impetus for the changing intellectual climate. Neo-Stoicism regenerated practical thinking about morality and individual conduct, while scepticism, which was in many ways linked to it, argued, in an age of reaffirmed faith, that the limitations of the human mind and perceptions made it impossible for mankind to arrive at any certain knowledge about anything. The works of Spanish sceptics were known and read abroad, but the constraints imposed by the Church and State upon the universities, and the action taken against individual scholars by the Holy Office, gradually isolated them from the current of rational and empirical philosophy being developed in other European countries by men such as Hobbes, Descartes and Gassendi, who had, along with others, set up a correspondence network to exchange and disseminate ideas. Despite early contact made through the efforts of the Jesuits, no Spanish philosophers are known to have participated in this correspondence.

The relevance of the arguments of scepticism, furthermore, was not lost on those humanist intellectuals still active at the end of the sixteenth century. Indeed, they were sometimes appropriated and adapted to the humanist offensive against the outdated thinking of conservative neo-Aristotelean scholars. It is not, therefore, surprising that a radical and heterodox thinker like Cervantes, whose background and education were formed by humanism, should, when writing *Don Quixote*, have applied the sceptical mode of thought to a series of questions relating to truth, history, fiction, falsehood, perception and judgement which reflected the preoccupations of the times. Across the years, Cervantes thus moves from the optimistic, tolerant tradition of humanist enquiry so evident in the more light-hearted Part I, to the relative pessimism and doubt typical of

Baroque scepticism that permeates Part II. What may astonish us, however, is the fact that Cervantes saw, almost from the outset of his work, that the kind of experimental fictional narrative that was beginning to emerge, free from the conventions of the familiar literary genres, could become an appropriate vehicle for the almost limitless exploration of all manner of social, philosophical and political issues of his day.

If we are to believe Cervantes' assertion that *Don Quixote* saw the light of day in prison, it would almost certainly locate the beginning of the book in 1597, when its author spent the last four months of the year in the Royal Prison in Seville. What became the writing of Part I of the novel occupied him until 1604. The protracted business of obtaining the necessary licenses and permissions for publication saw the book finally appear the following year. The sporadic writing of poetry, and work on the *Novelas ejemplares*, his collection of short fiction, also took up his time. This work, which included some stories that probably dated from the late 1580s, was finally published in 1613, followed in 1614 by his long, satirical poem *Viaje de Parnaso* (Journey to Parnassus) an attack on the declining artistic standards of poetry at the time, and the kind of example set by Lope de Vega.[1] It was also the year that Cervantes' feud with Lope became public knowledge. In 1615, the same year as the appearance of Part II of *Don Quixote*, Cervantes published what remained of his collected theatre, eight full-length plays and eight *entremeses* (one-act interludes).

The years between 1605 and 1612 had witnessed Cervantes become an international figure on the back of the popularity of the first part of *Don Quixote*. He had, temporarily at least, freed himself from the worst of his financial problems, had finally settled the long-running argument between himself and the Royal Treasury regarding the payment of taxes he had collected (the misunderstanding that had led to his imprisonment in 1597) and had followed the Royal Court's move back to Madrid from Valladolid. He also attempted to play a more prominent role in the Madrid literary academy. The precise date when he finally started work on the second part of his great novel is not known, but a fairly safe guess would be late 1611, dividing his time between this and the completion of the *Novelas ejemplares*. We can deduce that the *Novelas* were ready for the press and awaiting the completion of the necessary formalities and approvals by the end of 1612, and that the writing of the second part of the mad knight's adventures began in earnest at around the same time as the composition of *Viaje de Parnaso*.[2] Cervantes' last novel, *Los trabajos de Persiles y Segismunda*, was probably begun around the middle of 1612, with the collection and editing of his theatrical works taking place between 1613 and late 1614. Cervantes had evidently decided on this demanding schedule of writing for a reason. In 1614 he was sixty seven years old and his health was deteriorating. Yet he had acquired, late in life, international fame as a writer and was experiencing a period of unprecedented productivity and originality. Nevertheless, from this point on, while being determined to achieve the target he had set himself, he was clearly writing against time and the awareness of approaching death.

In the autumn of that year he had got as far as Chapter 59 of *Don Quixote* Part II when he was unexpectedly jolted by the publication in Tarragona of Alfonso Fernández Avellaneda's spurious sequel to Part I, entitled *Segundo tomo del Ingenioso Hidalgo Don Quixote de la Mancha*. This kind of plagiarism was not uncommon in early modern Europe, where the absence of copyright laws made it perfectly legitimate for one writer to appropriate the characters and plot made famous in a book by another, and to create a totally false sequel to it. (For example, after the success of the first part of *Guzmán de Alfarache* in 1599, its author, Mateo Alemán, was faced with two different false sequels before his own second part was published in 1604.) It was a risk run by authors of successful books of fiction that their work would be exploited and abused in this way. Indeed, in the prologue to his spurious second part Avellaneda gives the frequency of such plagiarism as a justification for what he has done, since, he claims, both he and Cervantes have the common aim of destroying the chivalresque romance. *Don Quixote* Part I had been on the crest of a popular wave since 1605, and in some ways it is remarkable to think that although some parodies and imitations of it had been produced shortly after its publication, no full-length, spurious sequel had been attempted until Avellaneda's effort. Perhaps by 1614, Cervantes had been lulled into a false sense of security over the matter, but there is little doubt that, when it did come, he found Avellaneda's false Part II particularly galling. He at once decided that the imposter would have to be answered in kind, and could not simply be condemned or dismissed.

The identity of Alonso Fernández Avellaneda has never been revealed, despite vigorous scholarly attempts to do so. Indeed, most scholars nowadays would probably support the view that it is a collective pseudonym that conceals a number of Lope de Vega's friends and admirers who shared his animosity towards Cervantes' views on literature, objected to his criticisms of Lope's standards, and – with Lope's direct encouragement – confected Avellaneda's *El Ingenioso Hidalgo Don Quijote de la Mancha* as an exercise in collaborative writing. Unlike many of its kind, the book is not an attempt simply to make money by exploiting someone else's talent, ideas and popularity. It is both a harsh personal attack on Cervantes, and – more importantly still – a pointed critique of where he stood on matters of literature, truth and morality. As such, Cervantes could not simply brush it off as an artistically inferior, superficial imitation (as many subsequent Cervantes scholars have tended to do). Avellaneda's criticisms demanded a different kind of response if Cervantes was to salvage the fifty-eight chapters that he had already written of his own Part II.

In his edition of *Alonso Fernández de Avellaneda. "El ingenioso hidalgo Don Quijote de la Mancha"* (Biblioteca Nueva, Madrid, 2000), Luis Gómez Canseco has summed up Avellaneda's intention as to astonish his readers while indoctrinating them in matters of the faith. In his review of Canseco's editorial work (2003) E. T. Aylward sums up Avellaneda's views as those of a religious as well as a social conservative, devoted to the rosary and obsessed with the moral decay that he saw as invading every aspect of Catholic Spain's society. Avellaneda clearly understood the radical, subversive nature of Cervantes' work, and set about replacing Cervantes' subtle social and cultural criticism with a rigidly orthodox agenda.[3] Canseco also argues, however, that Avellaneda had a reluctant admiration for what Cervantes had achieved:

> Avellaneda era consciente de que, a diferencia de las novelas pastoriles u otras narraciones con un género claramente definido en la tradición rena- centista, el *Guzmán de Alfarache*, y aún más el *Quijote* eran obras singulares, que rompieron con los modelos literarios conocidos y que debían su razón de ser a la originalidad de los autores.

> (Avellaneda was aware that, as distinct from the pastoral novels or other narratives whose genre was clearly defined in Renaissance tradition, *Guzmán de Alfarache*, and the *Quixote* even more so, were unique works which broke with the known models and owed their existence to the originality of their respective authors.)

Avellaneda was therefore obliged to arrive at a close understanding and appreciation of the literary merits of his target, and Canseco suggests that despite the fact that "aborreció con precisión matemática a Cervantes, supo apreciar su obrar narrativa y celebrar con su imitación episodios, personajes e invenciones de la primera parte,"[4] (Though [Avellaneda] hated Cervantes with an almost mathematical precision, he was able to appreciate his handling of narrative and to make his imitation celebrate episodes, characters and inventions from the first part of the book.)

James Iffland, another distinguished Cervantes scholar, who has devoted considerable attention to Avellaneda's imitation, has proposed a more far-reaching role for the book.[5] He points out that there are, despite the arguments of historicist critics, scant means to reconstruct the response to *Don Quixote* of the readers of Cervantes' own times. Most readers seem either to have accepted its popularity in a non-committal way or to have been openly hostile. (The latter seem to have been very much in a minority, their attitude often reflecting the petty in-fighting of literary circles and academies of the time.) In Avellaneda's continuation, however, we have a whole book that can be read as an example of the inimical, minority reception of Part I. In the course of his argument, Professor Iffland quotes Stephen Gilman's *Cervantes y Avellaneda: estudio de una imitación* (1951) where it is suggested that, far from being an untalented epigone, Avellaneda was a capable writer who felt a deep antipathy for the artistic and ideological "coordinates" of Cervantes' novel, and his counterreformation rejection of Cervantes' humanism, tolerance and relativism prompted him to produce a sharp, anti-Quixote retort.

Like most readers of Avellaneda's book, Professor Iffland points to the predominance within it of the comic, and the often cruel and crude nature of the humour extracted from it. He observes:[6]

> It is precisely there – in the type of laughter the work incites, and in the type actually depicted in its pages – where we find the true key to Avellaneda's ideological project more than in any other place.

Avellaneda possessed, Iffland claims, an acutely sensitive awareness for anything "oppositional" or "contestatory" in the *Don Quixote* of 1605, and seems to have realised that most of Cervantes' unsettling social and ideological message was transmitted (of necessity) indirectly through the work's comic mechanisms. Indeed, he fully grasped the liberating variety of carnivalesque laughter that Cervantes' combination of "wise madman" and "practical ignoramus" produces, including as it does the master/man relationship of the two chief protagonists, a relative egalitarianism between the classes, and the social and gender mobility that fills its pages. Furthermore there is the knight's madness, which casts a questioning ambivalence over the whole fictional world of the book. Avellaneda's riposte is made, inevitably, on the same terrain: the comic novel which Cervantes himself had virtually invented. However, we find that Avellaneda mobilises comic situations and the laughter of the characters (by extension that of the reader also) in a way that is methodically controlled from the top down by the aristocratic characters in the story, thus seeking to neutralise or re-channel Cervantes' worrying current of heterodox thought. Avellaneda systematically strips away from his version of the mad knight all vestiges of the *cuerdo* (sane, rational) with which Cervantes had so carefully balanced the *loco* (mad). The result is a two-dimensional, obsessive madman who lacks the capacity to charm and persuade us that Cervantes' character so frequently demonstrates.

One thing is, however, undeniable. Avellaneda's direct attack on Part I of Don Quixote exercised a major and disturbing influence upon Cervantes' second part of the book. Indeed, without that intervention, Cervantes' Part II might have been quite different from what it was. In his prologue to it, Cervantes makes it perfectly clear that he knew Lope was the moving spirit behind Avellaneda's novel. Also he realised that Avellaneda had accurately pierced the elaborate tissue of humour, irony and fantasy beneath which his heterodoxies had been disguised. Lastly he was aware that Avellaneda/Lope represented an inimical force with close links to the Church and the Holy Office that put him beyond Cervantes' limited reach.[7] If nothing else, Avellaneda's book fired a warning shot across his bows, and Cervantes decided that it was best to heed the warning. His response, however, was both considered and clever. He resisted the temptation to answer Avellaneda's attack by a direct counter-offensive. He thus set about demonstrating the fallacious nature of Avellandeda's text as part of his own story. It is in Chapter 59 of Part II that Don Quixote and Sancho learn of the existence of Avellaneda's book[8] when they overhear two fellow travellers discussing it in an inn (which for once Don Quixote has not – to Sancho's great relief – mistaken for a castle). Don Juan and Don Jerónimo are arguing about whether, after supper, to read more of the new second part of *The Adventures of Don Quixote de la Mancha*, because, as Don Jerónimo observes:

¿Para qué quiere, vuesa merced, señor Don Juan que leamos estos disparates, si a él que hubiere leído la primera parte de la historia de Don Quijote de la Mancha no es posible que pueda tener gusto en leer esta segunda?

(Why, your worship Don Juan, should we read that lot of nonsense, for those who have read the first part of *The Adventures of Don Quijote de la Mancha* could not possibly take pleasure in reading the second one.)

To which Don Juan replies with Pliny the Elder's classical adage: "No hay libro tan malo que no tenga alguna cosa buena." (No book is so bad that there is nothing of benefit in it.)

On hearing that in this new second part of his adventures, he no longer has Dulcinea del Toboso as his lady, and is now known as *El Caballero Desamorado* (The Unloved Knight) Don Quixote can contain himself no longer. He announces his presence and identity to the two travellers, and embarks – to their amazement – on the saga of Dulcinea's enchantment which can only be lifted by Sancho giving himself three thousand lashes on the buttocks. While his story leaves his audience wondering that such clarity of mind can give expression to such mad delusions, Don Juan and Don Jerónimo immediately recognise the Knight and his Squire from

Cide Hamete Benengeli's description of them in Part I, and dismiss Avellaneda and his creation as a fraud. Leafing rapidly through the traveller's copy of the book, Don Quixote delivers a handful of none too serious critical comments, both stylistic and factual, claiming that the language seems to be Aragonese, since it often omits the use of articles, and the author has mistakenly given the name of Sancho's wife as Mari Gutiérrez, whereas everyone knows it is Teresa Panza.[9] A historian who can make so grave an error is bound to have made others equally serious! At this point, Don Quixote makes a further decision that will show Avellaneda's book to be the inaccurate farrago that it is. Learning from Don Juan that in the false sequel Don Quixote goes to Zaragoza to take part in the annual jousting tournament held there, Don Quixote declares:

> Por el mismo caso . . . yo no pondré los pies en Zaragoza y así sacaré a la plaza del mundo la mentira de este historiador moderno, y echarán de ver las gentes como yo no soy el Don Quijote que él dice.

> (For that reason . . . I will not set foot near Zaragoza, and by not doing so I will expose this modern historian to the light of day and show people that I'm not the Don Quixote he says I am.)

The next morning sees the Knight and his Squire again on their travels, taking the most direct possible route to Barcelona in order to further show up the new historian who had told so many "lies" about them. There are three further occasions before the end of the book where Cervantes' characters comment directly upon the existence of the false continuation of the story. The first is to be found in the words, uttered with undeniable hyperbolic irony, with which Don Antonio Moreno's friends welcome Don Quixote and Sancho to Barcelona.

> Bien sea venido a nuestra ciudad el espejo, el farol, la estrella y el norte de toda caballería andante. . . . bien sea venido, digo, el valeroso Don Quijote de la Mancha; no el falso, no el ficticio, no el apócrifo que en falsas historias estos días nos han mostrado, sino el verdadero, el legal y el fiel que nos descubrió Cide Hamete Benengeli, flor de historiadores. (pp. 1019–1020)

> (A hearty welcome to our city for the mirror, the beacon and northern star of knight crrantry. . . . May he be welcomed, I say, the valorous Don Quixote de la Mancha: not the false, fictitious one, not the apocryphal version that the present time has seen fit to reveal to us in the form of fraudulent tales, but the true, legally certified and genuine one who Cide Hamete Benengeli, the flower of historians, has described to us.)

Don Antonio Moreno, a confidant and ally of the outlaw Roque Guinart, with whom the knight and his squire have just spent three weeks in his mountain hideout, is clearly bent on deriving as much amusement as possible from Don Quixote's madness. He flatters him and plays along with the knight's delusions very much as the Duke and Duchess did in earlier chapters. Nevertheless, despite this irony, which passes completely over Don Quixote's head, Don Antonio is well enough convinced that the lunatic who is a guest under his roof is the genuine article, the one whose adventures are recounted in Part I of *Don Quixote*, and not the false subject of a different story invented by a different author.

On the second occasion, shortly afterwards, Don Quixote visits a printer's workshop in Barcelona (Avellaneda's book was printed in that city by Sebastián de Cormellas) and witnesses an assistant correcting proofs of *La segunda parte del ingenioso hidalgo Don Quijote de la Mancha*, which he says is "compuesta por un tal, vecino de Tordesillas." (Written by someone or other from the neighbourhood of Tordesillas.). The knight immediately exclaims:

> Ya yo tengo noticia de este libro . . . y en verdad en mi conciencia que pensé que ya estaba quemado y hecho polvos por impertinente; pero su San Martín se le llegará como a cada puerco, que las historias fingidas tanto tienen de buenas o deleitables cuanto se llegan a la verdad o la semejanza de ella, y las verdades tanto son mejores cuanto son más verdaderas. (p. 1035)

> ("I've heard of this book," said Don Quixote, "and truth to tell it was firmly in my mind that it had already been burnt to ashes on the grounds of its sheer effrontery. But every pig's St Martin's Day comes eventually, for imagined stories are as good and enjoyable as they are close to the truth, or what appears to be true, and truth is at its best the truer it becomes.")

This criticism of Avellaneda's book for lacking verisimilitude is completely in line with El Pinciano's view that stories lacking either truth or verisimilitude are not literature but nonsense.

The last, and perhaps most daring, of Cervantes' direct references to Avellaneda comes in Chapter 72. Don Quixote, has been vanquished by the Knight of the White Moon (Sansón Carrasco in yet another disguise) and commanded to return to his village. Breaking their journey at an inn on their return, Don Quixote and Sancho encounter Don Álvaro Tarfe, who arrives with his servants on his way back to Granada, having taken part in the jousts at Zaragoza. One of the main characters in Avellaneda's sequel to Part I, Don Álvaro's friendship and influence is instrumental in saving the false Don Quixote, who has also gone to Zaragoza, from a number of punishments on account of his mad actions. But Don Álvaro is finally obliged to leave Avellaneda's protagonist committed to an asylum in Toledo in the hope of a cure.

Accosted by both the "real" Sancho and Don Quixote, who learn his name from one of his servants – it is one of their few recollections from their cursory view of the book in Chapter 59 – Don Álvaro readily admits that neither the genuine Don Quixote, nor the equally genuine Sancho, in any way resemble the pair of the same names that he left in Toledo. (Indeed, he additionally states that the Sancho Panza he has already encountered, though famed for his humour and comic banter, had failed to utter a single amusing word during their entire acquaintanceship.) Certainly, among Avellaneda's limitations as a writer – a deficiency Cervantes was quick to note and exploit – was his inability to create anything like the peasant humour and unselfconscious buffoonery for which Sancho is renowned, particularly in Part I. Though they frequently attract the laughter of other characters (and that of the reader him or herself) Avellaneda's protagonists are generally unsympathetic figures whom others laugh **at**, rather than laughing **with**. Before they part company, Don Quixote has no difficulty in persuading Don Álvaro to sign an affidavit to the effect that:

> No conocía a Don Quijote de la Mancha, que asimismo allí estaba presente, y que no era aquel que andaba impreso en una historia intitulada *Segunda parte de Don Quijote de la Mancha*, compuesto por un tal de Avellaneda, natural de Tordesillas. (p. 1092)

> (He [Don Álvaro Tarfe] did not know the Don Quixote de la Mancha, who was there present before him, neither was he the one who was now locked up in the history entitled *The Second Part of Don Quixote de la Mancha*, written by someone of the name of Avellaneda, a native of Tordesillas.)

The unexpected intervention into the story of a fictional character created by another author as part of another book is something of a masterstroke on Cervantes' part. This disconcerting yet very funny ploy is made possible, however, by reason of the fact that as early as Chapter 3, Don Quixote's conversation with the graduate Sansón Carrasco, gives him and Sancho a kind of "autonomy" as fictional characters. Sansón informs them that they are now famous throughout Spain and abroad, as a result of the success of the first part of their adventures, a history of the first and second *salidas* written by the celebrated Arab historian Cide Hamete Benengeli. From that point on, both the knight and his squire are aware of themselves as independent characters whose deeds and words are being recorded for posterity, and they express the hope that their wise chronicler will write only those things that truly happen. This complex reflexivity dissolves the frontiers between different literary texts, the reality of the time that separates them, and throws open the borders between imaginative literature and history.

The commonly held critical view of the impact upon *Don Quixote* Part II of Avellaneda's satirical attack on Part I can therefore be summed up as follows: faced in the autumn of 1614 with a spurious but inferior second part to his story by an unknown author (behind whom he clearly saw the hand of Lope de Vega) Cervantes was obliged, in the dozen or so final chapters that he planned for his own book, and some probable rewriting of parts of earlier ones, to take on the literary challenge that Avellaneda had thrown down. This he did by an ingenious and amusing means whereby he sought to show that the Don Quixote and Sancho who appeared in Avellaneda's book were imposters, and totally different from the genuine ones whose adventures had been chronicled by Cide Hamete Benengeli in Part I. It is also worthwhile, when considering the differences between Part I and Part II, to consider two further questions, namely: how far did Cervantes' feel obliged to change the ending he had planned for the book when, at Chapter 59, he learned of Avellaneda's sequel, and to what extent did he rewrite parts of earlier chapters to make his repudiation of the false *Quixote* possible?

Neither question can, of course, be answered with any certainty. But two quite plausible suggestions can be offered. These are that the whole of the Barcelona sequence that followed Chapter 59 was probably a rapid invention that took the place of the ending that Cervantes may originally have had in mind. Certainly he had now to avoid sending his characters to the jousts at Zaragoza, which he had first mentioned himself in Part I as a possible future destination for the mad knight, since Avellaneda had fastened upon this projected visit to Zaragoza as the setting for most of his version. Furthermore, with Don Quixote's face turned irrevocably towards Barcelona, how had the story to be ended? There seems to be every indication that from Chapter 3 on, Cervantes had it in mind to give Sansón Carrasco (a metaphor for the new Spain) the role of Don Quixote's nemesis; that is to say the instrument by which his career as a knight errant would be ended, and a "cure" for his madness brought about. After the shock of Avellaneda's attack, however, the only sensible option was to kill off his hero to prevent any third or fourth spurious parts appearing in the future. Avellaneda's challenge was thus a severe test of Cervantes' powers of imagination and narrative invention, which, in the end, he passed with flying colours. Nevertheless, the strong likelihood exists that the ending Cervantes gave Part II was not the one he might have originally had in mind, and was instead rapidly confected to meet the unexpected circumstances. To present his readers with a sane, repentant Alonso Quijano, who died at peace in the arms of the Church having repudiated everything he did under the influence of his madness, secured Cervantes against any new interest that Avellaneda's criticisms might have stirred up in the mind of the censor or the Inquisition. Additionally, the question arises of whether Cervantes found himself obliged to make changes to the original drafts of any of the chapters pre-dating Chapter 59, in order to accommodate his response to Avellaneda.

The answers to these questions must, of course, remain matters for speculation. As we have already indicated, Part II of *Don Quixote* contains three episodes – one in Chapter 3, another in Chapter 59 and the last in Chapter 72 – that distinguish it significantly from Part I. In this part, although Cervantes had, after Chapter 8, played continual games with the reader, hiding behind a fictional narrator and imagined sources that he insists comprise a genuine "history," and despite the dream the mad knight has, as he sets out on his first sally, that some sage, scholar or chronicler is following his every move, nothing had previously equalled the transitional force of this conversation with Sansón Carrasco. In something like half a page, Cervantes turns Part II into what is now called a "metafiction;" a self-reflexive narrative which constantly reminds the reader that what he or she is perusing is fictitious, and a work of literary art. From this point on, Don Quixote and Sancho (and all the other characters we are to suppose) are entities that are being written *about*; the subjects of a "historical biography" in fact, which the knight and his squire are thereafter conscious of. This realisation places them beyond the conventional control of their author, and they become "autonomous." The decisions and actions, "independently" taken by the characters themselves – as when, in Chapter 59, Don Quixote determines to avoid Zaragoza so as to give the lie to Avellaneda – are those which decide what the story line will be.

This is a major innovation in narrative convention which gives fictional creations the "freedom" to go beyond the restrictions of the literary work they inhabit; to occupy in fact the space of another novel, by a different author, without causing the reader to exclaim at the absurdity of the idea. Thus in Part II, Chapter 3, Cervantes laid the ground for the appearance in Chapter 72 of Don Álvaro Tarfe, totally outside the confines of Avellaneda's novel in which he originally featured. This situation may have been the result of a "happy accident": having altered the rules of narrative in Chapter 3, Cervantes felt perfectly free to act as he did in Chapter 72. On the other hand, it is just possible that Chapter 3, as we now have it, is one of a number of *post hoc* revisions, carried out to make Don Álvaro's entrance feasible. Whatever the answer to this question is, it is quite clear that Chapters 3 and 72 of Part II remind the reader that he or she is witnessing the making and unfolding of a complex piece of writing whose tendency towards self-reference establishes a metafictional line that Cervantes never quite crossed in Part I, though he comes very close to it in Chapter 8, where the first narrator breaks off his account in the middle of Don Quixote's fight with the Biscayan footman because his source manuscript has suddenly come to an end!

The effect that Avellaneda's text had on the second part of *Don Quixote* was therefore significant, but in many respects difficult, or even impossible, to assess as a whole. In writing Part I between the years 1597 and 1604, Cervantes had been free to pursue his ageneric, experimental journey more or less as his artistic and intellectual interests guided him, taking care only to avoid the attention of a censor who, in any case, probably took a relatively benign view of imaginative literature. It is, therefore, perhaps an oversimplification, but in no way a distortion, to suggest that the marked differences between Parts I and II stem from the fact that while being obliged to retain a common framework they pursue quite distinct topics and priorities. The humanist tradition in which Cervantes was brought up and educated, and which, in figures like El Pinciano was still very much a feature of Spanish intellectual life at the end of the sixteenth century, was the main driving force behind Part I, whose overall point of enquiry was the processes of writing and reading. This entailed an examination of how much actual, historical truth, or truth of the figurative or verisimilar kind, was necessary to make the Aristotelean categories of "history" and "poetry" viable in the early modern world. Part II, begun some eight years after the first part was completed, registers a shift in the author's thinking that can best be described as a preoccupation with truth as knowledge, and the capacity of the human senses to apprehend reality from pretence and falsehood. As Jeremy Robbins observes:[10]

> What all Spaniards share during the early modern period is a view of human perceptual fallibility and a concomitant belief in the need for sustained rational enquiry and perceptual scrutiny prior to any commitment to the external world, whether in word or deed.

These assumptions drove Spaniards to develop various "arts of perception," namely strategies designed to overcome the epistemological problems and to enable the individual to act effectively in the moral, political, social and religious spheres. This attitude of mind was largely fostered by the creative interaction between Scepticism and Stoicism in late sixteenth and early seventeenth-century Spain, and the contrasting concepts entailed in the dualities *ser/parecer* (being and seeming), and *engaño/desengaño* (deception and the repudiation of deception, or clarity of seeing). The antinomian attitude of mind, and the fascination for the play of opposites that this gave rise to, is mirrored in a great deal of Baroque art, since these concepts shaped virtually all types of discourse. Exercising a strong influence over questions of agency, morality, reasons of state, trust and honour, they fashioned a distinctive Spanish reaction to intellectual problems that were common throughout Europe. Indeed, Professor Robbins goes on to argue that:[11]

> Spain was affected by Scepticism, aware of its challenges to moral, political and theological certainties and to the Aristotelean *status quo*, and engaged in refuting, embracing, exploring and accommodating those challenges.

The militant nature of Counterreformation orthodoxy is often cited as the reason why Spain lagged behind the rest of Europe in the seventeenth century with regard to the development of modern science and philosophy. Certainly there was no doubt that scholars working in these areas tended to find their efforts blocked by the authorities and the Holy Office. Nevertheless, of all European nations at that time, it was Spain that most insistently confronted the questions of knowledge, truth, falsehood, certainty and perception that were at the centre of intellectual debate throughout the continent. The difference, Robbins points out, was that:

> Spain confronted these issues primarily through works of fiction. So obsessive are the questions of appearance and reality, of deceit and disillusionment in Baroque fiction that ... [it] ... can justifiably be viewed as Spain's major and distinctive contribution to the early modern preoccupation with knowledge.[12]

The two major works of fiction with which Robbins illustrates this point are *Don Quixote* Parts I and II (1605 and 1615) and Baltasar Gracián's *El Criticón*, Parts I, II and III (1651–57).

To read *Don Quixote* primarily as an exploration of, or response to, this intellectual crisis of the early sixteen hundreds, prompted as it was by the rediscovery of Scepticism and Pyrrhonism[13] in the later second half of the previous century, invariably strikes the reader as placing far too narrow a constraint upon a work. Nevertheless, beneath so many of the adventures and experiences undergone by the knight and his squire – including the more farcical and light-hearted – lurk the same fundamental questions: What is truth and what is falsehood? How can the one be distinguished from the other, and what is the extent and purpose of human knowledge? The changing nature of Cervantes' interrogation of these questions over the seventeen years between the start of Part I to the end of Part II, is probably the most fundamental explanation for the differences between them. In Part I of the book, the knight experiences a

series of "adventures" which largely arise because his madness causes him
to misinterpret the world around him. Thus he sees windmills as giants,
sheep as armies and a barber's basin as the legendary helmet of the hero
Mambrino.[14] Equally the reactions to him of those he confronts vary from
astonishment and bewilderment to prompt physical reprisal, as when the
shepherds, whose flocks of sheep Don Quixote has charged, pelt him with
stones from their sling-shots, knocking out his teeth.

From Chapter 25 on, beginning with his penance in the Sierra Morena,
and the introduction of the characters Cardenio, Fernando, Dorotea and
Luscinda, who are then joined by the Priest and the Barber from Don
Quixote's home village, the situation gradually changes. Although Don
Quixote remains, in a real sense, as mad as ever, and no whit less under
the spell of the novels of chivalry, he becomes the recipient of sympathetic
understanding on the part of people who decide to exploit his delusions
in order to return him to his home and hopefully a cure. An elaborate
charade is concocted, in which Dorotea poses as the Princess Micomicona
who is seeking the knight's aid to overcome a giant who has driven her
from her throne. While under the belief that he is accompanying the false
princess to her imaginary country to fight the giant, Don Quixote is
tricked, for his own safety, into travelling in a cage on the back of an ox-
drawn cart in the belief that he has been bewitched by a malign enchanter.

From the episode in the Sierra Morena to the end of the book, we see
a marked change in the reactions of the people Don Quixote encounters.
He is no longer a lone, misunderstood and potentially dangerous threat.
But instead he is surrounded by an entourage – the Priest, the Barber, and
the two pairs of upper class lovers – one of whom, Don Fernando, is an
aristocrat. These companions confer a status and respectability upon the
eccentric figure of the Knight which he had previously lacked. (Indeed,
Don Fernando's presence alone, and the class deference automatically
paid him, is enough to extricate Don Quixote from an embarrassing
encounter with the officers of the Santa Hermanidad.[15]) With the knight's
welfare in mind, this combination of old and new friends sets about falsifying still further the reality in which Don Quixote functions. They play
him at his own game by turning the rules of the imaginary, chivalresque
world he inhabits against him, and by pretence and role-playing
introduce a level of contrived deception into the story.

In the first part of *Don Quixote*, the fictional characters and the actual
reader are immersed in an ongoing narrative that questions the nature of
truth, and human perception of it. The Knight's misinterpretation of
external phenomena, whenever they appear to touch upon the world of
chivalreque fantasy that has become his chief frame of moral and social
reference is the chief means by which the truth is interrogated. His
madness transforms his distorted perceptions into a quasi-religious faith,

in which the writ of the chivalresque novel has become a spiritual and literal truth, replacing the teaching of the Catholic Church. In this question of unyielding faith, Don Quixote is therefore at one with the outdated Neo-Aristoteleans who embraced scholasticism and were a target of ridicule for the humanists. Both they and the knight adhered to a faith which obstructed and distorted the exercise of human reason. As a work, *Don Quixote* is permeated with a mixture of late humanist perspectivism, relativism and irony whose roots lay in Cervantes' naturally sceptical outlook, and to which the mental attitudes of both the Neo-Aristoteleans and the mad *hidalgo* of La Mancha were no better than nonsensical fun.

An important aspect of Cervantes' scepticism is his deliberate, often hilarious questioning of the authority and reliability of his own text (and by implication that of every other printed work). In Part I this is achieved by two principal means. The first, which is very familiar to all Cervantes specialists, is the "distancing" technique that he employs, to emphasise the artificial, "literary" nature of the narrative process. (The self-referential game of narrators and original sources is complicated, and will be examined in detail in a following chapter.) The second is the often-repeated but totally untenable assertion - and all the more amusing for it – that what we are reading is a "true history," taken from the Arabic text of the wise and learned chronicler Cide Hamete Benengeli. This record, having been translated into Castilian by an obliging *morisco*, is now being retold by the antiquarian and bibliophile who has discovered it among a bundle of manuscripts about to be sold in Toledo market. This, we are to believe, is the source from which the story is taken after Chapter 8 in Part I. The nature of the narrative, in which long conversations are recorded almost verbatim, and descriptive detail is supplied that only a close and present observer could have known, makes this claim a total, tongue-in-cheek impossibility. As such it also gives the lie to the most central of all conventions of literary fiction, namely that the narrator preserves a kind of god-like omnipresence which we all choose to accept by "wilfully suspending our disbelief," and thus allowing ourselves to become immersed in the story.

One of the things that Cervantes found himself obliged to do in Part I was to blur the lines between fact (history, truth or whatever form it might take) and fiction, the product of the imagination. This he sought to do in a way that allowed him to claim that a work of imaginative writing could powerfully demonstrate truth of a figurative or representative kind: always provided, of course, that it also showed an acceptable level of verisimilitude. It was a calculated defence of the kind of writing which he practiced against the attacks of its numerous opponents in early seventeenth-century Spain. But in Part II, Cervantes takes this process a step further. The events and experiences that both the knight and his squire undergo serve to confuse the line between reality and illusion – and similarly judgement and delusion - even more radically. For although Don Quixote's madness has in no way abated, a great deal of the world he encounters is itself being manipulated by other people for their own ends. This the Duke and Duchess, along with Don Antonio Moreno, Don Quixote's wealthy host in Barcelona, do for their own amusement, and Sansón Carrasco, does in his determination to find a rational cure for the knight's madness.

Of course, the clumsy but often hilarious pantomime that the ducal couple, together with their servants and courtiers, invent to amuse themselves at Don Quixote's and Sancho's expense, could never have deceived anyone of sound mind. But Don Quixote's derangement is such that he readily embraces this make-believe as reality (much as he had done Dorotea's impersonation of the Princess Micomicona in Part I). Sancho, on the other hand, though not in any sense mad, has allowed himself to be almost equally deluded by his ambition to become the governor of an island, and his native ignorance and deference to his social superiors. In Part I, he is "in on the act" that is used to inveigle Don Quixote into returning home. In Part II, however, he is as much duped and deceived as his master because it suits his desires to be so. All the while, the narrator, and through him the reader, look on as neutral though wondering observers who are invited to judge and compare the antics of the knight and his squire with those of the Duke and Duchess and their entourage, whose moral stature is shown to be so much less than that of their victims.

The philosophical view that saw life as an insubstantial dream, or the playing out of a predestined role upon a figurative stage (Calderón's *La vida es sueño* and *El gran' teatro del mundo* are, perhaps, the most developed artistic expressions of these ideas) was common throughout Europe, and was particularly fitted to seventeenth-century Spain. Both find echoes in Part II of Don Quixote, most notably in the experiences of both the Knight and Squire at the hands of the Duke and Duchess. Indeed, the gradual erosion of faith in the chivalresque ideals he had espoused in Part I are one of the direct consequences of Don Quixote's stay in the ducal palace, and an important element in distinguishing Part II from what had preceded it. In the first book, the reality of what the Knight believes he sees in the physical world – mediated as it is by magic, enchanters and all the conventional paraphernalia of the romance of chivalry – remains unshakeable. Central to this faith is his equally absolute subservience to the mental image of Dulcinea, who is his inspiration and justification. Throughout the book he shows no need to see her, and is perfectly content to limit his contact with the lady to a letter. He charges Sancho to take this missive to El Toboso, to speak to Dulcinea and observe her reaction to it, while he himself does extravagant penance in the Sierra Morena after the style of Amadís de Gaula.

Sancho's errand goes disastrously wrong however. He sets off forgetting the letter (which his master later found still in his pocket book) and soon met with the village Priest and Barber who were searching for Don Quixote with a plan to lure him back to his home. Sancho abandons his journey and returns with them and Dorothea, who they have encountered by chance in disguise, to the Sierra and his master. Later he is obliged to concoct a story to cover his omission. He admits to having forgotten the letter but says that having memorised its contents he asked a local sexton to write it afresh and duly delivered this to Dulcinea. Here, despite his ability to invent a credible lie, Sancho's imagination appears to fail him. He describes Dulcinea to the Knight in terms that are not a portrait of a high born lady in a palace, but of the real Aldonza Lorenzo, the strapping peasant girl he knows Dulcinea actually to be. He found her, he says, sieving wheat and working up a sweat with the effort. She, like Sancho, can neither read nor write, so she tears up the letter rather than allow someone else to read it to her, thus preventing another from learning her secrets. Despite the blinding discrepancies between Sancho's earthy description, and Don Quixote's idealised fantasy, the Knight manages to explain each one – at least to his own satisfaction – such is his unshakeable faith in Dulcinea's existence, and he accepts his Squire's story at face value. But in Part II, Sancho's lies come back to haunt them both.

Before setting out on his third sally at the beginning of Part II, Don Quixote restates to his friends the Priest and the Barber, at the end of what has appeared to be a very lucid and rational discussion about the state of Spain, that he is and always will be a knight errant whose mission it is to right wrongs, relieve distress and counter injustice; where necessary with the point of a sword wielded by his strong right arm. It would appear, therefore, that his madness has by no means abated when he and Sancho go off at dead of night to begin their new adventure by visiting Dulcinea at her palace in El Toboso – much to Sancho's misgivings – to ask her blessing for this new undertaking. Not surprisingly, they fail to find Dulcinea's "palace" in the darkened streets of the village, and at dawn Sancho persuades his master to retire to a nearby wood, while he returns to El Toboso to search by daylight.

Being fully aware of the impossibility of his task, Sancho spends the rest of the day trying to hit on a solution that will enable him to conceal his initial lie to his master. He finally decides, given Don Quixote's propensity to mistake inns for castles and windmills for giants, to deceive him a second time by swearing that three peasant girls on donkeys, who are going past the wood where the Knight is resting, are in fact Dulcinea and two attendants on horseback. But Don Quixote's perceptions are not misled. Despite Sancho's play-acting, he this time sees exactly what is in front of him; namely, three none-too-comely peasant girls mounted on asses. For an explanation he immediately resorts to magic: a malign enchanter has clearly cast a spell over Dulcinea so that he can no longer see her as she really is. He addresses the girl he takes to be his enchanted lady saying:

> Y tú, ¡oh extremo del valor que puede desearse, termina de la humana gentileza, único remedio de este afligido corazón que te adora! ya que el maligno encantador que me persigue y ha puesto nubes y cataratas en mis ojos, y para sólo ellos y no para otros ha mudado y transformado tu sin igual hermosura y rostro en el que de una labradora pobre.[16]

> (You, the highest point of value that can be desired, the ultimate of human gentleness and sole remedy for this afflicted heart which adores you, the evil enchanter who pursues my steps has put clouds and cataracts upon my eyes, by means of which, and by these only, your unequalled beauty has been changed and your face transformed into that of a poor peasant girl.)

Mystified and embarrassed by these attentions, the girl pricks the sides of her donkey which starts, throwing her off its back. Without assistance and in most unladylike fashion, she leaps to her feet, vaults onto the beast's back and all three girls set off as fast as their mounts can gallop. Don Quixote is left to bewail his misfortune at the hands of ill-intentioned magicians.

From this point on, the Knight's desire to break the spell on Dulcinea is a constantly recurring preoccupation, made even stronger by his vision in the Cave of Montesinos some chapters later. In his dream, Don Quixote again beholds Dulcinea in her "enchanted" form as a donkey-hopping peasant girl, who this time asks if he can lend her a few maravedís to purchase the necessities that she still needs in the world of gothic fantasy which she now inhabits. To his shame, Don Quixote – true to the example of knights errant – has nothing he can give her. Though his passion does not diminish, the Knight's faith in the truth of his vision of his lady is undermined, and the two Dulcineas thereafter stand as conflicting symbols in his mind. The artistic triumph of Parts I and II as a combination is, of course, built around the changes of character and perception that both Don Quixote and Sancho undergo as the narrative proceeds. It has often been observed that the episodic, arbitrary nature of the adventures through which they pass undermines the coherence of the story but, as A. A. Parker has pointed out,[17] the continuity resides in the effect of these experiences on Cervantes' two main protagonists, and the changes they bring about in both. In this respect, there is a strong link between the various, seemingly unrelated happenings and the impact they make, which exerts a measure of control over the immense expanse of the novel's two parts.

Professor David Quint takes this defence of Cervantes' method a stage further, in that he claims to be writing to refute critics who see in Don Quixote no clear unity and stress its episodic nature. He states that: "[The book's] episodes connect with, and comment upon other episodes, and they do so through a repetition of motifs, parallel actions and direct verbal echoes,"[18] and he goes on to argue that:

> In the very structure and narrative progress of *Don Quijote* Cervantes mimics and charts the arrival of the modern world that is beginning to succeed the feudal aristocratic order – the latter celebrated in the fantasy literature of chivalry that Don Quijote consumes and tries to re-enact. . . . [The book consists of] a master narrative of early modern Europe and the movement from feudalism to the new order of capitalism that will become the realistic domain of the modern novel: the genre this book does so much to invent.

It is the charting of this very process, Quint claims, that sees Don Quixote give up the greater part of the anarchic violence and aggression he has shown in Part I, and adopt in Part II a more moderate, peaceable and overtly Christian approach that is bound up with his recognition of the need to use money. This links him, in Part II, far more directly to the "moneyed classes," the new bourgeoisie – such as the Gentleman in the Green Overcoat – and the old aristocracy represented by the Duke and Duchess. Just how far he has changed by the end of the novel can be seen when he preaches Christian virtue to the bandit Roque Guinart. Part II nevertheless turns, in Quint's view, into a "biting satire" on the "knights" of Cervantes' own day, whose entrenched power and courtly idleness offer an explanation for the nation's decline under Phillip III.

We may therefore sum up, starting with the observation that the enduring reputation of *Don Quixote* as a "funny book" was well established in Spain and its colonies by 1612, and that this opinion of Part I continued to dominate public judgement of the work as a whole, even after the appearance ten years later of Part II. To some extent this must be attributed to public taste and reader expectation. Readers hoped – indeed they expected – to find in Part II the moments of hilarity and slapstick physicality that characterised Part I. For various reasons, however, although the familiar formula was not repeated to anywhere like the same extent, the established opinions on the nature of the first part were nevertheless imposed on Part II. These were unchallenged until the nineteenth century, when the alternative view of Don Quixote as an essentially tragic figure was put forward by the Romantic critics, based almost certainly upon a reassessment of Part II. A further distinguishing factor between the two parts inevitably arose as a result of the decade that separated the publication of Part I and that of Part II. From the death of Phillip II in 1598, by which time Cervantes had begun the story, to its completion in 1614 many things happened which affected both Cervantes' personal life, the history and destiny of Spain and the direction of Golden Age thought and art. The doubts about man's ability to perceive truth from falsehood fostered by the growth of Scepticism, and the ability of those with power to manipulate appearances to their own advantage, constituted a radical change of focus in Part II, shifting away from the humanist inspired rationalism that marks Part I, and moving increasingly towards a minutely observed social satire of the nobility and well-to-do.

4

Truth and Lies in History and Fiction

Don Quixote as a Defence of Imaginative Literature

Not even the most careless and superficial reader of *Don Quixote* is likely to remain unaware of the book's preoccupation with history and how it should be written. Cervantes took the matter seriously, showing himself ready, if not eager, to join in what had become a public debate in learned and literary circles. Despite the numerous direct and indirect references in the novel to the past and to historiography, it is nevertheless difficult to identify a specific set of ideas that could be said to represent an authorial opinion on the issues involved. This is mainly due to the comic irony and evasiveness with which the past is presented, and the absence of a fixed point from which might be judged. Instead the past emerges from the actions and exchanges between characters in the fictional "present" of the narrative, and is usually mediated through the amplifying lens of literature. Medieval chronicles and legends, the Spanish ballad tradition, novels of chivalry and the Moorish romance all provide Don Quixote with heroic models of the past, which he seeks to recreate within himself in his calling of knight errant. Thus Rodrigo the last King of the Visigoths, Ruy Díaz de Vivar (El Cid), Amadís de Gaula, Orlando of Ariosto's romance epic (better known as Roland, one of the legendary Twelve Peers of Charlemagne) form a rich mixture of fact, legend and fiction with which the chronicler, the historian (and ultimately, of course, the reader also) is left to deal. It would have been as typical of the muddled historic "vision" of the *lector vulgo* of the early seventeenth century as it was central to the mind of the fictional Don Quixote, disturbed as it was by his obsessive reading of romances of chivalry.

The majority of the examples of Renaissance historiography by Spanish and Italian scholars that Cervantes was most likely to have been familiar with were probably what Richard L. Kagan has termed "official histories."[1] Written with a political purpose, Professor Kagan describes such works as "approved" or "authorised," much as nowadays writers produce biographies of famous people which have received the stamp of approval of the subject or his/her surviving relatives. He makes a further distinction between general histories, which tell of the origins, deeds and achievements of a nation and its state policies (*historia pro patria*) and those which offer a more restricted picture of a ruler or powerful aristocrat which enhance his fame and reputation, deeds and policies, and generally promote his interests (*historia pro persona*). After Alfonso X (El Sabio) of Castile (died 1284) who personally involved himself in the compilation of the *General estoria* of Spain, Kagan notes a slow drift from the production of general or national histories to particular histories devoted to individuals, a phenomenon that was typical of historiography throughout Europe from the fourteenth to the seventeenth centuries, though the opening up of the wonders of the New World, and the flood of chronicles and official reports it occasioned, did see a partial return to the writing of general histories of the Spanish empire in the Indies.[2]

Because they served a largely political cause, official histories of any kind were frequently challenged on the grounds of inaccuracies and bias. Being appointed to the office of official historian was, according to some men of learning, akin to being authorised to tell lies. Those charged with the writing of official histories, given the obligations of their position, invariably cherry-picked their evidence and sources to suit their sponsor's purposes. This they did – though often with great skill – as a matter of course, but they rarely invented facts or deliberately distorted the past. Their main concern was to arrive at a version of past events which served the interests of their masters, while remaining credible and convincing to the general public. Some, for example, saw themselves in a similar light to Fray Juan de la Puente, a Dominican monk and historian to Philip III, who described himself as "la boca de la república" (a spokesman on behalf of the state).[3] Juan de Flores, meanwhile, a chronicler employed by Isabel I of Castile, defined his office as that of a "temporal evangelist," whose duty it was to immortalise the reputation of the monarch. There was usually no shortage of candidates for a post of official chronicler or historian. Those who served their sovereign in this way could count on a respected place at court, a regular stipend, good working conditions and access to state and private papers that would have been denied to unofficial historians. Nevertheless, their positions were not always straightforward, as Kagan reveals:

> The content and character of the writings of official chroniclers were generally determined by others, and in most cases their reports and narratives

were closely scrutinised and subject to review. Some official historians bristled at the thought of this kind of censorship, let alone the idea of sacrificing their Ciceronian notions of historical truth to political concerns. . . . two humanists, Juan Ginés de Sepulvéda and Pedro de Valencia . . . found it difficult to reconcile their personal notions of scholarly integrity with political exigencies and other constraints.[4]

Historians, furthermore, both official and unofficial, often suffered attacks and criticism at the hands of their enemies. Unsuccessful rivals for appointments, scholars with opposing views, those who felt they or their families and ancestors had been misrepresented, political rivals of those who employed them, all joined in the chorus of accusation that the works the official historians had written served only to pedal lies and inaccuracies. One victim of such attacks was the Italian physician, churchman and historian Paolo Giovio (1483–1552), accused not only of lies and inaccuracy but also corruption.[5] Another such historian was the Spaniard Francisco López de Gómara (1511–1566), who was chaplain to Hernán Córtes. Though he never went to the Americas, López de Gómara wrote a *Historia general de las Indias*, published in 1552. He had virtually unlimited access to Córtes, and to many other conquistadors who returned to Spain, and based his work almost entirely upon the various first-hand accounts he gathered up. His findings, however, drew howls of protest from many of the men who had accompanied Córtes to Mexico – including Bernal Díaz, who was himself working on his own version of the conquest – for being far too biased in Cortes' favour. Philip II was forced to have the book withdrawn from circulation, and it remained so for some twenty years.

Despite the clamour of disagreement and criticism that surrounded some historians and their works, the classical ideal of history as a truthful record of the past, remained very much alive in early modern Spain. But there were increasing doubts in the minds of many educated Spaniards about the possibility of finding and interpreting a truthful record of the past from the evidence available. Written sources were seen to be often of doubtful reliability, and even eye-witness accounts by different individuals of the same event were sometimes irreconcilable one with another. How, then, could even the most scrupulous historian, no matter how great his integrity, fasten upon the truth, which must by definition be absolute and exclude all other versions? However, despite the doubts that sceptics might have had about the truth inherent in history written by men who were prone to error, history that was carefully written, avoided rhetoric and weighed its sources in a balanced fashion, was at least an attempt to arrive at the truth, as distinct from the imaginings of poets and writers of stories and romances who had no such intention. Though historians might tell "lies" by accident or error, poets and fiction writers did so deliberately and as a matter of course, and fully deserved to be condemned for their untruths and dishonesty. Certainly this was the view of many Churchmen and neo-Platonists at the time who thought that poetry, and the writing of stories and romances, should be forbidden on moral grounds.

Their definition of what constituted lies was far-reaching and arbitrary. It ultimately included everything within a narrative or poem that was not a literal, observable or demonstrable fact, and not only applied to narrated events, characters and experiences that were the product of the imagination, but also the rhetorical devices of poetic and heightened language used to describe them. Although the often virulent arguments of the neo-Platonists and their allies were based primarily on moral criteria, there was also a political dimension to their condemnation of imaginative literature that was very much a product of Counter-reformation ideology. Both the state and the Church made every effort to embrace the arts through lavish patronage in order to channel artists into supporting the prevailing secular and religious orthodoxies. However, the capacity writers possessed to express heterodox or subversive ideas was a constant preoccupation, and made them potentially suspect in the eyes of those charged with establishing the moral and cultural authority of the time. After all, as long ago as 380 BC, Plato had excluded poets from his ideal republic for precisely those reasons! The response to these attacks of those who championed the arts and poetry was cautious and restrained. After all, their position was not a strong one. In practical and literal terms, although poetry – the epic in particular – might deal with historical (and therefore "true") events, the terms in which the deeds of individuals, and the happenings of which they were a part, were described were essentially poetic and a far cry from the veracities of detail that the anti-literature camp claimed on behalf of historians and what they wrote. Indeed, the debate took on an adversarial character. History, standing for "truth," was lined up against poetry, which represented "lies," as distinct and opposing modes of thought and language.

As an inveterate innovator in literary form and genre, who constantly sought to extend the scope of prose fiction, and to create an appropriate style for the purpose, it is hardly surprising that Cervantes should chose to join the debate on behalf of himself and his fellow authors. He did not, however, do so by producing one of the tentative essays of the time in defence of literature. Instead, as with his later demolition of Avellaneda's false Part II, he chose to make his a-generic novel *Don Quixote* into the vehicle for his arguments. These were original and ingenious, and comprised a central theme in Part I of the novel, which continues to be discussed, though with much less frequency, in Part II.

With regard to his views on literature, Cervantes was easily able to put himself on the side of the virtuous through his satirical deflation of the popular but moribund genre of the chivalresque romance, whose exaggerated fantasy and hyperbolic, artificial style had made these books the whipping boy of virtually all educated readers. Having made a familiar enough critique, however, which Cervantes did by a completely original and imaginative device – the invention of a mad hidalgo whose deluded belief that he was a knight errant stemmed from his incessant and misguided reading of these novels – he cleverly mounted his defence of literature by means of an ironic questioning of the truth and accuracy of written history.

The claim to truth that the Neo-Platonists and their allies made on behalf of historiography is ironically questioned by Cervantes' repeated claims, which he makes in considerable detail and with a perfectly straight face, that his story is itself a history, one written (at least after Chapter 8 of Part I) by the Arabic sage, scholar and historian Cide Hamete Benengeli, a copy of whose manuscript had been found in Toledo market by an amateur bibliophile and antiquarian. He employs a local *morisco* to translate the original Arabic into Spanish, having enjoined him to do so "sin quitarles ni añadirles nada" (without adding or taking away anything) and thereafter becomes the narrator for the remainder of the novel. His relationship with the original text, mediated by the translation of the unnamed *morisco*, is frequently brought into focus by his intermittent questioning of the accuracy of Cide Hamete's statements. Although he categorically states that the historian's job is to tell the absolute truth, he maintains that small errors do not matter so long as they do not detract from: "La verdadera relación de la historia, que ninguna es mala como sea verdadera" (The true relation of the history, for no history is bad so long as it remains true). Yet the narrator himself promptly questions his assertion of the true nature of Cide Hamete's account in the following words:

> Si a ésta se le puede poner alguna objeción cerca de la verdad, no podría ser sino haber sido su autor arábigo, siendo muy propio de los de aquella nación ser mentirosos.[6]

> (If anyone objects to this record on the grounds of truth, it can only be because its author was an Arab, it being the case that those belonging to this race are natural liars.)

Indeed, he embellishes this opinion still further with the observation that since Muslims and Christians are such committed enemies, Cide Hamete may well have been guilty of giving Don Quixote less credit than he deserved for his courage and many deeds, a fault in his character as a historian since:

> Me parece a mí, pues cuando pudiera y debiera extender la pluma en las alabanzas de tan buen caballero, parece que de industria las pasa en silencio: cosa mal hecha y peor pensada, habiendo y debiendo ser los historiadores puntuales, verdaderos, y nonada apasionadas, y que ni le interés niel miedo, el rencor ni la afición no se les haga torcer del camino de la verdad, cuya madre es la historia, émula del tiempo, depósito de las acciones, testigo de lo pasado, ejemplo y aviso de la presente y advertencia de lo por venir.[7]

> (For in my opinion, when the pen could and should exert itself to praise so worthy a knight, it appears to have routinely passed over his deeds in silence; a thing badly done and worse conceived since historians have to be, and should be, accurate, truthful and devoid of passion; so that neither self-interest nor fear, rancour nor affection may cause them to twist the path of truth – that truth whose mother is History – the emulation of time, the depository of deeds, witness to things past, example and adviser to the present and indication of what is to come.)

The ever-present ludic element of the novel, as distinct from the comedic one, lies in Cervantes' obvious enjoyment of the complex games he plays with the reader concerning the totally spurious origin he claims for his story, sowing doubt in his or her mind thereafter about what constitutes "truth" in historiography. He has his implied narrator comment frequently upon minor discrepancies in the text, and raise points stemming from comments made by the translator on marginal notes contained in the original. But at the same time, the narrator accepts at face value the wealth of detail and the almost verbatim records of conversations, which could only possibly have been known by the most attentive of eye witnesses with a superhuman memory and capacity for recording. The omniscient narrator was, of course, already a convention of narrative fiction that was universally accepted – part of what Coleridge later termed the reader's "wilful suspension of disbelief." But Cervantes' deliberate and ironical reminder of the impossibility of the omniscient narrator's task in real terms, by rejecting the narrative conventions of fiction and insisting that what his narrator is telling us is a history, whose records must be housed somewhere in the archives of La Mancha, not only raises questions about how history is written, but also subverts the conventions of narrative fiction. The question of how "factual" much of written history is, and how much the result of the historian's powers of imagination and interpretation, is purposely left hanging – provocatively and dangerously – in the air.

Cervantes' playful, self-reflexive exposure and questioning of the mechanics of narrative has long been recognised as subverting the very form with which he was experimenting, notwithstanding the fact that it contains the seeds of almost every literary resource and strategy that later novelists learned to use and exploit. For example, in his book *"Don Quixote:" An Anatomy of Subversive Discourse*,[8] Professor James Parr argues that though *Don Quixote* is regarded as a novel, there are strong reasons to see it instead as a menippean satire in the best tradition of Horace.[9] Parr rests his case for the subversiveness of *Don Quixote* mainly upon a study of its author's use of multiple narrative voices, of which he defines five. The first is the historian/editor who narrates the first eight chapters of Part I; the second is the antiquarian and editor who discovers Cide Hamete's manuscript and takes over the story from Chapter 9 of Part I to the end of Part II; then comes the morisco translator of the orginal Arabic manuscript, followed by Cide Hamete Benengeli, compiler of the original history from unknown sources assumed (by the second narrator) to exist somewhere in the archives of La Mancha. Finally, Professor Parr identifies a "supernarrator" whose voice intervenes and comments on the events of the story, often at the expense of the second narrator. Parr regards Cide Hamete as a joke played on the reader to follow on from the first joke – and probably one of the funniest in any literature – when the first historian abruptly runs out of material in the middle of the fight between the mad knight and the brave Biscayan footman at the end of Chapter 8, Part I. In Part II, Cide Hamete is referred to more often and becomes another non-present participant who belongs to a level of imagination comparable to that of Dulcinea del Toboso.

By contrast, though the supernarrator/editor emerges as a shadowy device, who has led the reader into believing that the narrator of Chapters 1 to 8 of Part I was (briefly) the central narrative voice, and that the second narrator who succeeds him, having discovered the manuscript and somehow being familiar with the opening of the story, would thereafter be the chief voice. The supernarrator serves as the necessary link between the first story-teller and the second one, who is the narrative voice for most of Part I and all of Part II. The question of which of these sources is reliable – i.e. a truthful narrator of what actually transpired – is a vexed one, and in the end Parr sums up his position as follows:

> The figure who makes his first appearance at the end of Chapter 8 takes charge of the narration from that point forward. Retrospectively we may assume that he has controlled the first eight chapters in a similar fashion, although his presence is not perceptible there. The dramatised reader of Chapter 9, is an episodic figure whose role is to parody the found manuscript device as well as the credulous common reader (*lector vulgar*) .

> ... The running editorial commentary on the found manuscript and the
> playful set phrase "the history goes on to say" and its variants, are all by the
> supernarrator, who refers to Cide Hamete in Part I, Chapter 52 as "the
> author of his [i.e. Don Quixote's] history" ... adding that the discreet reader
> should give Cide Hamete's manuscript the same credit he would give to
> books of chivalry, i.e. none at all![10]

Parr finally concludes his arguments by saying that:

> The supernarrator is the real wizard of this universe [i.e. the novel] not Cide
> Hamete, yet he is by no means always in total control, nor is he infallible. In
> his protean role, he is able to take on the characteristics of several lesser enti-
> ties. He can be as ironic as the historian of the first eight chapters, as
> exuberant as the second author and as deceptive as Cide Hamete.[11]

This is either brilliant self-parody on Cervantes' part or perhaps simply
carelessness. *Don Quixote* is not the "well-wrought urn" with a classical
generic model that *Persiles y Segismunda* attempted to be, but an immense
experiment in the writing of fiction, carried out over some seventeen
years, which established entirely new possibilities for that burgeoning
literary mode. Some inconsistencies and rough edges are inevitable.

The unavoidable question of what Cervantes had in mind when he
unleashed this plethora of voices and sources now becomes rather
pressing. Parr's view is that he intended to call into question not only the
waning authority of the books of chivalry, but also of translations and of
history itself as a reliable source of truth. This is the source of its potential subversiveness, since it suggests that a similarly sceptical attitude
could be taken to the reading of The Bible. Don Quixote himself, probably the most gullible and ingenuous reader of all time, declares that
giants existed in olden times because the Bible says so, and the Bible
"cannot err by one jot from the truth." The Bible is probably the greatest
example of faith in translation that the world has ever seen, but
Cervantes, always the responsible subversive, teaches us in *Don Quixote*
to read, discern and especially to doubt authority, beginning with the
authors of printed texts. To make the truth of the printed word relative
rather than absolute, and metaphorical rather than literal, Cervantes was
obliged to give his readers a work which subverted itself and thereby questioned the printed word in general. His network of deliberate
transgressions of genre, narrative time and place, and above all narrative
reliability, together with his ultimate appeal to the *lector discreto* (percep-
tive and discerning reader) are the means by which he does so.

On the other hand, how can Cervantes' warning against the credulous belief in the printed word of the *lector vulgar* (the ignorant and

naïve reader) be reconciled with a defence of literature and the debate on the purpose and importance of history in which *Don Quixote* engages? There can be little doubt that Cervantes held history in great respect as an ideal, or of the seriousness of his involvement in the public debate of the time on what history should be and how it should be written. Furthermore, despite the self-subverting characteristics of *Don Quixote*, Cervantes' clear belief was that virtually all literature – except, perhaps, the very worst – had some value and usefulness within it, which was not dependent upon the literal truth it contained of the kind found in the moral, philosophical and religious tracts of the age. Cervantes' view – one shared by numerous others – was that truth and moral value could be found in the symbolic and metaphorical verities implicit in good literature, provided writers abided by the principles of verisimilitude. That is to say that literature could speak of imaginary things that did not happen, but provided they resembled real life sufficiently for readers to accept that they *might* have occurred, the truths and moral lessons that literary works contained were as real and valid as any others, and would be understood by the *lector discreto* (the intelligent reader of good judgement).

Cervantes' reservations about literature and history as vehicles for the truth are, nevertheless, delivered even-handedly. His self-reflexive unmasking of the "narrative illusion" on which prose fiction was based may, like his attack on the chivalresque romance, have drawn some nods of approval from the Neo-Platonists, but his clever defence of literature was not, in the event, weakened by it. If literature had its faults and limitations as a vehicle for delivering the truth, history, whose chief purpose was to do so, was just as unreliable. Don Quixote's catalogue of the virtues that a good historian must display though ostensibly a face-value statement, is, in fact, a highly ironical assertion which implies that unless the historian can achieve an ideal state of perfection, he is unlikely to get any nearer the truth by means of the principles he practices than can a poet or novelist who exploits the tools of the trade that he has to hand. Certainly, the "archives of La Mancha" in which the original evidence of Don Quixote's career is presumed to lie, never reveal it.

In *Law and History in Cervantes' "Don Quixote"* Susan Byrne observes:

> In the late Middle Ages to the Renaissance, as law was using the tools of the trivium to reformulate and redefine itself, history broke out of its subservient role to this same scholastic triad. . . . Renaissance study of classical legal manuscripts was followed in short order by the research, translation and study of classical works from multiple fields, including history.[12]

She cites the Italian Paulo Giovio and the Frenchman Jean Bodin as the two crucial sixteenth-century figures in the development of history as an independent discipline. Giovio favoured the eye-witness approach to historiography, interviewing individuals who were involved or took part in events wherever possible, whereas Bodin favoured archival research as the best basis for writing history. In sixteenth-century Spain, history was appropriated by various vested interests to serve different purposes, and the debate over what these were was often acrimonious. Byrne says:

> Cervantes wrote *Don Quixote* as the pitched polemical battles over what Kagan studies as "perfect history," "official history" and "political history" were being waged.[13]

Cervantes was himself a serious student of history. He is thought to have had in his possession at the time of his death a copy of Juan de Mariana's *Historia general de España* (1601) and Pedro de Mantuano's critical revision of the work. He was almost certainly also familiar with Gines Pérez de Hita's two-part *Guerras civiles de Granada,* published in Zaragoza in 1595 and 1597. Part I, consists of the *Historia de los bandos de zegríes y albancerrajes.* It was purported to have been the work of an Arab scholar Aben-Harim of Granada. He was, however, fictitious, and the work is a historical novel almost certainly written by Pérez de Hita himself. The second part, *La Guerra de los moriscos* was based on the author's service as a soldier in the campaigns against the Moors between 1569 and 1571, and is highly autobiographical. Cervantes' humanist education and cultural formation would almost certainly have meant that he placed considerable importance on the authority of the past, but it would be rash to assume, on the evidence of *Don Quixote*, that this necessarily determined his view on history and the duty of the historian. Yet, as the Prologue to Part I of the novel indicates, he was faced with a major dilemma. He had produced what was an essentially "modern" text in an age where literature still sought legitimation in its appeal to a largely classical tradition. Humanism made great efforts to repossess the past in order to appropriate its authority for the cultural present. But this was, perhaps, asking more than history or historians could realistically deliver.

Cervantes' great novel thus found itself, despite its author's religious convictions, moving towards a state of "secularisation," which Anthony Cascardi has defined as:

> A conflict between two versions of cultural history and two versions of the authority on which those histories are founded, which, for simplicity, I will call the "humanist" and the "modernist." Whereas modernism represents an attempt to generate historical orientation for and from itself, humanism

reads the past in order to distil a rhetoric of values and a canon to sustain its cultural ideal.[14]

Professor Cascardi further points out that Golden Age writers often invented a vision of history that looked either to the past or the future as a way of fusing the contradictions between secular modernity and classical tradition. This produced imaginary worlds in which social and historical conflict did not exist. The chivalresque romance and the pastoral novel are probably the most recognisable examples of this "escape from history," which, as Cascardi indicates, provided "potent fuel" for the timeless present we usually associate with lyric poetry.

> It produces the nostalgic aestheticisation of the past that we see in works like *El Abencerraje* as well as Lope de Vega's *El caballero de Olmedo*. In a play like *La vida es sueño* it leads to the advancement of a politics of virtue as a way to quell revolution and to avoid more radical transformations of the social structure. . . . In relation to Cervantes, literature proves finally unable to deny its relationship with history. . . . Literature is the mode by which the present acknowledges its formulation and situation within the past, even as it seeks (as in the more idealising *Novelas ejemplares*) to transcend the conflicts of the present.[15]

Cervantes, however, chooses to combine these contending historical viewpoints in a single narrative whose action is then driven by the inevitable tensions between the two. Don Quixote's madness has caused the everyday, material world in which he is anchored to be replaced by the fantasies of the realm of chivalresque fiction, supporting his conviction that he is a knight errant in the mode of Amadís de Gaula and the host of other super-heroes of the genre. But the deeds he performs under this misplaced faith are either robustly opposed by others, shown to be mistaken or lead to his being beaten up, manipulated and ridiculed. Narrative time and space are similarly mixed. As scholars – notably L. A. Murillo – have shown, [16] the three sallies that the knight makes would probably have taken, given the distances travelled and the various delays along the way, some eighteen months to complete. Yet they take place in a single season of eternal summer. We are also asked to believe that, in the month or so that Don Quixote is said to rest at home between Parts I and II, recovering from his ordeals, the history of his adventures has been written, published and become the international success that Sansón Carrasco reports to Don Quixote and Sancho in Part II, Chapter 3.

These anomalies have given rise to numerous questions and some perplexity among critics. Are they intentional, or simply the result of carelessness on the part of a writer labouring under personal, economic and domestic pressures? As aspects of a narrative that lays down such a consistent claim to be a historical document, they are even more incongruous, unless, of course, they are understood as a general reflection on the lack of precise chronology often shown in contemporary historiography. It must nevertheless be recognised, that Cervantes has created a protagonist who, from the earliest beginning of his career as a knight errant, imagines himself as a historical figure, whose deeds will be written about. As he sets off at dawn on his first sally, Don Quixote muses to himself:

> ¿Quién duda sino que en los venideros tiempos, cuando salga a luz la verdadera historia de mis famosos hechos, que el sabio que los escribiere no ponga, cuando llegue a contra esta mi primera salida, tan de mañana de esta manera . . . ?

> (Who doubts but that at some future time, when the true history of my famous deeds comes to light, that the learned sage who writes it will describe this moment, my first sally so early in the morning, in the following manner . . . ?)

The manner that Don Quixote then imagines is couched in the hyperbolic style of the worst type of chivalresque romance, which serves also as a mordant parody of this kind of overblown writing with its vacuous classical imagery (the passage herewith repeated in a slightly different translation):

> Apenas había el rubicund Apo;o rendido por la faz de la ancha y espaciosa tierra las doradas hebras de su hermosos cabellos, y apenas los pequeños y pintados pajarillos con sus harpadas lenguas habían saludado con dulce y melíflua armonía la venida de la rosada aurora, que dejando a la blanda cama de su celoso marido, que por las puertas y balcones del manchego horizont e a los mortals se mostraba, cuando el famoso Caballero Don Quixote de la Mancha, dejando las ociosas plumas, subió sobre su famoso caballo Rocinante y comenzó a caminar por el antiguo y conocido campo de Monyiel.[17]

> (Hardly had the ruddy Apollo shaken out the gilded tresses of his beauteous hair before the face of the wide and spacious plain, or the little, painted birds greeted with the sweet, mellifluous notes of their harp-like tongues the coming of the rosy dawn who had left her jealous spouse's soft bed to unveil herself to mortals through the doorways and balconies which lined the Manchegan horizon, than the famous Knight Don Quixote de la Mancha, spurning the idle feathers of his mattress, mounted his renowned steed

Rocinante and began to traverse the ancient and familiar countryside of Montiel.)

By the opening chapters of Part II, the knight's desire to win recognition for his forthcoming deeds has ceased to be wishful thinking and become "fact," as Cervantes introduces into his fictional narrative the historical reality of the publication and international success of Part I of the book. The mechanism by which this is done is the character Sansón Carrasco. He is Don Quixote's eventual nemesis, a young man who typifies the new breed of graduate emerging from the universities of Counterreformation Spain. It is Sancho who breaks to his master the news he has heard from Sansón about the publication of their adventures:

> Me dijo [Sansón Carrasco] que andaba ya en libros la historia de vuesa merced, con nombre de El *Ingenioso Hidalgo Don Quixote de la Mancha*; y dice que me mientan a mí en ella, con mi mismo nombre de Sancho Panza, y a la señoraDulcinea del Toboso, con otras cosas que pasamos a nosotros a solas, que me hice cruces de espanto cómo las pudo saber el historiador que las escribió.

> ([Sansón Carrasco] told me that the history of your honour's deeds is doing the rounds in a book called The Ingenious Gentleman Don Quixote of La Mancha, and what's more that the book says a load of lies about me, and gives my name Sancho Panza, and about the Lady Dulcinea del Toboso, along with a lot of other things we experienced on our own, which really scares me as to how the historian who wrote them could have known about them.

To which Don Quixote replies gravely:

> Yo te aseguro, Sancho . . . que debe de ser algún sabio encantador el autor de nuestra historia, que a los tales no se les encubre nada de lo que quieren escribir.[18]

> I assure you, Sancho . . . that the author of our history must have been some wise enchanter, for to people like them nothing they want to write about is ever concealed.)

Throughout Part I, the knight's default response to situations that cannot be explained in terms of the fictitious world of the chivalresque that he inhabits is to attribute them to magic, to the work of enchanters, whether friendly or malign. This magical solution then reconciles all experience within the confines of the supernatural world in which he believes. The explanation is again invoked to explain Sancho's question. In this instance, however, its implication is very clear within the humorous game that Cervantes is playing with the reader by merging fact and fiction so adroitly. The warning that "to those of that kind, nothing they want to write about is ever concealed" is a direct criticism of historians who fill in the gaps between established facts with made-up details of their own.

Bias and misrepresentation, according to whether the historian's attitude to his subject is supportive or critical, is another of the weaknesses Cervantes observes in the work of his contemporaries, which can also be coloured by cultural and ethnic factors. This also passes through Don Quixote's brooding mind:

> Desconsolóle pensar que su autor era moro, según aquel nombre de Cide, y de los moros no se podia esperar verdad alguna, porque son todos embelicadores, falsarios y quimeristas.[19]

> (It disappointed him to think that his author was a moor, as indicated by the title Cide, because no-one could expect any truth from moors who are all fabricators, liars and fantasists.)

The popular prejudice against the moors as a nation of liars, which Don Quixote is made to share, can also be read as a veiled criticism of the tribe of historians whose "true" histories are no more reliable than the alleged dishonesties of the *moriscos*.

The following day's conversation with Sansón Carrasco, who recounts the popular success of the book, which invites the public to read it as each reader sees fit – irrespective of age or class – and to draw their own conclusions from it, goes further into the question of history and historiography, with Don Quixote commenting:

> No hay historia humana en el mundo que no tenga sus altibajos, especialmente las que tratan de caballerías, las cuales nunca pueden estar llenos de prósperos sucesos.[20]

> (There's no such thing as a human history without anti-climaxes, especially those which tell of affairs of knighthood, which can never consist wholly of happy and prosperous actions.)

To this observation, Sansón replies that there are clearly readers who would have been glad to have been spared some of the blows and beating that the knight had suffered, to which Sancho perceptively replies that this is what indicates truth in history. Don Quixote nevertheless observes that such details can nevertheless be omitted because:

Las acciones que no mudan ni alteran la verdad de la historia no hay para
que escribirlas, si han de refundar en menosprecio del señor de la historia,
A fe que no fue tan piadoso Eneas como Virgilio le pinta, ni tan prudente
Ulises como le describe Homero.[21]

(Actions that neither change nor alter the true path of a history need not be
written down, especially if they redound to the discredit of the subject of
the history. I'll swear that Aeneas was not as pious as Virgil paints him, nor
was Ulysses as wise as Homer would have us believe.)

This is a reasonable enough point, but although they were reputedly
writing about true events, both Virgil and Homer were poets, who offered
an artistic version of those long past happenings that were encased in
myth and legend, a point to which Sansón Carrasco promptly responds
with the conventional view that:

Uno es escribir como poeta y otro como historiador: el poeta puede cantar
las cosas no como fueron sino como debían ser; el historiador las ha de
describir no como debían ser sino como fueron, sin añadir ni quitar a la
verdad cosa alguna.[22]

(It is one thing to write as a poet and quite another to write as a historian.
The poet can sing of things not as they are but as they might have been; the
historian must describe them not as they might be but as they are, without
adding or omitting any part of the truth.)

While Sansón Carrasco here states the accepted Aristotelean position on
the difference between poetry and history, it is nevertheless expecting the
impossible from the historian, who can never be totally in possession of
all the details that pertain to any action or event. And even if he were to
be so fortunate, he would be obliged at some point to make major judgements of selection about which information to include and which to
dispense with for the purposes of the historic narrative. Finally Carrasco
launches into the well-known praise for the book's clarity of style, acces-
sibility and the fact that it contains nothing offensive in it, nor any
thought that is "menos que católico" (less than Catholic), to which Don
Quixote delivers the concluding remarks of the discussion:

A escribir de otra suerte . . . no fuera escribir verdades sino mentiras, y los
historiadores que de mentiras se valen habían de ser quemados como
moneda falsa; y no sé yo qué le movió al autor a valerse de novelas y cuentos
ajenos, habiendo tanto que escribir en los míos. . . . En efecto, lo que yo
alcanzo, señor bachiller, es que para componer historias y libros de

cualquier suerte que sean, es menester un gran juicio y maduro
entendimiento.... La historia es como una cosa sagrada, por que ha de ser
verdadera, y donde está la verdad, está Dios.[23]

(To write in any other way ... would not be to write truth but lies, and historians who set store by lies should be burned, like forged currency. Though
I don't know what moved my author to include in the book novellas and
stories that are not part of my history when he had so many of my deeds to
record. ... So finally, Mr Graduate, I would say that to compose a history
book of any kind it is necessary to have a great judgement and mature
understanding.... For history is like something sacred; it has to be true and
where truth is God exists also.)

If we gloss these words, and the preceding points in the conversation
between the knight and Sansón Carrasco on history and literature,
Cervantes' contribution to the great cultural debate becomes clearer. Its
stages are, however, by no means simple or self-evident. No one participant in the dialogue assumes a Socratic role which argues the view of the
author. Indeed, by turns both Sansón and Don Quixote put forward
opinions with which Cervantes may have agreed. On the other hand, both
also make statements from which he would have distanced himself, but
which were nevertheless part of the public debate of the time. Basically,
Cervantes seems to be working towards the argument that historians have
a moral duty to concern themselves with the truth; or, in historiograph-
ical terms, verifiable facts. These and these only must form the content of
written history, and everything that is not "true" in the strict sense should
be excluded from the narrative. This is what Don Quixote demands at the
end of the exchange, though it is an ideal that is unrealisable, something
that Cervantes himself was almost certainly convinced of. The truth (or
fact) of the matter is that the practicalities the historian encounters in
maintaining a consistent and credible narrative oblige him to deal with a
host of constituent problems, such as which facts are more relevant than
others in the search for the truth, and how true but trivial matters, which
have little bearing on the nature of the historical facts, should be
presented – if at all.

But notwithstanding all this, the reader has to bear in mind the essential irony of the situation Cervantes has created: this debate on history,
historiography and the moral duty of the historian is woven around a
fiction, a story which insists that it is a history, and therefore deals with
real protagonists – to the complete disbelief of everyone but the most
credulous and naïve members of the public. It can therefore be argued
that though he understood the problems faced by historians when
addressing the ideal that historiography sought to achieve, Cervantes was

not primarily putting forward a case on their behalf. Instead he was seeking to show in *Don Quixote*, by deliberately making fiction interact with historical fact, that the two modes of writing, distinguished one from another by Aristotelean precept, in fact had a great deal in common. Historians were obliged to become "novelists" at times when they found themselves having to speculate (or even invent) material to fill the gaps between demonstrable fact. By comparison, historical facts could form part of a fictional narrative whose imagined characters and events could comment upon, and lead to a better understanding of, the fact itself. Thus we see in key episodes throughout *Don Quixote* an in-principle critique of much of what was, at that time, history of the "official" kind. But by drawing history and narrative fiction together and stressing their common characteristics, Cervantes sought to achieve his chief polemical aim which was to mount a shrewd defence of imaginative literature against those who accused it of lies and immorality. He successfully demonstrated that the "lies" – the products of the writer's imagination inherent in literature – were virtually identical to much of the "truth" that passed for history in seventeenth-century Spain.

5

Justice, Law and Politics
Don Quixote as a Vehicle for Debate

The previous chapter has argued that Cervantes' reflections on truth and falsehood in history and literature, and his deliberate blurring of the divisions between them in *Don Quixote*, disguised a carefully conceived questioning of the conventional intellectual position of his time, and an argument in favour of literature as a purveyor of "truth" (at least in the sense of true understanding) by means of narrative invention. This discussion is just one of a number of debates that are taken up at various points in the book which should be seen as interrelated, since history, law and government were linked in the minds of most sixteenth-century scholars. For example, the foremost jurists of the day held that to pronounce authoritatively on the law and its application one needed also to be a historian, and a number of them straddled both disciplines. Similarly, political ideas and the art of successful government drew upon the lessons of historical *exempla*, and an appreciation of the law and its interpretation.

It has already been argued that one of Cervantes' intentions in writing *Don Quixote* was to use narrative fiction to join in the intellectual debates of his time. He does this, however, through the philosophical lens of scepticism, whose influence on Spanish thought in the sixteenth and seventeenth centuries was briefly referred to in Chapter 3 above. As Maureen Ihrie has shown, Pyrrhonist sceptical philosophy permeated *Don Quixote* and comprises an intellectual frame for the events of both parts of the book.[1] In Part I, the knight's mad delusions are responsible for his misinterpretation of everyday objects and phenomena. His inability to realise that windmills are not the giants of his imagination, and road-side inns are not castles, is a practical exploration of the *ser/parecer* duality already mentioned. While this confusion over the identity of objects in the external world continues to be a problem in Part II, the main difficulty Don Quixote and Sancho face is that other people are also manipulating and falsifying external realities in order to deceive them. Thus the play made by the book regarding scepticism's second duality of *engaño/desengaño* is brought to the fore. Don Quixote's journey throughout the third sally is towards ultimate *desengaño*. The realisation at the end of the book that he has been deluded, and his subsequent repudiation, on the point of death, of all his mistaken deeds as Don Quixote de la Mancha in the name of knight-errantry, is his moment of truth. The "scales fall from his eyes" permitting him to die a clear-sighted and repentant death as Alonso Quijano. Furthermore, by subverting his own narrative text, Cervantes echoes the view of Francisco Sánchez that written authority cannot serve as definite knowledge of a thing, since this can only be achieved by subjecting external phenomena to personal observation, experience and reason.[2] Needless to say, this inherently sceptical mindset infuses the debates that Cervantes takes up in the course of his story, and the conclusions to which his characters come as a result of them.

Cervantes would have had no lack of examples, both in poetry and prose, of various debates being conducted in literary form. Commonly these took the form of the dialogue, in which two or more characters discuss a topic, each taking a contrasting point of view, and argue out a conclusion, following the model of the philosophical dialogues of Plato. Indeed, a great deal of the novel is written as a "disguised" or informal dialogue in the shape of the ceaseless conversations and arguments between the knight and his squire, and the more occasional and formal exchanges between Don Quixote and a third party, or a group of listeners. These dialogue passages are regularly interrupted by the single voice of the narrator who recounts some action, event or adventure which carries forward the momentum of the story, and grants the reader a respite from the kind of engagement with the text that the dialogue passages often demand. (This dialogic element is almost completely lacking in Avellaneda's imitation of Part I, which becomes a somewhat impoverished, two-dimensional allegory as a result.)

Having ensured that his novel had been given the kind of structure appropriate to a central purpose of debate, Cervantes was free to introduce his topics for discussion as and when he chose in the lulls between the dramatic or comic action. In addition to the question of truth and falsehood in history and literature – already discussed in Chapter 4 – we find that our author ranges over matters as diverse as the law, justice, racial tolerance, government and politics, the place of women in society and the effects of love upon gender and social relations. In his treatment of these topics – all of them sensitive if not potentially dangerous – Cervantes displays a subtle judgement and the ability to diffuse arguments and conclusions among different characters. No one is privileged with special knowledge or experience, and issues are discussed as they arise from sometimes remarkable, but always credible, situations that could affect real people and which present social problems as well as moral and ethical examples. Cervantes' artistic masterstroke in all this was undoubtedly his decision to make the two chief parties to the debates, his mad but intelligent chief protagonist from the educated hidalgo class and an ignorant, illiterate peasant, whose practical wisdom is often undermined by his greed and ambition. The vast majority of other literary dialogues of sixteenth-century Spain were conducted between fictional and intellectual equals – namely, cultured people whose social and class view was similar, even if the opinions they were given differed. Sometimes the participants in a debate were even mythical characters, concerned at the vanity and corruption of contemporary society and institutions.[3] But in the conversations between the knight and his squire, a whole new dimension is opened up, revealing the struggle to overcome the social and cultural gulf between two important classes in Castilian society – the minor nobility and the peasantry. The friction of such an encounter, symbolised by Don Quixote and Sancho, inevitably affects both and serves not just as an opportunity for humour and social observation, but also as a revaluation of the class-based master and man relationship it represents. Cervantes' constantly reiterated message seems to be that serious discussion about Spain and the state of the country can only take place with the participation of the people, which implied a dialogue that closed the cultural gap between the educated minority and the illiterate majority.

Cervantes almost certainly shared the conventional intellectual view of his time that political thought and the law were closely linked, and that both were informed by examples from ancient and modern history. The evidence to this effect provided by the text of *Don Quixote* has occasioned a number of important recent studies, notably by Anthony J. Cascardi, Susan Byrne, Henry Higuera, Richard L. Kagan and Roberto González Echevarría, on which the present book draws substantially.[4] Although his paternal grandfather had been a lawyer and magistrate, Cervantes had no legal training as far as we can tell, but he had a number of reputable jurists among his friends and acquaintances, notably Gaspar de Baeza, who was also the Spanish translator of Giovio's *Histories*.[5] Inevitably, his personal experience and work as a civil servant would have given him a good knowledge of certain areas of the law and the frequent failings of magistrates to administer it correctly or fairly. At the beginning of the sixteenth century, Spanish law was a voluminous, complex and often contradictory thicket comprising *fueros* (traditional rights granted to people at different times, often with a local or regional application, which formed a kind of common law) and central laws promulgated by the kings and Cortés. To these were added royal decrees and administrative regulations. The attempt made by King Alfonso X (*El Sabio*) between 1251 and 1265 to reform and unify Castilian law – known as the *Siete Partidas* (Seven Registers)[6] remained a landmark for Spanish jurists of the Renaissance, a time which saw fierce debate between Italian and French jurists on legal reform and the application of Roman Law to sixteenth-century Europe. The Italians advocated the *mos italicus* (Italian social code) a system which applied Roman legal categories directly to early modern society, while the French championed the *mos gallicus* (French social code), arguing that the laws of antiquity needed to be revised and adapted to serve the purposes of Renaissance Europe. While they took part in this debate, Spanish jurists did not, however, propose a third way, or *mos hispanicus*.[7] Numerous revisions to the legal codes of Spain were undertaken in the sixteenth century nevertheless, usually referred to as *recopilaciones*.

Cervantes' treatment of history, law and politics in *Don Quixote* takes place within the narrative structure designed to promote debate. Political ideas tend to be explored through conversations, mainly between the knight and his squire in Part II Chapters 42 and 43; or, as in Part I, by means of impromptu diatribes like "The Age of Gold" and "Arms versus Letters," which Don Quixote delivers to different audiences. Discussions of points of law are, on the other hand, mainly indirect and not engaged in so openly. Instead, Cervantes chooses to place his characters in situations to which the law applies and then to observe how they behave and extricate themselves from the legal implications of their circumstances. (Don Quixote puts himself at odds with the law when he releases the galley slaves (Part I, Chapter 22) and throughout the first part of the book is pursued by the Holy Brotherhood.[8]) This throws the responsibility back upon the reader to judge the rightness, wrongness or injustice of what happens to the affected characters, or simply leaves the question open as to what the law will ultimately decide in their particular case.

It is Byrne who probably best sums up Cervantes' achievement in weaving together of the strands of history and law in a fictional frame in the following words:

> History as a perceptive commentary and justice as a thematic content are two key elements of Miguel de Cervantes' *Don Quixote*, as evidenced in the author's multiple references to contentious literary debates of his day, his use of formal and thematic aspects of contemporary historical questions, and his protagonist's exploration of the meaning of justice. Cervantes' masterpiece created a new paradigm.[9]

It is from this synthesis of empirical and fictional material Byrne claims, at a time when the boundaries between law, history and literature were fluid, that the novel emerges as a form, an argument that Roberto González Echevarría most persuasively makes in *Love and the Law in Cervantes* (2005).[10] However, in Cervantes' case she might, with good reason, have added political thought to the list. Political ideas, mainly centred on the conduct of rulers and their use of statecraft to maintain order and justice, were no less a subject for debate in sixteenth- and seventeenth century Spain than history and law. The position of the Renaissance prince or monarch as the highest fount of justice within the Christian state was generally accepted, and his ability to dispense it even-handedly and fairly through laws and pragmatics was a measure of his success as a ruler. This was a debate in which Cervantes was also deeply involved.

Humanists and writers of moral and philosophical tracts produced numerous treatises on politics and statecraft in Western Europe during the sixteenth and seventeenth centuries. Although Machiavelli's *The Prince* is the best known and most notorious of these documents (it was written in 1513 for Giuliano de Medici, who had seized power in Florence in 1512, but was not published until 1532) his notion of *ragio di stato* (reason of state) which overshadowed all other criteria for political action and the maintenance of power, was widely condemned as unchristian and immoral for the next hundred years. Published in 1516 in Basle, Erasmus' *The Education of a Christian Prince* faced the same problem that Machiavelli sought to counter – namely political turmoil and rivalry between ruling families in Italy, France and Spain – but propounded a completely opposite solution. Rejecting entirely Machiavelli's nostrum for a ruler who had seized power that it was better for him to be feared than loved, Erasmus commits himself entirely to the principle of hereditary monarchy which applied in most countries in Europe at the time, and urged that those who were born to rule should be educated to govern justly and benevolently, so that a prince's rule might never descend into tyranny or oppression. Like many of the works on this subject that were to follow, Erasmus emphasises the importance of governing according to underlying Christian principles, a theme that was to be taken up in the numerous political treatises that were produced in Spain over nearly a century and a half thereafter.[11]

Although very few of these treatises are read today – except by specialists – they were clearly popular in their time, a surprising fact given that Spain was rapidly becoming an absolute monarchy with aggressive imperial expansion in both the New World and the Old. From Erasmus' *The Education of a Christian Prince*, to Balthasar Gracián's *El politico* (The Politician) (1646) a succession of works appeared which were severally referred to as *guías* (guides), *relojes* (dials), *advertencias* (warnings) or *consejos* (advice and counsel), mostly designed to assist and advise particular monarchs on the course of their present and future roles. Erasmus' famous treatise was written as a set of precepts for the young prince Charles of Burgundy, soon to become Charles I of Spain and Holy Roman Emperor. Erasmus had formerly acted as a tutor and mentor to the young prince, and stressed the importance of the education and upbringing of a prince in order to prepare him to become a good and virtuous ruler, which, he claimed, Charles V represented, as had his father, the Hapsburg Philip The Fair who had married Juana (La Loca) of Castile. Although Charles publicly recognised the significance of the advice that the book contained, he did not reward Erasmus or make him a royal adviser, an appointment the Dutch scholar had probably hoped to acquire.

At the other end of the sixteenth century, Father Juan de Mariana SJ, a renowned theologian and doyen of Spain's historians, wrote what was to become the most controversial and notorious piece of kingly guidance when he published in 1599, his *De rege et regis institutione* (Concerning the monarch and royal institutions), It is thought to have been produced at the request of García de Loaysa, Archbishop of Toledo and former tutor to Prince Philip, son of Philip II of Spain, as a guide and encouragement to the young king who, though remarkable for his piety, showed little inclination for the burdens of state. The furore that was to surround this work arose from Mariana's discussion of the circumstances under which a people was justified in removing from power a tyrannical and unjust ruler. His conclusion that there was such a thing as justified tyrannicide, caused him to be compared with the immorality of Machiavelli, and the book was widely condemned by scholars across Europe. In France especially, where Henry III had been assassinated in 1589 by a Catholic fanatic, and his successor, the Protestant Henry IV, barely escaped the same fate during the St Bartholomew's Day Massacre, Mariana's "liberal" views were loudly condemned. The outcry led to *De rege* being withdrawn by the Spanish authorities, a decision almost certainly influenced by the growing disagreement between the Vatican and the Jesuit Order at the time. It would be almost unthinkable that Cervantes would not have been familiar with both these books and the widely read, though somewhat uncoordinated, *El reloj de principes* (A Dial for Princes), a guide written by Antonio de Guevara in 1525. Just how many of the other political works produced in the course of the century Cervantes might also have consulted is a matter for speculation, but a continuous train of developing political thought that follows similar lines can be traced which spans both parts of *Don Quixote*.

Given that in Part II of the novel, chapters 42 to 53, deal at length with the knight's advice to Sancho on how to govern the "island" that the Duke has promised him, and – between the interruptions of different story lines – an account of how Sancho thereafter carried out his administrative duties, it is perhaps surprising that the political aspects of *Don Quixote* have been so little investigated. Two major and relatively recent contributions to Cervantine scholarship have repaired this omission. The first is Henry Higuera's *Eros and Empire. Politics and Christianity in "Don Quixote"* (1995) and Anthony J. Cascardi's *Cervantes, Literature and the Discourse of Politics* (2012),[12] which throw a good deal of very different light into this previously dark and neglected corner.

Arguing that the portrayal of Man's love for God, from Plato to Saint Augustine, Dante and Fray Luis de Granada, was essentially erotic by nature, Higuera points out that by Cervantes' day the notion had become a literary and philosophical commonplace.[13] This Christian symbol was taken over by the Books of Chivalry and transformed into the spiritual inspiration that the lady who was the object of the knight's adoration provided for his heroic deeds, including imperial conquest. This idealised the lady into a semi-divine figure, and is the main *raison d'être* for Don Quixote's devotion to the largely imaginary Dulcinea, which underlay all his other aspirations to triumph, honour and conquest. Indeed, its impact upon the nature of his madness is crucial so that:

> Le parecía convenible y necesario, así para el aumento de su honra como para el servicio de su república, hacerse caballero andante y irse por todo el mundo con sus armas y caballo a buscar las aventuras y a ejercitarse en todo aquello que el había leído. ... deshaciendo todo género de agravio y poniéndose en ocasiones y peligros donde, acabándolos, cobrase eterno nombre y fama.[14]

> (It appeared to him to be both necessary and convenient, equally for the increase of his honour as for the good of the state, to become a knight errant, and to go throughout the world with his weapons and his horse seeking adventures and carrying out everything he had read about. ... righting all manner of wrongs and offences, and placing himself in situations and dangers which, by overcoming them, would redound to his eternal fame and good name.)

Higuera's conclusions are that *Don Quixote* contains the greatest novelistic portrait ever written of an important kind of would-be conqueror who, in his Christian manifestation, is a very complex phenomenon. He observes:

> Don Quixote wants to conquer the world out of love for Dulcinea del Toboso. ... His love for her, he thinks, inspires his whole imperial project. She has, he believes, divine attributes – beauty, might, perfect goodness – but she has also a low, earthly incarnation in a village lass.[15] Don Quixote's

belief in Dulcinea's perfections is based on his faith in the Books of Chivalry, his "Bible". . . . With Dulcinea, I have argued, Cervantes is portraying the Christian attempt to found a great politics on an erotic relation between the human soul and God; with Aldonza he expresses the relation between the Christian God and Christ himself; and with the Books of Chivalry he is examining many political and historical issues raised by the Bible.[16]

There is no denying that, in parallel with the desire for personal fame and honour in the service of his lady, together with the righting of wrongs and the dispensation of justice, there is in Don Quixote's motivation a strong element of ambition and desire for conquest on a grand scale. Even Sancho Panza is to be rewarded with the governorship of a city or island in the course of this "imperial project," which has inscribed within it an imperial politics also. Nevertheless, Professor Higuera's claim that this adds up to a "Christian attempt to found a great politics on an erotic relation between the human soul and God" may be a step too far.

Certainly Cervantes faced a challenge in the deployment of his chief protagonist. As the writer of a satirical novel which participated in the chief public debates of the time, he had to find a way to present the code of fictional medieval chivalry, and the aristocratic politics that the mad knight represented, with the contemporary concept of a nation state ruled by an absolute monarch; a Christian prince who was also heir to the intellectual and moral legacies of Plato and Aristotle as subsumed into Renaissance Christian thought. If it was Cervantes' intention to use Don Quixote's acting out of the role of knight-errant to illustrate the shortcomings of society in post-Tridentine Spain, the idealism and faith of his creation had to come into stark contrast with the daily realities of life in the reign of Philip III. Cervantes achieves this by having Don Quixote's cult of individualism and violent action place him outside the laws and conventions of his era, but also by making him a figure of fun. Thus, one fervently held faith – the mad knight's absolute belief in the truth of the chivalresque novels, the beauty, goodness and power of Dulcinea and the magical world in which they exist – contends sharply with the typical Spaniard's belief in the rightness of the country's Christian monarchy, its imperial and Catholic mission and the politics that went with it.

Anthony J. Cascardi's *Cervantes, Literature and the Discourse of Politics* engages much more directly with political ideas, and with Cervantes as a political thinker of an unusual kind. The book explores how literature can provide opportunities to rethink political ideas by creating fictional situations in which the practical application of political principles affects the conduct of individuals. He states:

I want to explore the specific ways in which *Don Quixote*…is itself involved in thinking about what the polis and political discourse might be. At stake is both a new understanding of one of the pillars of Modern European literature, and an alternative to "scientific" views of politics; an alternative that bears directly on how we ourselves might grasp the place of literature in the political sphere.[17]

This might well have been rephrased as "the interrelated places of literature and politics in the human sphere," for by the second decade of the sixteenth century Spain had become an immense, imperial power involved in administering policies and laws over a huge expanse of distant lands. The modern state, as envisaged by Spain's rulers, demanded collective and coordinated procedures for its control, and the means to enforce them. Early modern politics responded to these new administrative and ideological needs in ways that were vastly different from anything that classical political theory had dealt with. Recognising this, Professor Cascardi states:

Taking *Don Quixote* as my pivotal exhibit, I hope to show that literature in the early modern age was regarded as having the potential to think both speculatively and with critical scepticism about important political concerns of the day, but also to engage with the largest questions that politics might ask.[18]

The modern reader may therefore look to *Don Quixote* for reflections upon questions such as the nature of justice and how it can be brought about in the actual world. Who should govern the state and how? What sources of authority should underpin the law? Where does private interest end and the public sphere begin? What is it that constitutes political virtue? All these questions are, directly or indirectly, discussed in the course of the knight's adventures across both parts of the narrative.

Professor Cascardi's exploration of Cervantes' political discourse leads to a number of intriguing clarifications of passages in the text, not least the purpose of the two singular diatribes on which Don Quixote embarks in Part I. The first (Chapter 11) has as its subject the legendary Age of Gold, and is delivered to an audience of unlettered goatherds. The second, expounded to his companions and other guests at an inn, (Chapters 37 and 38) rehearses the familiar debate on Arms and Letters, or whether the career of a knight or soldier is of more value to society (or more honourable) than that of a man of letters. Despite the country's increasing need of soldiers, the nobility and hidalgo classes were increasingly avoiding a military career seeking instead a post in government service or in the Americas, or to secure a place at the royal court. These *letrados* (usually graduates in law and letters from the new universities) formed the main body of the growing bureaucracy that centralisation created, and fuelled the institutional corruption and nepotism that had, by the reign of Philip III, come to characterise it.

This being said, the interpretation of these two discursive episodes, placed relatively close to one another in narrative time, has in the past been anything but clear and certain. They do indeed constitute well-reasoned, largely familiar arguments set out in a recognisable, rhetorical form which emphatically emphasises the "sane" aspect of Don Quixote: his ability to talk with elegance and discretion on any subject which did not impinge upon knight-errantry, and to do so in a way that was quite at odds with his bizarre madness and appearance. There is, it is true, a major irony in the knight's choice of audience and moment, which exemplifies the lack of discernment he often shows. But this in itself hardly seems a sufficient reason for the inclusion of these episodes: a major piece of the puzzle is clearly missing, which is precisely what Cascardi's interpretation of them seems to supply. Professor Cascadi specifically argues that the legendary Age of Gold, of which Don Quixote speaks in Part I, Chapter XI, can be understood as an imaginary blueprint for a radically reformed state, of which equality is a defining characteristic. Indeed, Don Quixote's vision of chivalresque society, as he it explains to Sancho, is one where knights-errant fight to eradicate the injustices and inequalities that have, since those far-off times, overtaken the world, and to bring masters and men onto an equal footing.

> Quiero que aquí a mi lado y en compañía de esa buena gente [the goatherds] te sientes, y que seas una misma cosa conmigo, que soy tu amo y natural señor, que comes en mi plato y bebas por donde yo bebiere, porque de la cabellaría andante se puede decir lo mismo que del amor se dice: que todas las cosas iguala.[19]

> (I desire that you sit here at my side in the company of these good people, as one with me, your master and natural lord; that you eat from the same dish and drink wherever I drink, for one can claim as much for knight-errantry as one can for love: that it makes all things equal.)

It is difficult to understand how the knight can maintain his "natural" superiority as Sancho's master, while at the same time seeking to be equal in all other respects with his squire, and Sancho quickly rejects the idea, saying it would demand of him standards of behaviour he has never learned. His master's imagined world of chivalry remains a class-based society, but it nevertheless seeks to redress the inequality and social injustice that was a defining factor of early modern Spain.

Don Quixote's disquisition to the goatherds on the *edad de oro* provides numerous clues to the nature of the new society that suggests itself, even if man cannot return to the ideal of popular legend. In that imagined age, all property and land was held in common. People could sustain themselves without excessive labour on the bounties of nature, and peace and friendship reigned, since people were simple, eschewed conspicuous adornment and consumption, and spoke the truth without duplicity or falsehood. Crime did not exist, and natural justice prevailed without arbitrary judgement. Furthermore, women were not molested and coerced, and were free to make their own decisions. What the knight calls "nuestros detestables siglos," (our detestable centuries) where no woman can escape the "pestilence of love" (that is, presumably, to become the object of unwanted male desire) has brought into being the knight-errant, to which order Don Quixote claims to belong, to protect women, widows and orphans, to help the needy and to administer justice. If his purpose is to return the country to the social and moral ideal of the *edad de oro* by applying the code of chivalry to Counterreformation Spain, Don Quixote's aim is a totally impossible one, and Cervantes knows it. Yet as a restatement of a political ideal that feeds virtually all desire for beneficial social change, the mad knight's mission maps out an end to which all reasonable, Christian people should aspire.

The Age of Gold speech therefore seems to stand at the beginning of a series of interlinking political statements that are interwoven into Cervantes' narrative text, and is followed by the discourse on *Armas y letras* (Arms and Letters). Neither conforms to the usual political debate of the time, such as the differences between monarchies and republics, whether Christian legal principles should apply to the indigenous people of newly discovered lands, or whether a just war can be waged against a religious enemy. Instead, they draw upon myth and rhetorical argument to explore more general issues, many of which have classical origins; such as what is the best form of political life, who should govern and how they should be prepared for the task. Don Quixote's argument takes the form of a detailed comparison between the lives, privations, training and function of those who enter military service and those who study to be qualified in law. At the start of his peroration, he offers a eulogy about knight-errantry, and follows it with the statement:

Quítanseme delante los que dijeren que las letras hacen ventaja a las armas, que les diré, y sean quien se fueren, que no saben lo que dicen.

(Let me distance myself from those who claim that letters have the advantage over arms, for I shall tell them, whoever they may be, that they don't know what they are talking about.)[20]

His conclusion is that the greatness and stability of the state depends, first and foremost, upon the soldiers who defend and impose order upon it, not on the *letrados* who make and administer the laws, necessary though they are.

The importance and value of "armas" therefore outweighs that of "letras," though the speaker makes it clear that he is referring to "letras humanas, que es su fin poner en su punto la justicia distributiva y dar a cada uno lo que es suyo, y hacer que las buenas leyes se guardan" (the study of the humanities, whose purpose is to decide on the detail of how justice should be distributed, give to each what is theirs and to see that good laws are kept). Furthermore, the soldier runs the constant risk of losing his life, or being disabled, for little or no reward, while the lawyer, once established, has many means of enrichment (including bribes) at his disposal. By comparison, the soldier's aim is to secure "la paz, que es el mayor bien que los hombres pueden desear en esta vida." (Peace, the greatest good that men can wish for in this life). Cervantes has the knight end his speech with a statement of regret that he is a knight-errant in an age of artillery and gunpowder, which may deny him the fame his valour seeks, but which may also mean that his deeds are the better thought of, to which the narrator observes that:

> De tal manera y por buenos términos iba prosiguiendo en su plática Don Quijote, que obligó a que por entonces ninguno de los que escuchándole estaban le tuviese por loco antes, como todos los más eran caballeros, a quien son anejos las armas, le escuchaban de muy buena gana.[21]

> (In such a manner and in such fortunate terms did Don Quixote pursue his address, that, for the time being, it obliged all those who had formerly been listening to him, since most were gentlemen closely familiar with weapons and had heard him very willingly, to regard as him mad.)

The reminder, after his eloquent discourse, that the speaker is nevertheless insane, is Cervantes' ironical shield against objection to the sentiments expressed either by the reader or the censor. There is also a hint of irony in the narrator's assertion that the majority of the audience were "gentlemen closely familiar with weapons." With the exception of the Captive, it is hard to imagine that many of those present at the inn were fighting men in any real sense. Certainly Don Fernando and Cardenio do not strike the reader as belonging to that category, and this may indeed be a reference to the decline of the former military aspirations of the nobility, which was much more vehemently stated ten years later in Chapter 1 of Part II of the novel. In the discussion on the state of Spain between the recovering Don Quixote, the Priest and the Barber, Don Quixote complains:

Los más de los caballeros que agora se usan, antes los crujen damascos, los brocadas y otras ricas telas de que se visten, que la malla con que se arman; ya no hay caballero que duerma en los campos, sujeto al rigor del cielo. . . . triunfa la pereza de la diligencia, la ociosidad del trabajo, el vicio de la virtud, la arrogancia de la valentía y la teórica de la práctica de las armas, que solo vivieron y resplandecieron en la edad de oro y en los caballeros andantes.[22]

(The greater part of those who today call themselves knights prefer the rustle of the damask, the brocade and other rich fabrics that they wear to the crunch of the suit of mail with which they arm themselves. These gentleman knights no longer sleep in the open at the mercy of the heavens. . . . Laziness triumphs over diligence, idleness over hard work, vice over virtue, arrogance over valour, and the theory of war over the practical use of arms, all of which existed and shone only in the Age of Gold and among the knights-errant.)

And again Cervantes ends Don Quixote's sharp critique by having him bring the discussion back to the imaginary world of chivalry that he inhabits, thus reaffirming the knight's questionable mental state in order to avoid the pointing finger of the censor.

Don Quixote's madness is, however, evident from first to last in the final significant political discussion in Part I of the book. He is being returned by his friends to his village, locked in a cage and convinced that he has been bewitched by a malign enchanter when, in Chapters 47 and 48, he and the village priest fall into discussion with the Canon of Toledo, who is journeying through the countryside with a party of servants. Traditionally, critics have seen this episode as a discussion on literature and literary theory which continues, in much greater detail and refinement, the arbitrary debate on Don Quixote's library featured in Chapter 6. It has also been argued that the moderate views of the Canon reflect those of the author himself on the nature and function of imaginative literature. For Anthony Cascardi, however, the views expressed by the Canon represent a mainstream, official version of taste and critical judgement with which Cervantes' novel both interacts and questions. The Cannon is presented as a literary theorist in "thin disguise" who voices the post-Tridentine religious and political view of imaginative writing, including the opinion that the novels of chivalry are "perjudiciales a la república" (prejudicial to the republic). The Canon does not expand on this in any way, and Cascardi argues that it is unclear whether questions of truth and history, verisimilitude and unity, pleasure and the imagination – all questions to which his pronouncement gives rise – are a genuine part of his concern for the health of the republic.

Nevertheless, the Canon's view that political decisions have to be taken regarding which influences harm individuals, and by extension society at large, for which he takes as an example the novels of chivalry, hark back to Plato's *Republic*. Indeed, Cascardi claims that he wishes:

> To probe the possibility that the Canon's 'theoretical' considerations in fact stand at the centre of a crucial set of concerns about the political role of literature. . . . Indeed, the entire novel could be read as an exploration of Plato's concerns in the very different historical circumstances of the early modern age.[23]

Cervantes was clearly aware that the political discourse of his age was founded on a set of dominant ideas which reduced the possibility of a balanced debate. The term "republic" was common in contemporary discussions about the state, especially among humanists. The *república* features importantly in Antonio de Guevara's *El relox de príncipes,* as do ideas about which books should or should not be read. Some humanist writers looked to the classical notion of the *res publica* as a means of sharpening the definition of the *polis,* and grounding concepts like "society" and "community." But through the deluded idealism of his chief protagonist, Cervantes completely alters the terms of political debate. At the beginning of Part I, we find that Don Quixote looks forward to a new Age of Gold in which his fame and achievements will be recognised: "Dichosa edad y siglo dichoso aquel a donde saldrán a luz las famosas hazañas mías, dignas de entallarse en bronces." (Fortunate the age and happy the century in which the light will shine upon my famous deeds, deeming them worthy to be engraved in bronze.)[24] The fame that Don Quixote aspires to win by his heroic feats of individual action is a precondition for a most fundamental political change. He in fact imagines himself to be charged with restoring political and moral ideals of the kind portrayed in the novels of chivalry, precisely the kind of fiction that the Canon finds to be prejudicial to the modern state.

The canon's middle-of-the-road opinion, comprising principles culled from the irreconcilable classical authorities Plato and Aristotle, together with Horace, is a kind of conventional view that does not allow him to engage with the questions posed by the mad knight in the cage. Instead he puts forward a set of ideas which protect the prevailing wisdom regarding literature and the wellbeing of the state:

> Hanse de casar las fábulas mentirosas con el entendimiento de los que las leyeren, escribiéndose de suerte que, facilitando los imposibles, allanando las grandezas, suspendiendo los ánimos, admiren, suspendan, alborocen y entretengan, de modo que andan a un mismo paso de la admiración y la

alegría juntas, y todas estas cosas no podrán hacer el que huyere de la verisimilitud y de la imitación.[25]

(Lying stories need to be reconciled with the understanding of their readers, and be written so as to present the impossible in a believable way, playing down the magnitude of great things and creating wonder and astonishment in the minds of men so that they admire, suspend, enlighten and entertain in a manner which, with one accord, causes both wonder and delight. But the writer who eschews verisimilitude and imitation can achieve none of this.)

As Cascardi points out, the neo-Aristotelian adherence to verisimilitude, though Cervantes would have agreed with the need for it, also inhibits one of literature's most important features – the license to invent and hypothesise; to redraw the world as it might be in fact. Cervantes clearly realised from his own experience that life could throw up happenings as lacking in verisimilitude as anything that a writer could invent. Though necessary to ensure the reader's understanding and recognition of the fictional world, verisimilitude by itself is insufficient to draw a dividing line between fable and history.

Cervantes also seems to have been persuaded that the literature of his own day was, in a broad sense "politicised," since it was subject to the control of the state and the Church. His response to this in *Don Quixote* is to devise a way in which literary fiction could be made to speak the truth, notwithstanding the limitations and constraints placed upon it, and it is against this backdrop that the reader receives the Canon's discourse, which Cascardi sums up as:

The Canon begins with a concern about the health of the 'republic' and the role of literature within it, and concludes by assigning to literature a relatively circumscribed place within the discourse of politics, in part by accepting a narrow conception of the truth. The Canon's bargain is this: we can make literature 'safe' for the state if we constrain fantasy, if we restrict truth-claims to the realm of the plausible, if we limit its ability to touch the soul and if we demand that it adhere to the principles of 'good form.'[26]

The Canon's attempt to protect the state against the unhealthy influences of certain books, is however an ineffective shield against Cervantes' probing into the relationship between literature and political ideas, neither, as some previous scholars have suggested, do these views reflect the author's own opinions.

In Part II, however, we see political issues being drawn much more directly into the reader's purview, though still carefully masked under

layers of fiction. At the beginning of the book, Don Quixote, still conva-
lescing but rapidly recovering from the privations of his second sally,
discusses with admirable clarity a number of the political issues facing his
country with his friends the Barber and the Priest. His discrete summation of the position is, at the end of the conversation, completely
undermined by his re-assertion that he is and always will be a knight-
errant, proving that his madness, despite appearances, is as bad as ever.
But politics is taken up again between chapters 42 and 53 of the book in
an ingenious and unexpected way. Sancho Panza has, virtually since the
beginning of their adventures together, been partly persuaded to follow
the knight because he naïvely believes his master's promise that he will –
like many squires in the novels of chivalry – almost certainly become the
lord of a country, or the governor of an island which the invincible Don
Quixote has conquered. Sancho's reflections upon his future ascent to
power are both funny and embarrassing, as is his belief that he will be
perfectly capable of governing, once he gets a chance to show his mettle.
His opinion opens up a number of discussions between him and his
master. Among them, the issue of social class is an important one. In
Counterreformation Spain, public office was in the hands of the educated
classes and the nobility. (Only the Church provided a way for men of low
birth to rise to the top through ability and hard work, but Churchmen
usually played at best an indirect or advisory role in lay politics.)
Cervantes thus makes his characters – principally Don Quixote, whose
madness must always be taken into account – express some interesting
views at a time when the nobility of Spain showed itself increasingly
disinclined to provide the military and administrative leadership of the
country and its empire. The social edifice which, at the start of the
sixteenth century, had done so was being challenged by new, upwardly
mobile elements of the population, a situation upon which Don Quixote
is made to comment:

> Hay dos maneras de linaje en el mundo: unos que traen y derivan su descen-
> dencia de príncipes y monarcas, a quien poco a poco el tiempo ha deshecho,
> y han acabado en punta, como pirámide al revés; otros tuvieron principio
> de gente baja y van subiendo de grado en grado hasta llegar a ser grandes
> señores.[27]

> (There are two kinds of lineage in this world: those whose descent comes
> from princes and kings, and whom time has gradually undermined, so that
> they have ended up at the top of an inverted pyramid, and those who have
> their origins in the low-born, but rise from one rung of the ladder to the
> next until they become great and important men.)

Quite where Don Quixote, an impoverished *hidalgo*, would have seen himself located within the two kinds of lineage he describes is not clear. He is not of low birth, but evidently sees himself as about to achieve great things through his deeds of knight-errantry, which will catapult him to fame and position: to the point, in fact, where he might marry a princess, the daughter of a sovereign whose kingdom has been saved by his valour. On hearing this, Sancho's response is to reply: "Yo soy cristiano viejo, y para ser conde eso me basta." (I am an old Christian, and that should be enough to make me at least a count.) In sixteenth-century Spain, those without rank or status were at least able to lay claim to some intrinsic worth on the grounds of being a "cristiano viejo," that is to say, that their families bore no trace of Jewish blood over many generations. This fact alone, Sancho affirms, is sufficient grounds for him to be made a count when his master rewards him for his service.

Even at the beginning of Part II, where Sancho is arguing with his wife (now definitely called Teresa Panza) on the implications of his imminent elevation to the nobility, he states that his daughter Mari Sancha – now of marriageable age – will be wedded into the nobility when he becomes a governor. This news is much to the consternation of Teresa Panza, who insists that the girl should marry within her own class. Sancho will have none of it, but some forty chapters later, when he is being guided first by the Duke, and then by Don Quixote, on how he should govern when he reaches the Island of Barataria, much of the social presumption, and the confidence born of ignorance, that Sancho had previously demonstrated has been eroded by his experiences on the knight's third sally. Indeed, both are changed men. The change in Sancho, however, is the more clearly marked, and seems to have stemmed, to a considerable extent, from his imagined vision of the Earth, insignificant and tiny below him, as he flew through the heavens on the back of Clavileño, the Duke's "magical" wooden horse.

Previously Sancho had been brashly over-confident in his ability to rule due to his naivety and ignorance of what that entailed. Indeed, he had made it clear that once he had the power and authority of a governor in his hands, he would use it how he wished and to his own advantage. But now – as he believes – he is on the eve of the dream becoming a reality, his words to the Duke are those of a different man.

Venga esa ínsula, que yo pugnaré por ser tal gobernador que, a pesar de bellacos, me vaya al cielo: y esto no es por codicia que yo tengo por salir de mis casillas, ni de levantarme a mayores, sino por el deseo que tengo de probar a que sabe el ser gobernador.[28]

(As for the island, bring it on! I shall struggle to be the sort of governor who, despite being surrounded by rogues, may still get to heaven. And this is not for any desire on my part to get on in the world, or rise to great heights, but because I have a strong desire to get a taste of what it is like to govern.)

At this, the Duke is quick to point out that once Sancho has experienced power, he will not wish to cease giving orders and being obeyed, to which the squire replies: "Yo imagino que es bueno mandar, aunque sea un hato de Ganado." (I imagine it feels good to command, even if it is only a herd of cattle.) And to the Duke's warning that he has now to prepare himself, and try on the new clothes that he will wear as a governor, Sancho responds: "Vístame ... como quisieren, de cualquier manera que vaya vestido seré Sancho Panza." (Let them dress me ... however they like, whatever I wear I shall still be Sancho Panza.)

Sancho's newly-found humility makes him an attentive pupil for what follows in Chapters 42 and 43, where his master Don Quixote imparts some lengthy and detailed advice on how he should govern and conduct himself. Don Quixote's "advice to Sancho" has attracted its share of critical attention. These two chapters are a clear, but at times highly ironical, reflection of the numerous *guías* for kings and princes that were based on Christian principles, and published and read in Spain in the course of the turbulent sixteenth century. In Chapter 42, Don Quixote spells out to Sancho a list of moral and ethical principles which he describes as "documentos que han de adornar tu alma"[29] (Precepts that must adorn of your soul). The first is the injunction that Sancho should at all times fear God, for only in doing so will he derive the wisdom to govern justly and well. It is followed by the instruction that he should, above all, strive for self-knowledge, so as to avoid gaining a false estimation of himself through ambition. From this point on, however, Cervantes' *guía* takes a rather different direction from its predecessors. Addressed, for the most part, to individual kings and rulers, these works, from Erasmus' *Institutio Principii Christiani* (1516), to Fr. Juan de Mariana's *De Rege et Regis institutione* (1599), took as read the status, nobility and power of the prince they sought to guide and impress.[30] Cervantes' brief handbook on government is, however, addressed to an uneducated peasant, and is based on the assumption, voiced by Sancho, that: "No hace al caso que no todos los que gobiernan vienen de casta de reyes"[31] (It doesn't matter that not all those who govern are descended from kings).

In becoming a *gobernador*, Sancho is not, of course, being elevated to kingship or any other kind of high authority. His role is far more that of a local or regional magistrate, who administers the law in his area of jurisdiction and is responsible for the safety, good order and behaviour of the communities under his authority. Even if his governorship were a genuine one, instead of a monstrous joke organised by the Duke and his servants, Sancho has been "appointed" to the position by the Duke himself, whose vassals the inhabitants of Barataria are. Cervantes' brief political and moral guide would therefore seem to be aimed not at monarchs and princes, but at middle-ranging functionaries in the state apparatus who were increasingly unlikely to be recruited from the aristocracy. They came instead from among the numerous and ambitious, young *letrados* – Sansón Carrasco is an obvious example – issuing from Spain's burgeoning universities. This new generation of educated Spaniard came from a variety of backgrounds, and sought their fortunes mainly as lawyers, civil servants and administrators, either in Spain or its American colonies. These "meritocrats" were, nevertheless, despite sometimes having lowly ancestry, educated men trained in law and administration, not illiterate peasants like Sancho Panza, whose aspirations to govern his fellow men and women would almost certainly have seemed funnier and more absurd to Cervantes' seventeenth-century Spanish readers than they do to those of the present century.

Yet these middle and lower levels of officialdom, as Cervantes knew well from personal experience, had become a cornerstone of inefficiency and corruption within the state bureaucracy of both Philip II and Philip III, notably where the administration of the law was concerned. Lawyers often manipulated court proceedings so that they could extort higher fees from their clients, while judges, magistrates and officials frequently accepted bribes (from those who could afford them) to administer the law in their favour. It is therefore scarcely surprising that two of the valuable nuggets of advice that Sancho receives from his master are firstly, that he should not be ashamed of his lowly origins, and secondly to pursue virtue and seek to do good deeds, since:

No hay para qué tener envidia a los que por padres y abuelos tienen príncipes y señores, porque la sangre se hereda y la virtud se aquista, y la virtud vale por sí sola lo que la sangre no vale.[32]

(There is no reason to envy those who have princes and great lords for their fathers and grandfathers, for while blood is inherited, virtue is acquired. Virtue is valuable for itself alone while blood is not.)

Virtue in this context, it would appear, is the determination to seek out the truth of every matter: "por entre las promesas y dádivas del rico como por entre los sollozos e importunidades del pobre" (that which lies beneath the promises and gifts of the rich man and the sobs and importunings of the poor). And Don Quixote follows this with the exhortation that: "Si acaso doblares la vara de la justicia, no sea con el peso de la dádiva, sino por con el de la misericordia" (If, by chance, you do bend the rod of justice, make sure that it is the weight of pity not that of a bribe which is the cause.)[33]

Cervantes' "philosophy" of politics is therefore rooted in the principle of good government by an upright ruler through the fair administration of laws that provide equity for all. Justice must be administered even-handedly, but pity and compassion should be allowed to temper the severity of a sentence. These humane views were almost certainly not unique to Cervantes, but the inference that, for a Christian prince, politics and good government were primarily a matter of ensuring that secular factors did not interfere with social justice, was possibly a fresh contribution to the debate. Cervantes' insistence that the law be dispensed with understanding and compassion had its foundation in the Christian doctrine of original sin, a point which the theologians like Erasmus and Mariana also emphasised. Don Quixote's advice concludes, in this chapter, with the words:

Al culpado que cayere debajo de tu jurisdicción, considérale hombre miser-able, sujeto a las condiciones de la depravada naturaleza nuestra, y . . . . muéstrátele piadoso y clemente, porque aunque los atributos de Dios todos son iguales, más resplandece y campea a nuestro ver el de la misericordia que el de la justicia.[34]

(Consider the guilty man who falls within your jurisdiction to be a miser-able sinner, bound by the condition of our depraved human nature, and . . . show pity and clemency towards him. For though the divine attributes are all of equal value, in our eyes mercy outshines and achieves more than justice.)

Having handed down the precepts for a good governor, Don Quixote turns in the next chapter to a parody of the other kind of guide that was popular reading among aristocratic and court circles in the sixteenth century, namely, the conduct manual for courtiers and the nobility. Its model was Castiglione's *Il Cortegiano* (1528) which became famous throughout Europe as the work which created the ideal for the Renaissance gentleman and courtier as a fusion of the chivalric and neo-platonic codes. Of noble family, the prototypical courtier must first be a soldier with all the necessary military skills to play a leading role in battle, but he was a modest, compassionate warrior, who was also a lover who showed unimpeachable conduct towards court ladies; also a poet and musician with an educated appreciation of the classics. *Il Cortegiano* and its imitators were concerned with the process by which the self-fashioned courtier was formed, and placed great importance on speech and appearance in impressing his ruler and his fellow men and women. Cervantes' parody of one of the most influential books of the previous century clearly questions the role and life-style of the courtier which, by the beginning of the seventeenth century, was clearly changing, particularly the commitment to military activity in the service of the king.

However, instead of a body of sophisticated advice on how young men of noble birth might achieve the ideal of the courtier, who was a soldier, lover and scholar of unsurpassable finesse, courtesy and sensitivity, we find Don Quixote imparting a number of very down-to-earth instructions – with which Sancho frequently argues – about how an illiterate and uncultured peasant should behave to avoid offending others. This amusing catalogue requires Sancho to keep himself and his house clean, to cut his nails, and to keep himself tidy, since "vestido descompuesto da indicios de ánimo desmazalado" (untidy dress is a sign of a disorganised mind). Sancho is furthermore warned to reward his servants discreetly and avoid ostentation, with the example that "Si has de vestir seis pajes, viste tres y otros tres pobres, y así tendrás pajes para el cielo y para el suelo" (If you have six pages to clothe, let three be finely dressed and the other three be poorly attired; that way you will have pages for both Heaven and Earth). If Sancho brings his wife to live with him, he must treat her respectfully but not let her show him up, and if she dies he should think of re-marrying a woman of suitable social status. Other than this, he must avoid eating onions and garlic, dine sparingly and drink little, since wine encourages indiscretion. A point of some hilarity is the knight's injunction that Sancho should avoid chewing on an over-full mouth, and above all "ni de erutar delante de nadie" (do not eructate in front of others), at which Sancho says: "Eso de *erutar* no entiendo" (I don't understand what "eructate" means). There follows a homily on the fact that "erutar" is an acceptable word in polite company for the common usage "regoldar" or "belch" which is a vulgar affront to the Spanish language. Just as the books of etiquette usually dwell on the importance of how the ideal courtier should be dressed, Don Quixote also gives Sancho instructions about what to wear.

> Tu vestido será calza entera, ropilla larga, herruelo un poco más largo, gregüescos, ni por pienso, que no les están bien a los caballeros ni a los gobernadores.[35]

> (As for clothes, you should wear full breeches, a long coat, and a cloak of slightly greater length, knee breeches most certainly not, for they are not appropriate for either knights or governors.)

Finally, Sancho complains that his master has told him so many things that he can't possibly remember them all, and suggests that they be written down. Although he cannot read, he promises to give the paper to his confessor who will then din them into his thick skull. This brings forth a torrent of complaint from Don Quixote, on how unacceptable it is that a governor should be unable to read and write, for this shows either that his origins are indeed of the lowest, or that he is a time waster. At least, he suggests, Sancho should learn to sign his name. To this, Sancho replies that when he was steward of his confraternity in his home village, he learned to make some shapes which people said spelled out his name. In any case, if he was a governor then he was the boss and would do what he liked, including pretending he had hurt his right hand so couldn't write with it. In the argument that follows, Sancho launches proverb after proverb to support his argument, which drives his master to distraction having just advised him not to speak in this way when he is a governor. Indeed, Don Quixote seems finally overcome by the fear that, despite his endeavours to counsel him, Sancho will make a disastrous mess of governing anyone. At this, Sancho restores the knight's faith by saying:

> Sólo vuestra merced me ha puesto en esto de gobernar, que yo no sé más de gobiernos de ínsulas que un buitre, y si se imagina que por ser gobernador me ha de llevar el Diablo, más me quiero ir Sancho al cielo que gobernador al infierno.[36]

> (It is you, your worship, who started me on this business of governing, because I know as much about governing islands as a vulture. So if you think that the Devil will carry me off for being a governor, I can only say that I'd far prefer to go to Heaven as Sancho than to Hell as a governor.)

Don Quixote, in great relief, exclaims that Sancho is fit to rule over a thousand islands, because: "buen natural tienes, sin el cual no hay ciencia que valga" (You have a good nature, without which no knowledge is worth anything).

Cervantes' view therefore seems to be that good government is more likely to result from the moral standards of the ruler than from his capacity for political manipulation. Only "good" people can be expected to manage the affairs of the state and its citizens well. Social status, education and experience are, by themselves, insufficient for the task if humility, a benign nature, adherence to the truth, a sense of justice and adherence to Christian teaching are lacking. Controversially, he also maintains that these qualities are as likely to be found in people of lowly birth as among the aristocratic and well-off classes. However, Cervantes' excursion into the realm of politics is not limited – as is the case with most of the guides to princes – to a theoretical discussion of how a ruler should conduct himself and be educated for his role. Instead he goes on to offer the reader, in five further chapters, a number of examples of Sancho's practical "wisdom" in dealing with the challenges that the Duke's servants invent to trip him up. These episodes are interspersed, between Chapters 45 and 53, with events that recount Don Quixote's encounter with Doña Rodriguez, the pretended wooing of the knight by the Duchess' maid Altisidora, and exchanges of letters between the Duchess and Teresa Panza, Teresa and Sancho, and "Governor" Sancho and his master Don Quixote. This is a comparatively new narrative tactic on Cervantes' part, which his narrator claims was adopted by Cide Hamete to create variety while avoiding the inclusion of material which had no part in the actual history of the knight and his squire. It also enables him to avoid the temptation to stray into unrelated diversions, something he had been criticised for doing in Part I.[37] Certainly the ploy of keeping his two protagonists apart for a few chapters gave him a temporary opportunity to build two separate story lines with proliferating developments, and to briefly reintroduce Sancho's wife Teresa and his daughter Sanchica.

At the start of Chapter 44, Cervantes' narrator leaves the reader in no doubt that Sancho's departure for Barataria, in his governor's clothes and accompanied by a retinue which includes his beloved donkey, now frees him to tell of the further doings of Don Quixote.

Deja, lector amable, ir en paz y enorabuena al buen Sancho, y espera dos fanegas de risa que te ha de causar el saber cómo se portó en su cargo, y en tanto atiende a saber lo que pasó a su amo aquella noche. . . . los sucesos de Don Quixote o se han de celebrar con admiración o con risa.[38]

(I pray you gentle reader, to let the good Sancho make a fortunate and peaceful departure and to await the barrel of laughs you will surely get from knowing how he acquitted himself in the course of his duties, and for the time being attend to learning what happened that night to his master. . . . for the affairs of Don Quixote can only be greeted with wonderment or laughter.)

Here, however, the order must be reversed. I propose to follow Sancho's brief and remarkable "governorship," and its political and moral implications, and to leave the Duchess's attempt to undermine the mad knight's idealised love for the imaginary Dulcinea, and his "righting of wrongs" in the real world until a later chapter. Despite the humour of both these narrative threads, however, Cervantes deliberately places his two main protagonists in situations where each is being tested in a fundamental area of their faith in themselves: Don Quixote's adherence to the codes of chivalry as a means of combating the failings of Spanish society, and Sancho's effort to bring honesty and natural justice to the rule of law.

Sancho is sent on his way to Barataria at the beginning of Chapter 44, and we return to the affairs of his governorship at the beginning of Chapter 45. Barataria, we learn, is a village of some one thousand inhabitants which, Sancho is told, makes up the island of the same name, and the Town Council comes out to greet the new governor when his party arrives, the narrator slyly observing:

> El traje, las barbas, la gordura y pequeñez del nuevo gobernador tenía admirada a toda la gente que el busilis del cuento no sabía, y aún a todos los que lo sabían, que eran muchos.[39]

> (The new governor's clothes, beard, corpulence and smallness of stature astonished all who weren't in on the secret, and even the considerable number who were.)

Immediately Sancho is ushered into the church and from there to the Governor's rooms where he is placed upon the judgement seat. Discovering that facing the chair is an inscription commemorating the inauguration as Governor of "Señor Don Sancho Panza," he immediately objects, saying that he has no title and nobody in his family has ever laid claim to one either. He says, furthermore: "Podrá ser que si el gobierno me dura cuatro días, yo escardaré estos dones, que por muchedumbre deben de enfadar como los mosquitos." (If this job of governor lasts five minutes, I will do away with these "dons" who, on account of their numbers, must be as troublesome as mosquitoes.)

There follows straight away the first case which the Governor is required to judge. It has been brought by a labourer against a tailor. The labourer has provided the tailor with a length of cloth from which he has made him agree to make five hoods. The tailor does so but the hoods are no bigger than finger stalls, which fit on the fingers and thumb of one hand. The tailor claims that he has kept his word, and that not so much as a scrap of cloth has been left over. Sancho quickly states that the case does not need to be resolved according to the law – of which he is in any case ignorant –but according to common sense and fairness. He very quickly decides that the labourer should forfeit his cloth, and the tailor should lose the hoods he has made from it, which will be given to the inmates of the local prison. This case is immediately followed by a more complex one between two old men. One of them claims that he has leant ten gold *escudos* to the other, who leans heavily on a cane, which the borrower has refused to return, claiming that he has already repaid it. However, the lender says he is prepared to accept the borrower's word if he will swear on oath before the Governor that he has truly repaid the loan. The borrower hands his stick to the lender, draws himself to attention and swears on the cross that forms the head of the Governor's staff of office that regarding the ten escudos "Se los había vuelto de su mano a la suya, y que por no caer en ello se los volvía a pedir por momentos."[40] (He had returned the loan, from his own hand to that of the lender, who, forgetting he had done so, kept on demanding its return.) Having sworn, he takes back his cane and leaves the room.

But after a moment's thought, Sancho calls him back and asks for the loan of the man's cane. He then hands it to the crestfallen lender saying that he is now fully repaid. "What?" cries the old man, "is this cane worth ten gold *escudos*?" Sancho asks for the cane to be split open, and there inside, to everyone's amazement, is the money which is now handed back to the lender. Sancho explains to the astonished bystanders how it was he deduced that the money was hidden in the cane, and "de donde se podía colegir que por los que gobiernan aunque sean unos tontos, tal vez les encamina Dios en sus juicios, y más que él que había oído contra otro caso como aquel al cura de su lugar."[41] (From that one could infer that those who governed, even if they were complete fools, sometimes had their judgements guided by God, and besides he had once heard the priest in his home village recount a case that was very similar.)

Next, Sancho is taken to a banqueting hall where a splendid dinner has been set out. But the ravenous Sancho is promptly forbidden to sample any of the dishes on offer by the Governor's official doctor, on the grounds that they will damage his health. (Sancho's propensity to overeat is such that abstinence on health grounds would have been be particularly galling for him, and this is obviously one of the torments that the Duke has thought up for him.) After a fourth dish has been refused him on some trumped-up medical grounds, Sancho, still trying to be reasonable, asks the doctor what things he could be allowed to eat without taking harm. The reply is:

Lo que ha de comer el señor gobernador ahora, para conserver su salud y corroborarla, es un ciento de cañutillos de suplicaciones y unas tajadicas sutiles de carne de membrillo, que le asisten el estómago y le ayuden a la digestión.[42]

(To preserve and fortify his health, his honour the Governor should now eat a hundred or sothin wafers, and some finely cut slices of quince, which will settle the stomach and aid the digestion.)

In mounting anger, Sancho asks the doctor his name and qualifications, receiving the reply that his name is Pedro Recio de Agüero, from the village of Tirteafuera, between Caracuel and Almodóvar del Campo, and that he is a doctor from the University of Osuna.[43] Finally gubernatorial wrath explodes! Pedro Recio is told to remove himself immediately from the Governor's sight, for although Sancho states that he reveres good and learned doctors, bad ones are no better than public executioners. At first glance, then, the laugh continues to be on Sancho, who is still completely deceived by the elaborate charade around him. But the incident has greater significance as a general critique of ignorant doctors who impose unfounded and dangerous theories upon their unfortunate patients.

At this point, the Duke stirs the pot by sending Sancho a letter warning him that mutual enemies are plotting to attack the "island" and assassinate the governor. On having the letter read to him by his secretary, Sancho comments that the first person to lock up should be Dr Pedro Recio, who will certainly kill him by starvation if he gets the chance. If he is going to have to fight a battle, he needs to do it on a full stomach because "tripas llevan corazón, que no corazón tripas." (The stomach sustains the heart, but the heart does not sustain the stomach.) Any hope that Sancho might have entertained about eating is, however, dashed by the request from a suitor to lay an urgent request before the governor. The man is admitted, and at considerable length requests the Governor to sponsor the marriage of his only daughter who, as he describes her, is the ugliest and most unsuitable candidate for marriage imaginable, to the equally dubious son of a rich neighbour, and to give him several hundred ducats to set up house for the couple. Sancho's patience is promptly exhausted by this request – no doubt helped by the pangs of hunger – and he sends the suitor away threatening to break a chair over his head. But later Sancho realises he has learned a lesson:

> Ahora verdaderamente entiendo que los jueces y gobernadores deben de ser o han de ser de bronce para no sentir las importunidades de los negociantes, que a todas horas y todos tiempos quieren que los escuchen y despachen, atendiendo sólo a su negocio venga lo que viniere.

> (Now I truly understand that judges and governors ought to be – indeed have to be – made of bronze so as not to feel the importuning of men of affairs, who at all times of day demand that they listen to them, do things for them and devote their attention only to their business, no matter what else might be happening.)

Sancho therefore emerges as a man who, despite his lack of education, is able to learn quickly from personal experience, and to win the confidence and loyalty of those around him by his simplicity and integrity. On the promise of food in future, Sancho patches up his misunderstanding with Dr Pedro Recio, and announces that he will make a tour of Barataria to find out what living conditions are like and what needs to be changed. Indeed, it is his intention to:

> Limpiar esta ínsula de todo género de inmundicia y de gente vagamunda, holgazanes y mal entretenida. Porque quiero que sepáis, amigos, que la gente baldía y perezosa es en la república lo mismo que los zánganos en las colmenas, que se comen la miel que los trabajadores abejas hacen. Pienso favorecer a los labradores, guardar sus preeminencias a los hidalgos, premiar los virtuosos y, sobre todo, tener respeto a la religión y a la honra de los religiosos. ¿Qué os parece de esto, amigos? ¿Digo algo o quiébrome la cabeza?[44]

> (Rid this island of every type of vileness and idle, ne'er-do-wells who misspend their time. For I wish you to know, my friends, that idle wasters within the state are no different from the drones in a hive, who eat the honey that the worker bees make. I intend to favour the labourers, to safeguard their value above that of the minor nobility, reward the virtuous and, above all, to respect religion and reputation of monks and the clergy. What do you think of that my friends? Have I said something sensible or am I cudgelling my brain for no good reason?)

Sancho the Governor is, it seems, someone who rules by consensus, not by autocratic pronouncement, and listens to his advisers. Far more important, however, is the content of Sancho's words. They amount to the most direct statement of political intention in the book, and a radical one at that, which sees the peasantry and rural labouring classes as something other than workhorses to be taxed, while a largely idle hidalgo class escapes work and taxation almost entirely. To Sancho's question, the major-domo then replies:

> Dice tanto, vuesa merced, Señor Gobernador. . . . que estoy admirado de ver que un hombre tan sin letras como vuesa merced, que a lo que creo no tiene ninguna, diga tales y tantas cosas llenas de sentencias y avisos tan fuera de todo aquello que del ingenio de vuesa merced esperaban los que nos enviaron y los que aquí venimos. Cada día se ven cosas nuevas en el mundo: las burlas se vuelvan en veras, y los burladores se hallan burlados.[45]

> (Your Honour the Governor has said so much that I stand amazed that a man so unlettered as is Your Honour which, as I believe, adds up to a complete lack of learning, should say so many things full of judgement and advice, that are far beyond anything that those who sent us here, and those

who accompanied you, expected. Every day the world beholds new things: deceptions turn into truths and the deceivers are themselves fooled.)

This whole-hearted response from the major-domo, one of the Duke's principle servants and the main organiser of Barataria charade, not only expresses surprise that an illiterate labourer can dispense wisdom and justice in the way Sancho has done, but is also a tacit agreement with the principles of government that he has just propounded. The major-domo's comment that he is witnessing tricks which give rise to truths, so that the joke rebounds on those who conceived it, is more than just a personal statement. It reflects far more pertinently upon the Duke and Duchess, who invented the deception for their private amusement, and their moral assumptions in doing so.

Governor Sancho's next decision is to make a tour of the "island," which clearly serves as a metonym for Spain itself, together with his chief officials and scribes to see at first-hand how the people live and what reforms are needed. On their first tour of the streets, which takes place at night, the Governor's party comes upon a knife fight between two men over the winnings of one of them in a nearby gambling house. Having dealt with the affray, Sancho reflects on whether to close down the gambling house, only to be advised not to. It is owned, he is told, by a man of great local importance, and despite the huge sums of money won and lost over the tables, is run according to the law and is not a hotbed of other crime like many of the poorer gambling establishments. These are the ones that the Governor should begin by closing if it is his intention to control gambling. While Sancho is considering this advice, two more cases are brought to him in short order by the officers of the watch. One is a witty young wag who enjoys poking fun at authority, and who is dismissed with a warning, the other is a girl dressed as a young man, who is soon joined by a young man – her brother – who is dressed as a woman. While very much the stuff of theatre or popular fiction, the episode high-lights a situation about which Cervantes himself clearly felt strongly; the tendency for girls of marriageable age to be confined to the family home by their parents, and to lack any knowledge of the world outside it. The girl in this case has disguised herself so that she can go out and discover what the streets actually look like, having been confined to the house by her strict father since she was a small child. The difference between this unnamed girl and the relative freedom of Sancho's daughter Sanchica, a robust, fourteen year-old peasant lass, who we meet in the next chapter, could hardly be more evident.

There follows the account of Don Quixote's continuing trials at the Duke's palace, an exchange of letters between Sancho and his wife Teresa, a letter from the Duchess to Teresa, with which she sends her some cloth and a necklace, both delivered by a handsome page, a missive from Don Quixote to Sancho and Sancho's reply. Governor Sancho's tour of his domain continues, though he is still tormented by Dr Pedro Recio's "dietary sophistries," and he is approached in the street by a man who presents him with yet another legal conundrum, purportedly from some local judges in another part of Barataria who have requested the Governor's advice. Apparently, the estate of an important man is divided by a river across which a bridge has been built, with a courthouse and a gallows at one end of it. Four judges apply the local laws, one of which states that anyone wishing to cross the bridge must swear on oath where he comes from and where he is going. Those who swear truthfully are allowed to pass over the bridge, but those who lie about their point of departure and destination are sentenced to be hanged at the gallows. A traveller has arrived, however, who has said on oath that his destination is to be hanged on the gallows. The judges have reasoned that if they let him pass he would have lied and therefore incurred the death penalty. On the other hand, if they hang him, he would have spoken the truth and should instead have been allowed to pass. On being asked what the judges should do with the man, Sancho replies that the part of him that spoke the truth must be allowed to pass, while the part that lied should be hanged. The questioner protests, that this was not possible since the body cannot be divided in two. To this, Sancho's answer is:

> Este pasajero ... tiene la misma razón para morir que para vivir y pasar la puente, porque si la verdad le salva, la mentira le condena igualmente; y siendo eso así, como lo es, soy de parecer que digáis a esos señores que a mí os enviaron que, pues están en un fil las razones de condenarle o de absolverle, que le dejen pasar libremente, pues siempre es alabundo más el hacer bien que mal. Y esto le diera firmado de mi nombre si supiera firmar.[46]

> (This traveller ... has the same reason to die as he has to live and pass over the bridge, since the truth saves him equally as much as a lie condemns him; and this being so, I am of the opinion that you should tell the gentlemen who sent you to me that since the reasons to acquit him or condemn him are of equal weight, he should be allowed to pass freely, since it is far more praiseworthy to do good deeds than bad ones. And I would hand you down this judgement signed with my name, if I knew how to write.)

Two letters from Teresa Panza follow hard upon the heels of this judgement, one to the Duchess and the other to her husband, which are read out for the amusement of the Duke's court. They explain the effect of disbelief in the village – notably on the parts of the priest, the barber and Sansón Carrasco – at the news that Sancho has been made a governor, and describe the jealousies that have immediately been aroused, and how much Teresa is looking forward to leaving the village in a carriage to visit her husband at the Duke's court and get one up on her neighbours. Hard on the heels of this comes the end of the joke at Sancho's expense, as he is relieved of his governorship in a feigned attack on the Governor's residence by pretend enemies.

But this is not before Sancho has spent a busy afternoon making bye-laws for the improvement of Barataria. He orders that food should only be sold by those who produce it, that wine can be imported from anywhere, provided its place of origin is stated and a fair price fixed according to quality, and that watering it down was punishable by death. He lowers the price of footwear, places an upper limit on servants' wages, imposes penalties for singing bawdy songs in public, and decrees that the miracles sung of by blind ballad singers should be limited to those for which there was evidence that they had actually happened. Lastly he creates the post of overseer of beggars, to ensure that those who asked for alms were genuinely unable to work, and not displaying various deceptions and fake injuries. Indeed, the narrator informs us:

> Ordenó cosas tan buenas que hasta hoy se guardan en aquel lugar, y se nombran "Las constituciones del gran' gobernador Sancho Panza."[47]

> (He decreed so many good things that even today in that place they are still called "The Constitution of the Great Governor Sancho Panza.")

Just how great a legal legacy Cervantes thinks these laws amount to, despite the fulsome praise of the narrator, is of course entirely open to question, for throughout the book carefully moderated irony is never far from the surface of any observation. But the extent to which Sancho's homespun "wisdom" is often superior to the letter of the law in bringing about justice has, I suggest, to be taken at face value.

But what is the wider political message that the example of Sancho's brief governorship offers? Characteristically, Cervantes erects several layers of defence to safeguard himself against criticism. Sancho is a figure of fun and the object of an elaborate practical joke. In reality he has no kind of authority, and the cases that he "judges" are fictions acted out by those who are party to the deception. He therefore rules over a world of total pretence where nothing is what it seems. The policy he adopts could therefore have been passed off as deluded make-believe, along with every-thing else, if the censor had chosen to question it. Sancho's example and stated political aims nevertheless form a model in the reader's mind. The first serious point that Cervantes seems eager to make is that those in authority need to possess a good moral character, honesty, a lack of pretension, human understanding and trust in God. Furthermore it is better to be governed by someone who is totally unlettered, provided he possesses these qualities, than by an educated man who does not. Secondly, Cervantes appears to suggest that government should rest on a basis of consensus, since no-one possesses authority unless it is entrusted to him by others. Thirdly, that in the resolution of human grievances and disagreements, understanding and natural justice are more important than the technicalities of the law.

A governor, magistrate or government official who conducts himself in the recommended way nevertheless needs a policy to guide him. The one that Sancho advocates is short and simple, if somewhat idealistic. It is to rid Barataria of wrong-doing and crime, to expel work-shy wastrels and vagabonds, to reward the virtuous and protect the position of the labouring masses against exploitation by the *hidalguía*. He is also determined to maintain the position and reputation of the Church and clergy. If texts like *De rege* and *The Education of a Christian Prince* were written as handbooks for kings and princes, the history of Sancho's governorship, and his preparation for it, is aimed at a lower, far more numerous but equally vital target. It is a manual for local magistrates, judges and administrators with whose frequent failings Cervantes was only too familiar at first hand, both as a private individual and as government civil servant. Nevertheless, a political message can be deduced from it. Namely, that no matter how carefully the head might be cultivated, if the limbs and extremities are inefficient and corrupt, the body politic will suffer, as will the reputation of the prince himself. (A case in point was the damage done to the good name of Philip II after the failure of the Armada, and the subsequently uncovered peculation and corruption which marred its preparation and provisioning.)

The examination of Cervantes' "political discourse" in *Don Quixote* can however be taken further. In the various discussions and declarations that pass between the mad knight, his squire and a host of other characters, it can be pointed out that we encounter little that is new in terms of political "philosophy." Like the vast majority of his European contemporaries, Cervantes seems to have accepted without question the institution of rule by a hereditary monarch, provided that the power given to one man was not misused, and was dispensed with justice, mercy and adherence to the principles of the Christian faith. But this acceptance, and the provisos that accompanied it, applied not just to heads of state. The qualities that distinguished a Christian Prince should be found also in his ministers, advisers, governors, judges, tax collectors and law officers. Those who made the laws and applied them comprised a large body of state authority which determined how people lived and behaved, both as individuals and towards one another. The law was thus a broadly political means by which the monarch, his ministers and the ruling classes – in Cervantes' day the landed nobility and the Church – channelled the activities and labour of the populace in the directions their rulers deemed necessary, although these were periodically challenged by the people. But in general, the greater the fairness and justice with which laws were made and administered, the greater the willingness of the people to preserve the *status quo*.

Where, despite his constitutional conservatism, Cervantes' ideas differ from mainstream political discourse in seventeenth-century Spain is in his constant questioning of the social effect on people's lives of politics and the law. Although Cervantes was unenthusiastic about the style and form of the picaresque novel, it undoubtedly influenced the type of social and political critique that runs through *Don Quixote* and a number of his *Novelas ejemplares*. The law, and how it is applied across all classes of people, is of far greater importance than overarching political theories. These were, in any case, almost redundant in a world where the accepted norm was a nation state ruled by a hereditary monarch or prince, which guaranteed a certain level of safety, peace and order to its citizens under the moral and spiritual guidance of the Catholic Church. (Only in a few places where Lutheranism, Calvinism or some other form of the "Protestant heresy" had gained a strong, popular hold, were alternative political models introduced or debated.)

The evidence we have so far presented in this chapter indicates that Cervantes pursued, as an important and recurrent thread in the fictional narrative of his great novel, a clear political debate (or discourse) with his reader. His main concern was a politics of social justice, and the implications of political decisions which, once translated into law, were administered by a professional bureaucracy of the kind in which he had himself served. The *letrado* class, in Cervantes' eyes less honourable or necessary than the armed forces, now held sway in a country which had fallen far below the ideal the mad knight had described in his speech on the Age of Gold. But only a madman like Don Quixote, dedicated to his lone crusade to restore honour and justice through a code of chivalry that was a literary myth rather than a historical reality, had the vision to try to change things for the better. Similarly, it is the unlettered peasant Sancho Panza, who manages to achieve a degree of honesty and justice in his short-lived stint as a local governor, even though his governorship was purely a hoax played upon him by two high aristocrats with time and money to waste in the pursuit of amusement.

By constantly manufacturing fictional circumstances that ask questions about how fairly people are dealt with by the authorities, and how well or badly they are able to treat each other, Cervantes asks his readers to make judgements in passing on a stream of "political" questions which reach into nearly every major aspect of life in Counterreformation Spain. From the disparity in the application of the law to the rich – who usually secure favourable treatment and the poor who seldom do – to the treatment of women and gender relations, the expulsion of the *moriscos*, the activities of bandits, the treatment of servants and apprentices, sending criminals to the galleys, and the increasing neglect on the part of the privileged nobility of military and other services to the king, Cervantes' political discourse is an integral part of his creative genius as a novelist. It may well be argued, and probably was by many of his contemporaries, that despite Cervantes' protestations to the contrary, the novel may feed off history but reveals little by way of truth in return. The history that Don Quixote and the picaresque novel both truthfully, though not literally, portray is that of the world which their fiction imitates, with all the social, moral and political problems which that world contains. This is a challenging role for the writer to take upon himself and one that, in its turn, challenges established attitudes, practices, ideas and morals.

6

Humour, Irony and Satire in
Don Quixote
Public Merriment and Private Laughter

There is a well-known anecdote that, on hearing one of his courtiers suddenly burst into a peal of spontaneous laughter, King Philip III of Spain commented: "He must be reading *Don Quixote*." The question of humour in Cervantes' novel – what kind it is, its centrality to the book's conception and how the author chooses to employ it – has had its fair share of critical attention since its infectious influence began to spread across Western Europe and the New World. But since the early 1960s, when P. E. Russell's important and controversial article "*Don Quixote* as a Funny Book" appeared,[1] a keen, historicist light has been shed on the subject. Professor Russell's argument was that Cervantes himself regarded his experimental narrative to be an inducement to laughter, and that there was no evidence that either its author or its international readership, in the seventeenth and eighteenth centuries, saw it otherwise – in short, it was universally regarded as primarily a source of amusement.

To a significant extent, this view, which was shared and developed by a number of Cervantes specialists, notably A. J. Close, questioned the assumptions behind the Romantic school of Cervantes criticism which had dominated the period from 1830 to 1920. Indeed, Close's influential work *The Romantic Approach to "Don Quixote"* (Cambridge University Press, Cambridge, 1979) effectively challenged the basis for symbolic readings of the book which turned its mad protagonist into a tragic figure – the idealist ultimately defeated by a cynical and materialistic world. But in the process, both Russell and Close raised some necessary questions about humour in *Don Quixote*, namely, what did Cervantes and his contemporaries regard as funny, and how far could humour and hilarity be exploited in a fictional narrative without causing offence? Close's investigation of these questions in his study entitled

Cervantes and the Comic Mind of his Age (2000)[2] provided a number of detailed and well-researched answers.

But laughter, particularly in the literary sphere, is a notoriously two-edged weapon. It is almost always subversive, even when sympathetic, because it banishes seriousness and strips away dignity and authority from whatever it is directed at. A "funny book" is always likely to exploit the laughter of its readers for some particular end, often doing so in the form of satire. The things that made Cervantes' contemporaries laugh are mostly familiar enough to the post-modern reader. The incongruous, the ugly or misshapen – including human beings – often excited mocking, ribald merriment. Accidents and physical mishaps might also be greeted with laughter, much to the probable chagrin of the victims. Obscenity and scatological humour were – and still are – commonplace among ordinary people, as was parody, iconoclasm and almost any kind of irreverence directed by the masses at their social superiors. These were all mainly "vulgar," spontaneous forms of humour, which, along with wordplay, slang and thieves' cant, made up the popular "carnavalesque" tradition so brilliantly defined by Bakhtin. These were the cultural patrimony of all classes, notwithstanding their social position. But the culture of written language, still relatively new as the printing industry and book trade expanded, was a very different matter. The printed word was the basis of learning and entertainment for the more prosperous, educated classes, and its contents and standards – unlike the spontaneous oral tradition – were strictly monitored by the twin guardians of Spanish society, the State and the Church.

In *Cervantes and the Comic Mind of his Age*, A. J. Close offers a thorough discussion of the two key aspects of what the Spanish reading public looked for in good writing. These he describes as *propriedad* (appropriateness or decorum) and *discreción* (wit), both powerful elements in Cervantes' notion of the poetics of comedy. Close comments:

> Cervantes practices what he preaches [in relation to *propriedad*] employing euphemism for sexual and scatological matters, and attributing indecent language, when used, to low characters like Sancho and the innkeeper's wife. ... [*Discreción* or wit] is a quality of mind with which the wit of Cervantes' humourists, including Sancho, is repeatedly associated. ... It includes such things as taste, tact, fundamentally a sense of occasion, all of which lean naturally in the direction of *propriedad*.[3]

In Cervantes' case, there is an overlap between his idea of "good comedy" and his conception of good linguistic usage. (Even comic absurdity gives greater pleasure when guided by wit and expressed effectively.) But is Cervantes' insistence on *propriedad* typical or exceptional? His reservations about the picaresque genre are well-known, and there is a good deal of difference between his use of language and that of the picaresque authors. Close's observation on this question is informative:

> He [Cervantes] transformed comic fiction either by purging its tradition-ally base subject matter – clever seductions by randy friars, ingenious confidence tricks, confusions in dark bedrooms, mishaps in privies – or by presenting it from a central perspective which is, however comical, basically enlightened or honourable. From that basic shift, much though modern Cervantine criticism has been reluctant to accept the consequences, exem-plariness naturally follows; it pervades narrative viewpoint, atmosphere and ethos, metaphoric connotations, rhetorical slant and characterisation.[4]

If Cervantes himself makes any statement, direct or indirect, on his theory of comic fiction it is probably to be found in his Prologue to Part I, where the perplexed "author" is advised by "friend" not to follow the pretensions of other authors by trying to impress readers, in the intro-ductions and epilogues to their works, with quotations, marginal notes, and eulogies in prose and verse from scholars, noblemen or other founts of wisdom. Instead he should imitate life as he sees it, since the truer the imitation the better the writing is likely to be, and concentrate on his chief aim of debunking the iniquitous novels of chivalry, on which no classical authority has ever pronounced judgement. Furthermore, he should seek to make his history of the deeds of Don Quixote as appeal-ing as possible to all sorts and conditions of readers:

> Sólo tiene que aprovecharse de la imitación en lo que fuere escribiendo, que, cuanto ella fuere más perfecta, tanto mejor será lo que se escribiere. . . . Procurad también que, leyendo vuestra historia, el melancólico se mueva a risa, el risueño la acreciente, el simple no se enfade, el discreto se admire de la invención, el grave no la desprecie, ni el prudente deje de alabarla.[5]

> (All that is needed is to take advantage of imitation in whatever you write, for the more perfectly you imitate life, the better the writing will be. . . . Try also to ensure that, when reading your story, the melancholy individ-ual is moved to laughter, he who laughs easily laughs even louder, the simple-minded does not get bored, the reader of good judgment admires its wit and imagination, the serious-minded don't look down on it, nor do the prudent withhold their praise.)

This advice from the unnamed "friend" probably spells out the bones of Cervantes' theory of comic narrative as clearly as anything in the ensuing twelve hundred pages. Indeed, Close observes, in relation to this passage,

> This insistence on merriment, unpretentious style and educative purpose brings *Don Quixote* firmly into the sphere of the Classical art of comedy which aims to purge emotions through laughter . . . and portrays, in easy and familiar language, the ridiculous foibles of ordinary folk in order to teach them prudence in the conduct of their private lives.[6]

A principal aim of *Don Quixote* – in fact, the *only* one stated in the Prologue to Part I - is the demolition of the waning genre of the chivalresque romances, which were still a popular source of entertainment and diversionary reading for all classes of people in sixteenth-century Spain. To mount a general attach on an entire genre required both imagination and the command of a suitable method of attack. Inevitably this was furnished by the satirical mode, but in which of its numerous forms was something over which Cervantes must have deliberated. Satire is an ancient form of criticism and attack with venerable classical roots and examples. It frequently employs a manifest fiction which can be levelled at almost any target – an individual, a group, a state of affairs, customs, manners and moral standards, political manipulation and ideology, cultural standards, tastes and scholarship – indeed, very few aspects of human life, including ideas and religion, have escaped its barbs over the centuries. The satirist assaults his target primarily by devaluing it; by making it seem ridiculous, hypocritical or mistaken in the eyes of his readers, and he uses humour in one or other of its rhetorical forms to do so. He thereby incites laughter at the target's expense, with irony, parody, paradox and metonymy being the most frequently employed means of doing so. Gilbert Highet argues for the existence of three main forms of satire.[7] These are the diatribe, where a first person speaker addresses the reader; the parody, where an existing work of literature, form or genre is ridiculed by the creation of an incongruous imitation which distorts its style, ideas and content; and lastly satirical intent contained in a non-parodic fiction. In sixteenth-century Spain, the "dialogue," a debate between two or more people – as used by Plato to expound philosophical ideas – was also adapted by humanists to serve as a vehicle not only for discussion of contemporary topics and issues, but also for satire.

Cervantes did not begin his literary career as a satirist or a comic writer. His first novel, the pastoral romance *La Galatea* (1585) more or less followed the generic formula of a neo-platonic debate on love, conducted by numerous idealised characters within an equally unreal natural setting. Shortly after, however, Cervantes began to write for the theatre. Though most of his plays have been lost, those that remain, particularly the *entremeses* – short, comic scenes, often with music and songs, which were performed in the intervals between the acts of a *comedia* – show a sharp ear for dialogue, good characterisation and a flair for comic invention. By 1597, when it is thought that Cervantes began *Don Quixote*, life and experience had inevitably changed him. He had begun to adopt a more philosophical, ironic and critical perspective on life, which seems to have sharpened his imagination, inventiveness and sense of the ridiculous. Furthermore, his time in government service, during the later years of the reign of the ageing Philip II, seems to have imbued him with a strong sense of the political, imperial and spiritual failings of his country, and an awareness of its growing social injustice. These factors clearly influenced the tone of his mature writing, including both parts of *Don Quixote*. It is in a number of the later stories of the *novelas ejemplares*, and in *Viaje de Parnaso*, his long, satirical, mock-epic poem which criticises the literary tastes and standards of the day, that we see the emergence of Cervantes the satirist.

The ideological clash between humanism and scholasticism in the sixteenth century, and the movement for Church reform championed by scholars like Erasmus of Rotterdam, had led to the regeneration of satirical writing of all kinds in the early to mid-sixteen hundreds in Spain and Italy, while Rabelais' immortal *Gargantua et Pantagruel* marked the high point of a sophisticated style of satire that exploited the grotesque realism and fantasy of the medieval parodists and folk humour. In works like *Lazarillo de Tormes*, and a number of other writings by humanists and *conversos*, many of which circulated in Spain in the second half of the century in manuscript form only, the spirit of opposition and criticism remained very much alive. Whether or not Cervantes knew of these works, he was able to draw inspiration from this current of heterodoxy which he channelled into Part I of his experimental narrative. It heralded also Cervantes' concern for what literature could achieve outside the parameters of the accepted genres and conventions. Had it a role, like that of "righting wrongs," which Cervantes' mad protagonist had abrogated to himself in his reincarnation as a knight errant? Could it function as a corrective to the failings and injustices of the age? It is the belief behind this study that Cervantes' natural tendency towards playful irony, his talent for clever parody and his gift for extravagant physical humour were all called into play to allow him to pursue these questions. Any extended fictional narrative, especially one like *Don Quixote* that lies outside any recognised genre, is an inclusive form which, while offering numerous opportunities to employ satire, is not limited to the satiric mode. Within the encompassing story therefore, Cervantes found freedom to manoeuvre his satire in a number of different directions, or to suspend it altogether.

Although this discovery grew out of what the author's creative imagination perceived as his story unfolded, the pieces did not come together all at once. As the novel opens, an omniscient, if ironical, narrative voice claims the role of historian who tells the story of an impoverished hidalgo, whose fortune, life-style and appearance are briefly but deftly sketched in, save for the exact place in La Mancha where he lives. This information the narrator chooses to withhold, but he is also purposely vague about the character's name, which might be "Quijada" or "Quesada."[8] But everything we learn about the hidalgo's straightened circumstances, diet and way of life presents us with a ironical parody of the declining class of small landed gentry and petty nobility from which he comes. We next learn of this gentleman's passion for books of chivalry, of which he had become an obsessive reader, so much so that it turned his mind, and in his ensuing madness he believed himself to be a knight-errant of the kind who had filled his dawn-to-dusk reading hours.

Parody thus pervades the tone of this opening chapter and that of the following seven. We follow the deranged hidalgo as he invents a suitably chivalresque name for himself (Don Quixote de la Mancha), improvises armour and weapons, makes ready and renames his ageing skeleton of a horse, conjures up from his imagination, based on the memory of a local peasant girl he had secretly admired, a lady fit to be worshipped by a knight-errant of the courtly tradition, and embarks on his first adventure. As he sets out at daybreak, he muses upon how some wise scholar will record his first setting out (when the true history of his adventures comes to be written) in words that are a comic pastiche of the overblown style that had come to represent that of the genre as a whole.

> ¿Quién duda sino que en los venideros tiempos, cuando salga a luz la verdadera historia de mis famosos hechos, que el sabio que los escribiere no ponga, cuando llegue a contar esta mi primera salida tan de mañana, de esta manera? "Apenas había el rubicundo Apolo tendido por su faz de la ancha y espaciosa tierra las doradas hebras de sus hermosos cabellos, y apenas los pequeños y pintados pajarillos con sus harpadas lenguas abían saludado con dulce y meliflua armonía la venida de la rosada aurora, que, dejando la blanda cama del celoso marido,[9] por las puertas y balcones del manchego horizonte a los mortales se mostraba, cuando el famoso caballero don Quixote de la Mancha, dejando las ociosas plumas, subió sobre su famoso caballo Rocinante y comenzó a caminar por el antiguo y conocido campo de Montiel."

> (Who could question but that in times to come, when story of my famous deeds sees the light of day, but that the wise magus who wrote them would, when he comes to tell of this, my first sallying-forth, so early in the morning,

do so in the following words?: "Hardly had the ruby-cheeked Apollo cast the golden locks of his beauteous hair over the wide and spacious face of the land; or the small, painted birds greeted with the sweet, mellifluous sound of their harp-like tongues the coming of the rosy dawn, she who stealing from the soft bed of her jealous spouse now showed herself to mortals in the doorways and balconies which lined the Manchegan horizon, than the famous knight Don Quixote de la Mancha, leaving behind the idle bed feathers to mount his celebrated steed Rocinante, began to cross the ancient and familiar landscape of Montiel.)

Everything that describes Don Quixote's preparations for his role as a knight-errant makes him a figure of fun and debases the fictitious ceremonial that might have accompanied the emergence of an Amadís de Gaula or Palmerín de Inglaterra in the books of chivalry. At a run-down country inn frequented by muleteers, Don Quixote keeps vigil over his arms and is "knighted" by the innkeeper in a made-up ceremony devised to humour the madman who had descended upon him, claiming the inn to be a castle, the innkeeper its chatelaine, and hailing the inn-servants and prostitutes who frequented it as noble ladies. By making the mad knight a figure of sympathetic fun (sympathetic at least to modern audiences, though Cervantes' contemporaries were probably a good deal more pointed in their laughter) and a blatant anachronism, who seeks to impose his misplaced delusions of chivalry upon the modern nation state of Spain, Cervantes underlines the fantastic irrelevance of the books of chivalry to real life. As the knight's first adventure clearly shows, when he intervenes on behalf of the farm boy Andrés, who is being ill-treated by his master, neither moral nor even metaphorical truths can be drawn from this outdated, fictional code which Don Quixote follows to the letter.

The parodic attack is continued in Chapter 6, in which Don Quixote's library is inspected by the village priest, the barber, the knight's housekeeper and his niece, all of whom blame the books for Don Quixote's madness. On seeing some hundred volumes ranged on shelves, the housekeeper immediately fetches a jar of holy water for the priest to sprinkle in case the books bewitch those present. The niece insists that the entire contents of the library be destroyed without more ado, and:

Lo mismo dijo el ama, tal era la gana las dos tenían de la muerte de aquellos inocentes; mas el cura no vino en ello sin primero leer siquiera los títulos.

(The housekeeper was of the same opinion, so strong was the wish of the two for the death of those innocent volumes; but the priest could not bring himself to do so without even reading their titles.)

There follows a conversation between the priest and the barber about the worth of each volume taken off the shelves, with the priest pronouncing judgement largely on the basis of his personal tastes and hearsay about the books' contents and style. The collection comprises chivalresque romances, pastoral novels and poetry, and the handful that is saved contains some interesting choices. The grounds for consigning them to the flames are equally interesting. But among the fortunate few *are Amadís de Gaula, Palmerín de Inglaterra* and *Tirante el Blanco* among the books of chivalry, and from the pastoral novels *La Diana* by Montemayor, Gil Polo's *Diana enamorada*, and with Cervantes' own *La Galatea* – after some deliberation about the author and whether he will finish the story. Two collections of poetry are also spared, and the priest carries off *Los diez libros de fortuna de amor* by Antonio de Lofraso for himself.[10] Everything else is hurled into the courtyard to be burned, and the door to the room is bricked up.

The first thing to note about the examination of the library is that none of the volumes on Don Quixote's shelves would have found their way onto the Index of Forbidden Books. All those mentioned are works of literature – prose fiction and poetry – that were well known and which circulated freely, despite the criticisms aimed at them by certain groups. The episode is a critique of the ways in which a society views literature, and a parody of the way in which the censors assessed, approved or condemned books. Don Quixote's library is not subjected to a search for heretical, irreligious or morally dangerous content. Instead the books are arbitrarily saved or condemned to the flames on a hasty judgement of their literary merit – very much as the average reader might do. Even so, the impression is given that few contemporary literary works would have met Cervantes' stylistic and aesthetic criteria for literary worth that would merit their preservation.

Deflation of the chivalresque by means of parody continues until the end of Chapter 8. Accompanied by Sancho Panza, as his squire, Don Quixote sets out on his second sally and is almost at once involved in the adventure that has come to symbolise the book as a whole: his bruising encounter with the windmills which he mistakes for giants. The knight's painful recovery from the unsuccessful assault is followed immediately by the adventure that ends Chapter 8. His madness causes him to believe that a group of mounted priests wearing San Benitos,[11] and escorting a carriage carrying a group of ladies, is a gang of malefactors abducting damsels in distress, and he charges to the rescue. For his impetuosity, he is challenged to a fight by the hot-tempered Biscayan footman of one of the carriage occupants. As the footman, astride a mule and with a cushion for a shield, faces the emaciated knight with motley armour on his broken-down horse, the reader is treated to a hilarious travesty of a confrontation between the knights of the romances. But just as the adversaries come together with raised swords, we are astonished to be informed by the narrator historian that:

> En este punto y término deja pendiente el autor de esta historia esta batalla, disculpándose que no halló más escrito de estas hazañas de don Quijote, de las que deja referidas. Bien es verdad que el segundo autor de esta obra no quiso creer que tan curiosa historia estuviese entregada a las leyes del olvido, ni que hubiesen sido tan poco curiosos los ingenios de la Mancha, que no tuviesen en sus archives o en escritorios algunos papeles que de este famoso caballero tratasen; y así, con esta imaginación, no se desesperó de hallar el fin de esta apacible historia, el cual, siéndole el cielo favorable, le hallo del modo que se contará en la segunda parte.

(The author of this history leaves the outcome of the battle dangling at this very point and moment, on the excuse that he has been unable to uncover any details of the deeds of Don Quixote, beyond those already recounted. It is certainly true that the second author of this present work refused to believe that so curious a tale should be consigned to oblivion, nor that the able and intelligent men of La Mancha could have been so lacking in curiosity that they did not retain in their archives or desk drawers more papers relating to this famous knight. So inspired by this idea, he did not give up hope that he might come across the full ending to this pleasant story which, by Heaven's grace, he found in the manner that is recounted in the second part of this book.)

This is probably one of the most outrageous jokes at the reader's expense in the history of literature. To many present-day readers it is also very funny. However, the question remains as to why Cervantes should have chosen, at such an early point in the story, to play a joke on his public that entirely changed the structure of the narrative. This is probably best answered by assessing just what he achieves as a result of his gamble. The most obvious and immediate change is that the satirical first-person biographer/historian who began the narration is summarily ditched. The two final paragraphs of Chapter 8 are clearly spoken by an unannounced, different voice which informs the reader that the first narrator has run out of material at this point, and has ceased to write. A second one, however, has unearthed the continuation of the story which will be presented in the next chapter. The new narrator introduces himself at the start of Chapter 9, and briefly recounts how he discovered an Arabic manuscript in Toledo market that contained the full account of Don Quixote's adventures. He had this manuscript, the work of Cide Hamete Benengeli, an Arab historian, translated into Spanish by a willing *morisco* for three bushels of wheat and two stone of raisins, instructing him to leave nothing out and to add nothing of his own to the text. It is from this translation that the second narrator now continues the tale of Don Quixote and Sancho Panza, from time to time questioning the accuracy or credibility of what Cide Hamete states, but otherwise showing himself to be a naïvely acquiescent follower of the knight's deeds.

At some early point in his writing, Cervantes must therefore have realised that a first person narrator, who was himself satirising the events and characters he describes mainly through parody, was too limiting. It may well have been that he initially had in mind a short work of similar length to the Italian *novelle* he was familiar with, an example of which he offers us in the Priest's reading of the story *El curioso impertinente* in Part I, Chapters 33 to 35. If this had been the case, the initial narrative method might have been adequate. But having successfully created his insane protagonist, and set him upon his hopeless quest with considerable hilarity, Cervantes was unwilling to rewrite the opening section of the book after he realised the scope his idea offered. Instead of a narrowly satirical attack on a single literary genre, he found himself at work on a book which – while retaining its focus upon the original intent – was taking on a scope that was almost open-ended. What was beginning to emerge was an ageneric, comic epic set in contemporary Spain, which imitated the life of the people while also encompassing elements of established fictional genres. Furthermore, its tone could oscillate between slapstick comedy, parody, moral instruction, social observation, serious debate upon truth, reality and imagination, and the roles of literature and history while at the same time mediating between them.

The hiatus in the fictional "historical sources," the change of narrator and the introduction of Cide Hamete Benegeli, as the new chronicler from whose original version the story is taken, completely changes the tone and thematic scope of the narrative that follows. And with it, we also see a change in the nature of the humour. The helter-skelter series of mad adventures that the knight had experienced ceases temporarily. Instead the reader is carried along at a more sedate pace by a conversation between the knight and his squire, leading to a situation couched entirely in the pastoral genre. A chance encounter with a group of friendly goatherds leads to a lengthy interlude in which the knight delivers his address on the Age of Gold to this rustic and largely uncomprehending audience. This is followed by the news of the death of Grisóstomo, a scholar poet who had fallen in love with Marcela, who though from a rich family has chosen the life of a shepherdess. Marcela's indifference to Grisóstomo's courtship is blamed for his death, and his friends have gathered to attend his funeral. Don Quixote and Sancho decide to join the mourners, and on the way to the graveside have a conversation with one named Vivaldo, who questions the conduct of knights-errant as described in the books of chivalry. While Don Quixote is countering his arguments, they arrive at the burial site. From this point until the end of the episode, the knight and his squire are removed from the centre of the action and assume the role of passive spectators.

The burial given to Grisóstomo is, in line with the conventions of the pastoral novel, a pagan one. His friend and fellow student Ambrosio pronounces a funeral oration and Vivaldo reads to the assembled mourners a long poem, the dead man's last work, entitled *Canción deses-perada* (Song of Despair) in which he laments the cruel indifference of Marcela, the object of his love who has brought about his untimely death.[12] Though both Ambrosio and the dead man's last *coplas* have placed the blame for his demise upon her, Vivaldo has cautiously questioned their right to do so. At this moment, Marcela herself appears on a ridge of high ground overlooking the grave, and proceeds to defend herself, saying that she is not to blame for the fact that she could not return Grisóstomo's passion, and has dedicated herself to a solitary, independent existence tending her sheep. As she departs, Don Quixote springs into life once more, urging those present not to follow her, though he tries unsuccessfully to do so himself. At this point he abruptly leaves the pastoral world he has temporarily inhabited for the past few chapters, and returns to harsh reality. As a result of Rocinante's interest in some mares being driven by a group of men from Yanguas he receives yet another beating.

This process of interpolation is, in fact, fundamental to the narrative strategy of Part I of the book, and operates on more than one level. Primarily it involves the insertion into the story of events and incidents concerning characters who are entirely coincidental to the main narra-tive, or are not even "real" in as much as they are characters who inhabit the story of the *Curioso impertinente* (The Man of Impertinent Curiosity) read by the Priest to the company at an inn. The tale told by the Captive and the presence of Zoraida, his Moorish wife-to-be who wishes to become a Christian, is a further example, and one similar to the funeral of Grisóstomo, in that the knight and his squire are at best passive witnesses of it. The *Curioso impertinente* story belongs to a different but well-known genre of the time, the secular romance of love and intrigue which came from the Italian *novelle*. There is a hint of further borrow-ings from it in the introduction of the two pairs of lovers – Don Fernando, Dorotea, Cardenio and Luscinda – whose tangled relationships are resolved in the company of Don Quixote, Sancho, the Priest and the Barber during the interlude in the wilds of the Sierra Morena. Certainly Fernando, Cardenio and Dorotea enter fully into the main action and play an important part in deceiving the mad knight and enticing him back to his village. Nevertheless, they remain, because of their circumstances, very much like stereotypical characters from a secular romance playing stock parts – interpolation at one remove in fact.

In the first part of the novel, we therefore find a constant balancing of humour, satire and parody, with contrasting interludes of seriousness, which Cervantes manipulates by a process of narrative insertion and interpolation. But not all of his readers were happy with this technique. Some readers took exception to often lengthy episodes – such as the Captive's Tale and the story of *El curioso impertinente* – which lay outside the main story line and diverted the reader's attention from it. Indeed, Cervantes had Sansón Carrasco make clear to Don Quixote and Sancho at the beginning of Part II, that this has been one of the few criticisms levelled at Part I,[13] and it is clear that the author had decided to treat his narrative structure differently in Part II: to provide variety but to keep it much closer to the arc of his two chief characters. It must be said, however, that Cervantes interrupts the Priest's reading of *El curioso impertinente*, with the episode of Don Quixote's nightmare in the room above, which saw him engage in the monumental battle with the "giants" that were the innkeeper's wineskins, thus briefly restoring the presence of his chief protagonist as a figure of mayhem and fun.

Change in Part II comes as much from within the characters themselves as from the fictional world in which they are placed. Yet Cervantes does not entirely forsake interpolation or situations where the knight and his squire return to the role of passive witnesses of events in which they can play no meaningful role. The episode where they are the guests of the outlaw Roque Guinart, and go finally to Barcelona with his assistance is one example. The sea adventure and love plot surrounding the returned *morisca*, Ana Felix, is another. Cervantes also allows Don Quixote and Sancho to grow in their own ways by separating them to let them have individual adventures and experiences – the knight in the Duke's castle, and Sancho governing his island. Also, the knight and his squire find themselves at odds in their interpretation of happenings, such as the descent into Montesino's cave and their "flight" through the heavens on the back of Clavileño, the magical wooden horse.

But with the exception of the incidents of the enchanted boat, the freeing of the lions, the destruction of Maese Pedro's puppet theatre and the two encounters with the disguised Sansón Carrasco, posing as a rival knight, there is a marked absence of the kind of incidents and adventures that made Part I such a success. Indeed, even the interventions of Sansón are calculated happenings, elaborate deceptions – like those devised by the Duke, the Duchess and their servants both at the castle and Barataria, or Don Antonio's talking brass head in Barcelona. Indeed, the spontaneous, hair-raising scrapes into which Don Quixote enthusiastically flung himself in Part I no longer occur with any frequency, almost certainly because Cervantes realised that too much repetition of this formula would be restrictive for him and tedious for the reader. The evidence seems to indicate, therefore, that in Part II – and probably in Part I also – laughter was a means to an end, not an end in itself. *Don Quixote* was a work whose broad purpose depended upon humour, but was not a "funny book" in the sense proposed by Peter Russell. This being the case, the forms of humour employed were chosen in relation to the changing trajectories of the main characters, and through them the author's probing explorations into contemporary Spanish society, as seen through the lens of his deepening philosophical scepticism.

7

The Novel as a Mirror to Society
Women, Class and Conflict in
Don Quixote

When Henry Fielding, who some have hailed as the father of the English novel, published *Joseph Andrews* in 1742, he claimed that the novel was written "in imitation" of Cervantes and *Don Quixote*, which was at the height of its fame and influence in England at that time. Fielding's knowledge of the book was almost certainly based upon one or more of the four English translations that were then available.[1] Nevertheless, his understanding of Cervantes' literary intentions, though partial, was accurate. In his introductory chapter to Book 3 of *Joseph Andrews* ("Matter Prefatory in Praise of Biography") he states:

> I declare here, once and for all, I describe not men but manners; not an individual but a species ... not to expose one pitiful wretch to the small and contemptible circle of his acquaintance; but to hold a glass to thousands in their closets, that they may contemplate their own deformity, and endeavour to reduce it, and thus by suffering private mortification, may avoid public shame.[2]

Fielding thus gives notice that he intends Joseph Andrews to be a satirical book, but also comic; one that would hold up to ridicule the faults of mankind and society in general, rather than mounting an attack upon an individual. This could also be a description of the attitude of mind that Cervantes had adopted in writing the work that Fielding claimed to be imitating. Does not a book, Fielding demands of his reader, which records the achievements of the renowned Don Quixote de la Mancha deserve to be called a history, just as much as Mariana's great *Historia de rebus Hispaniae*? It is obviously does not, because it is entirely fictitious, but in this Fielding was clearly relishing (and reiterating) Cervantes' ironical humour in maintaining that his novel was the history of a real person.

Maybe mention Fielding

But Fielding continues by saying that it merits the title "history" because the universality of *Don Quixote* records the behaviour of the human race every bit as much as works of history, which can result in very different interpretations of the same sets of facts. He asks:

> Is there in the world such a sceptic as to disbelieve the madness of Cardenio, the perfidy of Ferdinand, the impertinent curiosity of Anselmo, the weakness of Camilla, the irresolute friendship of Lothario? Though, perhaps, as to the true time and place where those several persons lived, that good historian may be deplorably deficient.[3]

As, indeed, is the good historian at the beginning of Part I of Don Quixote, who is unsure of the knight's true name, and has intentionally forgotten the name of the village in which his subject lived.

Fielding's invocation of Cervantes doubtless added authority to his own first serious foray into prose fiction. Neither can there be much doubt that Fielding was very much at ease with what he perceived to be Cervantes' formula for writing. He had no difficulty, furthermore, in seeing the characters that Cervantes presented as metaphors, even stereotypes, for universal patterns of behaviour and human nature. But while Fielding may have been quite certain that his own intention in writing *Joseph Andrews* was to hold a mirror up to society, and may even have seen in *Don Quixote* an example of this kind of social comment, Cervantes himself made no claim to do so. Instead he asserted, in his *Novelas ejemplares*, that the stories contained nothing that might harm the reader. By "harm" he was almost certainly referring to ideas or imagined events that might give the reader any cause to question some aspect of Catholic doctrine or faith. Yet virtually all the stories of the *Novelas* place their characters in circumstances which pose moral and social dilemmas, and do so in a way which challenges a number of contemporary social and moral attitudes. Since the *Novelas ejemplares* and *Don Quixote* were coeval, it follows – narrative form apart – that they probably shared the same conceptual, social and moral framework. Both were also written under the shadow of the same censorship.

Was Fielding correct, then, in thinking that Cervantes' target in *Don Quixote* was not limited to the destruction of the chivalresque romance, and the bad writing for mainstream taste that it entailed, but that it also included a broad-based critique spanning all classes of Post-tridentine Spanish society? The answer to this question suggested earlier in this study is that this was precisely Cervantes' aim, though probably not an initial one. The book begins with the knight's deluded actions creating opportunities for debate on philosophical and moral questions. But the possibilities of a broader satirical examination of Spain's social and political life soon became apparent as the first part of the story developed, and took viable form after the events of the Sierra Morena. By the time Part II came to be written, the book's function as a "Menippean satire" had overtaken in importance the attack on the virtually defunct genre of the romance of chivalry. Cervantes genuinely objected to this type literature on literary and aesthetic grounds, but this opposition was shared by many, including numerous prominent churchmen, who argued that this kind of fiction also did moral harm to its readers. Cervantes thus not only used this widespread criticism of the novels of chivalry as a justification for writing *Don Quixote*, but also as a veil for a broader exploration and critique of Spain's recent history and the attitudes of its people.

From the first page of the book, Don Quixote emerges as a character who the author has fixed in his particular class and social circumstances with the uncompromising certainty of a naturalist pinning a specimen in a glass case. His class, habits and material way of life are sketched in by the author, locating him in the lower levels of the *hidalguía*, a member of the petty nobility who owns a small, impoverished estate, who does not work, and for whom, like the rest of his class, military service to the monarch is a relic of a previous generation. All this we are told before we learn of his passion for reading books of chivalry which has affected his mind. It was a mark of genius on Cervantes' part to couple this cultivated madman in a master and man relationship with Sancho Panza, an illiterate, rural labourer from a nearby village that is part of Don Quixote's dwindling domain. The endless conversations between the knight and his squire, as they travel the roads of La Mancha in search of adventures, reveal them to be products of very different social classes and cultures trying, and often failing, to understand one another. John Rutherford's statement in the introduction to his translation of *Don Quixote*, throws an interesting light on this:

> One of Cervantes' many innovations is his exploration of linguistic register, to give all his characters, even those who make the briefest of appearances, their own distinctive voices.[4]

This observation points not only to Cervantes' originality in the use of spoken language in narrative fiction, but also to his uncannily good ear for class and regional variations of speech which he recreated on the printed page.

Cervantes not only gives his characters their own distinctive voices, but also designates their social class by the way they are made to speak. Furthermore, especially in Part II, he continually extracts humour from the mistakes made by the uneducated in the presence of their social superiors. Sancho Panza is the main source of this kind of social comedy in his frequent conversations with his master and the Duchess and the Duke. The often extravagant courtesies used by the nobility and the educated towards one another in Renaissance Spain are also captured with precision. Indeed, they are at times also cleverly transformed into flattery and irony, and in Part II become part of the elaborate game of humouring the madman, that characters like the Duke, Duchess, Don Antonio Moreno and their servants play upon Don Quixote. The potential for social, political and moral comment – whether satirical or not – is greatly increased by the inclusion of a number of characters from differing backgrounds, who are brought together by the ingenuity of the author. This happened relatively little in Part I, and was managed, at times in a somewhat contrived fashion, through the interpolated episodes, such as the appearance of the Captive and his Moorish bride in a country inn,[5] the fiction within a fiction of the story of the *Curioso impertinente*, the pastoral interlude of Crisostomo's unrequited love for Marcela, and the personal back-stories told by Cardenio and Dorotea.

But in Part II, Cervantes rang the changes in response to the criticisms that Part I had attracted. He decided to cut out the interpolations, to cut down the number of adventures in which the knight becomes involved, and to introduce a much broader range of characters, while allowing some of his original cast to reprise their roles. Thus we meet, for a second time, Don Quixote's niece and housekeeper, occupying the same roles as in Part I, and have two a brief glimpses of the Barber and the Priest. Their role in pursuing Don Quixote, with a view to returning him safely home and curing his madness, falls to a new character, Sansón Carrasco, a recent graduate from Salamanca University, who is well-intentioned but rather full of himself. Sancho's wife Teresa is also introduced, her conversation with her husband revealing that Sancho's judgement may be little sounder than his master's, since he still expects to raise the standing of the family by being made the governor of somewhere as a result of one his master's deeds of valour. The innkeeper, his wife, his mischievous daughter and the inn servant and prostitute Maritornes also duly make their reappearances, as does Ginés de Pasamonte, the galley slave who Don Quixote released in Part I, but this time avoiding the law by posing as Maese Pedro, the owner of a travelling puppet theatre and a fortune-telling ape. The stream of new characters contains Don Diego de Miranda, a prosperous *hidalgo*, his son, a would-be poet, the Duke, the Duchess and the various members of their household, notably Altisidora, the Duchess's maid, Doña Rodriguez a duenna, her daughter and the footman Tossilos, together with a number of officials and citizens of Barataria, who set up the extravagant deception of Sancho's governorship. Sancho himself also encounters his friend Tomé Cecial disguised as the squire of the Knight of the Mirrors (Sansón Carrasco also in disguise), and another old acquaintance, Ricote, the illegally returned *morisco* who is dressed as a pilgrim. Add to all this Ana Felix, Ricote's daughter, who, posing as a pirate, is captured by a Spanish galley while attempting to rescue the man she loves from imprisonment in Algiers, the Catalan bandit Roque Guinart, his friend Don Antonio Moreno and the unfortunate Doña Claudia Jerónima, and we begin to see a cast of surprising size and diversity. The appearance of Don Álvaro Tarfe, who has been "intertextualised" from Avellaneda's *Segundo Tomo del Ingenioso Hidalgo Don Quixote de la Mancha*, and who signs an affidavit stating that the Don Quixote and Sancho that he had known in Zaragoza were imposters, is, perhaps, the icing on the cake.

Yet the person who exercises the greatest influence on the story, Dulcinea del Toboso, does not appear in it, and does not even exist – except as an idealised figment of Don Quixote's over-heated imagination, far removed from his recollection of the actual peasant girl which prompted him to create Dulcinea as her ideal counterpart. Since human perfection is impossible, it is scarcely surprising that no reader, or character in this story, is ever able to share the knight's vision of his lady. On the other hand, no reader could forget the picture of the real Aldonza Lorenzo that Sancho Panza paints for his master, when he tries to conceal the fact that he has not visited Dulcinea in her castle at El Toboso as instructed. This Dulcinea is strong, loud-voiced and sweating, as she sieves a pile of wheat on the threshing floor. While Sancho relates his imagined experience, his master makes laughable attempts to reconcile the rough physicality of the working peasant girl his squire describes with the notions of ideal grace and beauty with which he himself has endowed his vision of Dulcinea.

Dulcinea serves a number of purposes in Cervantes' story. She exerts an ever-present moral and spiritual influence over the deluded knight, both in her ideal form, and after she has been transformed by enchantment into a peasant girl. As the former, she represents the high point of beauty, grace, wisdom and purity to which humanity can aspire, and it is in her honour that Don Quixote sets out to wander the world righting wrongs, redressing grievances, punishing the wicked and dispensing justice by his strength and valour. It is axiomatic to the code of chivalry that a knight errant must love and serve a lady who is his moral and spiritual lodestar. Don Quixote's passion for Dulcinea, he constantly asserts, is pure and platonic. This fact preserves his chastity and makes any kind of liaison with a flesh and blood woman impossible, as Altisidora discovers, to her eventual fury and the reader's amusement, when her feigned attempts to seduce the knight are all rebuffed. The modern reader is never quite certain whether to applaud the knight's moral fortitude, condemn his lack of sympathy, or look upon him as a serious case of sublimated libido – even as someone who suffers from a genuine fear of women as sexual beings.

Yet what enraptures Don Quixote most about his imaginary lady is the unequalled beauty that his disturbed mind has endowed her with. Female beauty is evidently something upon which Cervantes and his contemporaries placed a high value, and was frequently regarded by neo-Platonists as being an outward sign of virtue, spirituality and wisdom. Certainly, Don Quixote states that Dulcinea possesses all three in abundance. This feminine ideal, however, is the creation of a madman, which is tantamount to saying that she could not exist in real life, and is therefore a major irony. Furthermore, does the beauty and majesty of Dulcinea inspire her knight to accomplish great deeds? Don Quixote's adventures are either the result of mental delusions or are contrived by others in order to deceive him. Despite the adoration, discipline, determination and courage that he displays the knight achieves nothing but comic mistakes, perhaps because the source of his inspiration is as fallacious and misplaced as his mission of chivalry. Cervantes, it appears, offers this idea as something for the reader to reflect upon, but it also has a great deal to do with the literary portrayal of women and the social contexts in which they were viewed in seventeenth-century Spain.

The varied gallery of female characters that Cervantes offers to his readers has little in common with the ideal that is Dulcinea. While a number of these – for example Marcela, Dorotea, Luscinda, Zoraida and Ana Felix – give the impression of being largely the products of literary convention, they are primarily driven by recognisably human desires, emotions and practical necessities. On the other hand, others, like the Duchess, Altisidora, Doña Rodriguez and the humbler creations – Don Quixote's housekeeper and niece, Teresa Panza, Sanchica, the innkeeper's wife and daughter, Maritornes and the array of other brief appearances – are, sketched from life. They blend easily and naturally into the narrative, and are not inserted by some kind of device, plot or coincidence. With the exception of Dulcinea, who can *only* be understood as a metaphor or symbol, there is a sense of the real and also a certain exemplariness about Cervantes' other female characters.

The most "literary" of all is Marcela, lifted entirely from the conventions of the pastoral novel. A counterpart in real life to this episode would have been unthinkable, yet Marcela's fictional situation and courageous defence of her conduct in her speech at Grisóstomo's graveside, raise important questions about gender relations, freedom of choice, and the conventions and constraints under which women were placed in Spain at the time. These were restricted, with only two real alternatives: marriage and the convent. Widows and unmarried women from less well-off families, like Cervantes' sisters Andrea and Magdalena, often scraped a living by their own labours as dress-makers, laundresses, shop and stall keepers, rural labourers and servants. Education for girls was rare, and usually consisted of private tutoring at home for the better-off. The universities and the professions were closed to women. Even opportunities to own or inherit property were limited, since what a woman owned became her husband's property on marriage. In a patriarchal society of this kind, Marcela's refusal to marry Grisóstomo because she did not love him, and preferred an independent existence, would have been completely unrealistic, and only a woman who possessed inherited wealth could have considered it. To live independently and make a living from her sheep, which Marcela claims she intends to do, would only have been possible within the highly unreal and stylised pastoral world from which she comes.

Yet, as Don Quixote and even some of Grisóstomo's friends begin to think as they listen to Marcela's words by the graveside, all the rational arguments lie with her. No woman should be forced into marriage against her will; no woman should be condemned for rejecting the attentions of someone they did not love; and a woman who chose to live independently supported by her own work and resources should be free to do so without criticism and in safety. This side of the "question of women" was not unheard of in Spain, and had been widely debated in France during the fifteenth and sixteenth centuries under the title "la querelle de femmes" (The case for women). But for most people in Spain – notably the Catholic Church – it was not a popular topic, and the abundant moral literature of the time, mostly written by churchmen, frequently addressed the matter of female conduct and how the ideal wife should behave. The moral and spiritual standards thus promulgated left little room for departure from the strictures of the *status quo*. Drawing upon his own experience, and doubtless also that of his sisters and mother, Cervantes clearly took a more open and equal view of gender relations than that advocated by the prevailing Church wisdom and the social conventions of the aristocratic and more prosperous classes. Without claiming that he was some kind of proto-feminist, it can be argued that Cervantes' liberal attitudes towards women and marriage would have been seen as tendentious and subversive had they not been expressed in terms of the familiar conventions of the pastoral novel.

The characteristics that Marcela shares with Dorotea, the other important female character in Part I, are intelligence, independence and courage, none of which would have readily been associated with women in seventeenth-century Spain which placed a premium upon beauty and virtue. Dorotea is also gifted with a ready ingenuity, which she employs both for herself, in her pursuit of Don Fernando and the restoration of her honour, and on behalf of Don Quixote when she impersonates the

Princess Micomicona in order to entice him back to the safety of his village. Dorotea, like Marcela, is also a "literary" creation; the kind of heroine found in an Italianate novel of intrigue. Deceived by the man she loves, she is determined to win him back and restore her reputation through marriage. She therefore sets out in pursuit of him, disguised as a boy, an unconventional means to a conventional dénouement. In Dorotea's case, however, there is an added complication. She is the daughter of a rich farmer, whereas Don Fernando is the younger son of a high aristocrat. The gulf in social class is therefore a further factor with which she must contend, and which, it is hinted, may have contributed to Don Fernando's initial unfaithfulness. We also learn from the suffering Cardenio, who had isolated himself in the Sierra Moreno, that Don Fernando his former friend, had married Luscinda, the woman to whom Cardenio himself had been secretly married. A disbelieving spectator at the wedding, Cardenio had fled the city half way through it, out of his mind with grief. He learned later that Luscinda had fainted a few minutes afterwards, and that a note was found on her unconscious body stating that she was secretly wed to Cardenio, and intended to kill herself after the ceremony, to which she had only agreed so as not to shame her parents. Don Fernando who leaves the failed wedding in a fury is thus shown, in the eyes of others, to be an untrustworthy and callous young aristocrat with little thought for anyone but himself and his own honour.

With a timing that only a romance of intrigue could have got away with, Cervantes has Don Fernando, his face concealed by a travelling mask and accompanied by servants, arrive at the same inn that Cardenio, Dorothea, Don Quixote and the rest of their party have just entered. What is more, he does so in the company of the veiled Luscinda. Their unexpected meeting with Cardenio and Dorotea, once their features have been revealed, is followed by speeches from Luscinda and Dorotea, both addressed to Don Fernando, the former urging him to release her so that she can join her true husband, and the latter eloquently arguing her love and her right to marry him, in which she completely sets aside any impediment about nobility of blood.

> Y si te parece que has de aniquilar tu sangre por mezclarla con la mía, considera que poca o ninguna nobleza hay en el mundo que no haya corrido por este camino, y que la que se toma de las mujeres no es la que hace al caso en las ilustres descendencias, cuanto más que la verdadera nobleza consiste en la virtud, y si ésta a ti te falta negándome lo que justamente me debes, yo quedaré con más ventajas de noble que las que tú tienes.[6]

(And if you think your blood will be destroyed if you mix it with mine, bear in mind that few or none are the noble families that haven't gone down the same path, and that the woman's blood is not taken into account in an illustrious descent. Besides which, true nobility consists of virtue, and if you lose that by denying me what I am so rightly owed, I shall have a greater claim to nobility than you.)

Don Fernando immediately softens, admits the rightness of Dorotea's many arguments and releases Luscinda to rejoin Cardenio. Thereafter, he shows himself to be quite the reverse of the person the reader had imagined him to be, and ready and willing to help the mad knight's friends to return home with him. Whether because of his rank, his courteousness or his natural tendency to command, Don Fernando soon establishes himself as the *de facto* leader of the now enlarged group surrounding Don Quixote. While Dorotea continues to play the part of the Princess Micomicona with his blessing, he embarks on a short character arc of moral and emotional rehabilitation under her influence.

The reconciliation of the two pairs of lovers, now returned to their true partners, brings a restoration of harmony to the narrative, which is almost immediately broken again by the arrival at the inn of the army Captain, and former prisoner in Algiers, who has escaped, bringing with him his Moorish wife Zoraida, who is seeking conversion to Christianity. In another interpolated episode, the Captain relates his story to the assembled guests, which includes a vivid description of the suffering of Zoraida and her father when she eloped from Algiers leaving her family and renouncing Islam in order to go to an "enemy" country. Zoraida, we are told, had a Christian nurse – also a slave in Algiers – from whom she learned the rudiments of Christian belief and the cult of the Virgin Mary. Cervantes' slightly melodramatic narrative, with its familiar literary trappings, is based upon a strongly traditional outlook on the moral implications of relations between men and women, but it nevertheless asks a number of questions about love, marriage, women as a gender and their place in contemporary society which can be seen as opposing mainstream attitudes. Despite the fact that all of his reputable, upper-class female characters are given a rare degree of physical beauty (possibly an ironical criticism of contemporary literary convention) it is clearly an attribute which, for Cervantes, only impresses at first sight. More important in all four women are virtue, courage and intelligence, which they show in different ways through their actions. This is particularly true of Zoraida, both in her secret wooing of a Christian slave – the penalty for which might even have been death if she had been discovered – but also for her decision, on religious and amorous grounds, to leave her family, set aside her Muslim faith and embrace the culture of an enemy country as a foreign woman married to a Spaniard, a huge sacrifice made for love and religious faith. Furthermore, as Dorotea makes clear to Don

Fernando, if virtue is expected of women in their dealings with men, their family and husbands, it should be equally expected of men in their dealings with women.

In Part II, however, we see Cervantes adopt a different approach to the subject of women and gender relations in Spain. The tendency towards literary idealisation of upper class female characters is for the most part avoided. He also discards the temptation to transform them into exemplary figures in the moral sense. Indeed, Claudia Jerónima and Ana Félix, the only two women in Part II whose cameo appearances towards the end of the book present both as "larger than life" creations from the pages of romance fiction, are presented to the reader as legal and political case histories on which to reflect, with no definite judgement given at the time. How should society treat an unfortunate woman like Claudia Jerónima who has been deceived and committed a crime of passion? Alternatively should Ana Félix, a Christian woman born in Spain, who is on a mission to rescue Don Gregorio, the man she loves, from captivity in Algiers, be punished because she is an illegally returned *morisca*? Are both not cases where natural justice would be very different from what will be meted out by the law?

In Part II, we find the more important female characters located in a single context – the household of the Duke and Duchess, beginning with the duchess herself, and descending through the duennas, ladies' maids and servants that surround her, and who observe a strict order of seniority and status. These are, of course, not to be confused with the Countess Triffaldi, and various other unfortunate ladies of rank – all of whom are impersonated by men of the Duke's service – who come to ask for Don Quixote's assistance as part of the deception organised to provide amusement for the ducal couple and their court. Outside this circle are the more lowly folk, including Don Quixote's niece and housekeeper, Sancho's wife Teresa and his daughter Sanchica. These, together with the inn-keeper's wife and daughter and the inn-servant Maritornes, make brief but significant reappearances from Part I, and serve as unchanging points of reality outside the world of fantasy and deception in which the knight and his squire are immersed, thus maintaining the continuity of the narrative in the actual world.

It has already been pointed out that the overarching female presence in Part I of the novel is the imaginary Dulcinea de Toboso whose beauty, wisdom and grace completely possess the mind of her inventor, Don Quixote. Just as his delusions of knight-errantry are unwavering, despite the constant challenges of the contemporary world, so is the ideal of his lady constant and unshakeable. She is his impregnable spiritual and moral fortress, and while she so remains a cure for the knight's madness is impossible. It is interesting to note that Sansón Carrasco, the newly graduated *letrado* from Salamanca, is nevertheless determined to find a cure by playing Don Quixote's game of chivalry and turning the rules against him; to challenge Don Quixote, defeat him in a show of arms and then order his defeated opponent back to his village for a year. (This may be seen as a typically rational and scientific approach by an example of an educated mind of the time.) By comparison, it is the Duchess who intuitively realises that Don Quixote's malady depends as much upon his faith in Dulcinea as it does upon his reading of books of chivalry, and is determined to explore this avenue further. Her intention is not, however, to find a cure for the knight's madness, but rather to find a way of extending the joke that she and her husband have decided to play on Don Quixote and his squire, whose rustic witticisms have so amused her. Neither is her aim entirely without malice, since any undermining of Don Quixote's faith in his lady, or compromise of his loyalty to her, is bound to have a serious effect on him.

Yet it was Sancho who sowed the first seeds of doubt surrounding Dulcinea in his attempt, at the beginning of Part II, to cover up the lie he had told his master in Part I about having visited Dulcinea in her village, and witnessing her response to the letter that the knight had sent her. Don Quixote's decision at the start of Part II to go at night to El Toboso and ask Dulcinea's blessing for the third sally, on which he was about to embark, was a mission which naturally failed. He found no trace of the palace in which he believed she lived. This was compounded by a second ruse on Sancho's part to cover up his first lie. Having persuaded his master to rest in a nearby wood, Sancho undertakes to return to El Toboso and search the village by daylight to find Dulcinea's palace, which he knows does not exist. He then returns to the knight to say that Dulcinea and two attendants have come out to meet him, and points to three peasant girls on donkeys who are riding along the road behind him. But on this occasion, Don Quixote's capacity to see castles where there are country inns and giants where there are windmills, fails Sancho's intentions. The knight does not behold the beauteous Dulcinea and two attendants resplendent upon richly caparisoned steeds, but sees only what is there in front of his eyes – three very ordinary peasant girls on donkeys – one of whom, having fallen off her mount when he approaches her, leaps to her feet, vaults with remarkable agility onto the back of the retreating animal, and gallops off along the road as fast as she can. Both Don Quixote and Sancho (for different reasons) are forced back upon their usual explanation for phenomena that do not appear to add up: Dulcinea has been enchanted. The anxiety this possibility awakes in the knight's confused brain is subsequently confirmed by his dream in Montesino's Cave, during which he encounters Dulcinea changed into a peasant girl, who tries to borrow money from him for "necessary expenses." Thereafter, his enduring mission is to find a way to break the spell, and restore Dulcinea to her previous state.

Having wormed the truth out of Sancho about his deceptions and their unexpected outcome, the Duchess is able to invent a deliciously elaborate scheme that will also see Sancho paid back for his trickery. The astonishing night-time theatre that she and the Duke arrange in the open country after a day's hunting sees Dulcinea (impersonated by a handsome page) accompanied by the figure of Merlin appear to Don Quixote, Sancho, the Duke, Duchess and hunting party, to deliver the news that the enchantment upon Dulcinea can only be broken if Sancho gives himself three thousand three hundred strokes upon his bare buttocks. This time Don Quixote swallows the deception entirely, and Sancho appears to do so, while protesting with bad grace at the severity of the punishment he must administer to himself. Some of the funniest scenes in the remainder of the book involve Don Quixote's efforts to persuade Sancho to flog himself, and Sancho's ingenuity at avoiding or feigning self-flagellation.

The second barrel of the Duchess' stratagem is to present Don Quixote, whose nervousness where women are concerned she has already noted, with the temptations posed by a flesh and blood female admirer. Her maid Altisidora is therefore ordered to pretend to be infatuated with the knight and make advances to him. The reader assumes that Altisidora accepts this role enthusiastically, since she is described as being sharp-witted and brazen, and is clearly enjoying the joke being played by her master and mistress. The exchanges between the knight and Altisidora, she protesting her "love" and he rejecting it on the grounds that his heart belongs to another, take place in song and verse, another source of humour which happens while Sancho is absent governing Barataria after his own comic, down-to-earth fashion. But Sancho's return from his short-lived governorship helps his master to make up his mind to leave the ducal palace and pursue his adventures. The two "missions" he had agreed to undertake while there, the deliverance of the bearded duenna Countess Triffaldi, and the restoration of the honour of Doña Rodríguez's daughter, had both been somewhat doubtfully resolved, so that nothing required his continued presence while the attentions of Altisidora argued for his prompt departure. Altisidora's last desperate song of love is sung in public as the knight and his squire depart the palace, Don Quixote taking the view – not unlike that of Marcela in Part I – that he is not to blame for what might befall the girl as a result of her misplaced passion.

The final scene in this thread of the story – the "resurrection" of Altisdora having died of a broken heart – is played out later. Despite his gladness that Altisidora has returned to life, Don Quixote remains as unmoved as ever by her suit, provoking a sudden, angry and even vicious outburst in reply. If Altisidora was only playacting her love for Don Quixote, as the Duchess had instructed, why should she react to her rejection with a fury that only someone genuinely in love might have been capable of? Cervantes is, I suggest, showing the reader a certain side of the character of a woman who is self-confident, well-born and used to moving in the highest aristocratic circles, as well as being clever, talented and bold. Even though it was pure pretence, Altisidora had, at her mistresses' bidding, set herself the task of seducing the mad knight, as part of the charade in which most of the ducal household was involved, and in the full knowledge of her fellow servants and companions. To be seen to fail in such an uncompromising manner was clearly a considerable loss of face and one which was both embarrassing and infuriating for her. Especially as her "rival" was a non-existent figment of Don Quixote's imagination. Cervantes clearly knew a good deal more about the strengths and weaknesses of female psychology than he was prepared to reveal openly, but only occasionally do we catch a direct glimpse of its less positive features.

The Duchess is portrayed as an equally mixed character. She is charming, sympathetic, outgoing and considerate in her dealings with all classes of people, but has a malicious sense of humour and gives short thrift to those who do not play the game according to her rules. In short, her position gives her power which she is very willing to use. In her dealings with Sancho Panza, despite her amusement at his rustic wit and utterances, the Duchess shows interest, generosity and a common touch which reassures him and gains his confidence. She appears to do so again when, with Sancho dispatched to the governorship of Barataria, she sends a page to visit Tereza Panza, his wife, with letters from Sancho and herself, and the present of a coral necklace. The friendliness of the Duchess' letter, telling Teresa how well Sancho is governing the island that the Duke her husband has given him appears to be a reflection of her outgoing nature, but is nothing more than a cynical extension of the ducal duplicity being used at Sancho's expense. The Duchess knows that the governorship will be brief, and has no compunction in making Sancho's wife and daughter part of the joke, and a laughing stock in their village, by raising their social expectations, which the well-rehearsed page reinforces with his flattering comments.

The use of letters to bring into the main narrative characters who are a good distance from the action is an interesting introduction. Cervantes uses the device effectively but briefly at one particular juncture of the story, but does not adopt it anywhere in his writing as a major vehicle for narrative. The late seventeenth and eighteenth centuries in France and England was to see the emergence of the "epistolary novel," a fictional tale told entirely in the form letters between different characters, which became popular in both countries. Epistolary novels fell out of fashion soon after, probably because though they presented a number of different points of view on the fictional world they created, they were narrower and less dynamic as narrative forms, than the ubiquitous, impersonal narrative voice, or first person narrator that characterised the Romantic period and the great novels of nineteenth-century realism. Cervantes, however, wishes to maintain the fiction within a fiction that Don Quixote is a real history, and his narrator makes frequent passing reference to Cide Hamete Benegeli, and the original translated manuscript in which he impossibly records the knight's deeds. Letters serve, therefore, as admissible evidence in the writing of histories, and consequently have a recognisable place in the work of Cide Hamete.

But letters are also personal statements that can reveal a lot about their authors, even when written by a scribe on their behalf. Sancho's two letters, one to Don Quixote and the other to Teresa, and Teresa's missive to her husband and her reply to the Duchess are all of this kind. In Teresa's letter to Sancho we see her unbridled delight at Sancho's elevation to a governorship, and her down-to-earth expression of it. But we also see the surprise that is mingled with the joy, and the immediate quickening of the social ambition that, in Part II, Chapter 5, she had been at pains to restrain. Then, having no faith in the possibility that the deeds of her husband's mad master might see the gullible Sancho raised to governor's estate, she had rigorously dismissed any such possibility, and had argued with her husband against the notion of marrying their daughter Sanchica into a noble family, or lording it over her neighbours with her new-found status. But having received what she believes to be proof that Sancho's wild ambition has indeed been realised – namely the Duchess's letter and the promptings of the artful page who is in on the joke – her point of view rapidly changes. Her joyful but respectful reply to the Duchess indicates that nobody in the village believes that Sancho has become a governor, for which reason, she says: "Estoy determinada, con licencia de vuesa merced, de meter este buen día en mi casa, yéndome a la corte a tenderme en un coche, para quebrar los ojos a mil envidiosos que yo tengo"[6] (With your ladyship's permission, I am determined to use this fortunate moment for the good of my house by going to court, stretched out in a carriage, which will be one in the eye for the many who already envy me).

Her letter to Sancho, by comparison, is one of unbridled, down-to-earth delight:

> Yo te prometo y juro como católica cristiana que no faltaron dos dedos para volverme loca de contento ... cuando yo llegué a oír que eres gobernador, que me pensé allí caer muerta de puro gozo, que ya sabes tú que dicen que

así mata la alegría súbita como el dolor grande. A Sanchica tu hija se le fueron de aguas sin sentirlo de puro contento.[7]

(I promise you, and swear to it as a Catholic Christian woman, that I was within an inch of going mad with happiness ... when I heard you have been made a governor. I thought I was going to drop dead with pure pleasure, because they say, as you know, that sudden happiness can kill just like great pain. And as for your daughter Sanchica, she wet herself from sheer delight without realising it.)

Teresa has, she says, to put up with the disbelief of the Priest, the Barber, the Sexton and Sansón Carrasco and her neighbours, but her faith is unshaken, and she asks Sancho about whether she should come to court in a carriage, and that he should provide a good dowry for Sanchica so that, as the daughter of a governor, she can marry well. The Teresa we now find reflecting upon how she should assume the airs of a lady, and the cost of her new lifestyle, is far removed from the woman who earlier in the story had tried to temper her husband's aspirations with peasant common sense. Cervantes thus shows that pride, ambition for power and social status which earns the respect of others is close to the surface of Spanish society. Sancho willingly walks away from his brief period of false office with a clean conscience when he comprehends the price he will have to pay for the privilege of exercising power, not having enriched himself by a penny. But he does so, it would seem, without a thought for the effect on his family, whose hopes have been raised and then dashed within a few short days. But Sancho's desire for high office comes from his wish to prove himself capable of the task, despite his background and lack of education, rather than a love of power and self-aggrandisement for their own sake.

Between Don Quixote's conclusion, in the wood outside El Toboso, that Dulcinea had been turned by enchantment into a peasant girl, and his encounter with the Duchess, the adventures and encounters of both the knight and his squire follow one another in rapid succession. The outstanding adventures concern the wagon-load of actors going to perform *The Parliament of Death*, Don Quixote's encounter with the Knight of the Mirrors, whom he defeats in battle, Don Quixote's attempt to challenge the lions, the affair of Camacho's wedding, the knight's descent into Montesino's Cave and Maese Pedro's puppet show. Important though these adventures are, the characters in whose company Don Quixote pursues them are just as significant, but for a quite different reason. They introduce us, among others, to Don Diego Miranda (the gentleman in the green overcoat), Basilio and Quiteria, who have used Camacho's intended wedding to trick their way into marrying one another, Basilio's cousin the learned Humanist, the Licenciado and the Bachiller, and the former galley slave Ginés de Pasamonte now unrecognisable under his new identity of Maese Pedro. They also show us another side of Sansón Carrasco in disguise as the Knight of the Mirrors and Tomé Cecial, posing as his squire. All these characters play cameo roles which add to the rapidly building picture of contemporary Spanish society, and more will follow, but it is at this particular point of the story that Cervantes seems to develop a taste for creating brief appearances by fictional creations who are also satirical objects.

Referring only to the examples of Don Diego Miranda and the Humanist Cousin, we see how Cervantes pokes fun at two social types which would have been easily recognisable to his own readers. Shortly before Don Quixote's mishap with the helmet full of cheese curds, when he is about to challenge the lions being transported in cages along the road, Don Diego has given us a lengthy account of himself that is the polar opposite of the first narrator's laconic sketch of Don Quixote himself.[8] With appropriate self-regard, Don Diego announces:

> Soy un hidalgo natural de un lugar done iremos a comer hoy, si Dios fuere servido. Soy más que mediamente rico y es mi nombre Don Diego Miranda. Paso la vida con mi mujer y con mis hijos y con mis amigos; mis ejercicios son el de la caza y la pesca, pero no mantengo ni halcón ni galgos, sino un perdigón manso o un hurón atrevido. Tengo seis docena de libros, cuáles de romance y cuáles en latín, de historia unos y de devoción otros; los de las caballerías aún no han entrado por los umbrales de mis puertas. Hojeo más los que son profanos que los devotos, como sean de honesto entretenimiento, que deleiten con el lenguaje y admiren y suspendan con la invención, puesto que de éstos hay muy pocos en España. Alguna vez como con mis vecinos y amigos, y muchas veces los convido; son mis convites limpios y aseados y nonada escasos; ni gusto de murmurar ni consiento que delante de mí se murmure; no escudriño las vidas ajenas ni soy lince de los hechos de otros; oigo misa cada día, reparo mis bienes con los pobres, sin hacer alarde de las buenas obras, por no dar entrada en mi corazón a la hipocresía y vanagloria, enemigos que blandamente se apoderan del corazón más recatado, procuro poner en paz los que sé que están desavenidos; soy devoto de Nuestra Señora y confío èn la misericordia infinita de Dios Nuestro Señor.[9]

> (I am a hidalgo, and a native of the place where, if God be served, we shall eat today. I am more than moderately rich, and my name is Don Diego Miranda. I pass my days with my wife and children and with my friends; my main activities are fishing and hunting, though I don't keep a falcon or greyhounds, preferring instead a tame partridge and a bold ferret. I pos-

sess some six dozen books, some in romance languages and others in Latin, some of them histories and others books of devotion, but romances of chivalry have not yet crossed my threshold. I tend to peruse the profane books rather than the devout ones, always on the understanding that they contain honest entertainment in which the language delights and the invention provokes admiration and wonder, though there are not many like that in Spain. Sometimes I dine with my friends, and more often I invite them to dine with me, since my tables are always neat and clean and lack for nothing. I don't like gossip and don't allow people to gossip in my company; I don't pry into other peoples' lives, and I don't keep a sharp eye on what others do; I go to mass every day and share my goods with the poor, but without making a show of my good deeds so as not to let either hypocrisy or vanity gain entry to my heart, since both are enemies which gently take possession of it. I try to leave in peace those who I know are quarrelsome, I am devoted to Our Lady and I trust always in the infinite mercy of Our Lord God.)

At first glance, these may all seem fine attributes; certainly Don Diego seems happy enough to lay claim to them. But though he may be rich and well-respected among his acquaintances, Don Diego clearly represents, in Cervantes' eyes at least, the decline of the old petty nobility, whose privileges were traditionally earned by giving military support to the King whenever it was needed. As Philip II knew to his cost, this kind of service was no longer provided by the second half of the sixteenth century, either by the *hidalguía* or the higher aristocracy, though they jealously retained their privileges. Even Don Diego's *ejercicios* – fishing and hunting – are of a diminished kind, hunting partridges (with a tame decoy bird) or rabbits with a ferret, just as any peasant or labourer might. This immediately impugns his courage, since his game offers no threat to his own comfort of safety. Indeed, when Don Diego remonstrates with the knight for his foolhardiness in trying to take on the lions in combat, Don Quixote tartly replies:

Váyase vuesa merced, señor hidalgo ... a entender con su perdigón manso y con su hurón atrevido, y deje a cada uno hacer su oficio. Éste es el mío, y yo sé si vienen a mí o no estos señores leones.[10]

(Go, Sir Hidalgo Your Honour, and take care of your tame partridge and bold ferret, and let everyone do his own job! This one is mine, and I know whether or not these gentlemanly lions will come for me.)

Not surprisingly, Don Diego is taken aback by the appearance and speech of Don Quixote, and decides that he is obviously a total madman.

However, further exchanges result in the hidalgo saying that he has a son in whom he is somewhat disappointed, and who, having been sent to university to learn Greek and Latin, has refused to go on to study Law or Theology as his father wanted, but spends all his time reading and discussing classical poetry. This is the cue for another of Don Quixote's literary speeches. He replies to Don Diego, urging him to let the young man study whatever subject he likes best and is best at, and follows this with some observations on how he might ensure the best outcome for his son's output of poetry. Don Quixote recommends the young man be discouraged from writing satires that are aimed at individuals in favour of poems which condemn human vices generally, saying: "Si el poeta fuere casto en sus costumbres, lo será también sus versos; la pluma es lengua del alma." (If the poet is chaste in his behaviour his verses will be also, and the pen is the soul's tongue.) The knight's good sense and literary knowledge immediately oblige Don Diego to adjust his opinions; the knight is clearly not as mad as one might think.

Despite the affair of the lions, which immediately follows this conversation, Don Diego invites Don Quixote and Sancho to stay at his house and introduces them to his wife and son, Don Lorenzo. The aspiring poet is also determined to make a judgement about whether the knight is mad or sane, and they begin an interesting discussion in which Don Lorenzo enquires what subjects Don Quixote has studied. The knight replies that he has studied knight-errantry, which includes all fields of recognised knowledge, including medicine and a knowledge of curative herbs, not to mention the practical skills of shoeing a horse, repairing saddles and bridles and swimming. But furthermore a knight errant must:

> Guardar la fe en Dios y en su dama; ha de ser casto en los pensamientos, honesto en las palabras, liberal en las obras, valiente en los hechos, sufrido en los trabajos, caritativo con los menesterosos y, finalmente, mantenedor de la verdad, aunque le cueste la vida en defenderla.[11]

> (He must have faith in God and in his lady; he must have a chaste mind, speak with honesty, be liberal in his works and valiant in deeds. He must be long-suffering in his labours, charitable with the needy and, finally, he must always maintain the truth, even if he has to give his life to defend it.)

This may be the pronouncement of a madman, but it is evidently an ideal to which Don Quixote believes he is trying to conform in his capacity of knight errant, and one which surpasses, as Don Lorenzo observes, any science or discipline taught anywhere, though he expresses the doubt that there were ever knights errant who could have displayed all these virtues and qualities. Don Quixote replies that Don Lorenzo shares this doubt with the vast majority of people in the world, as he has himself found out, but all they have to do is ask themselves how necessary knights errant would have been in past ages, and how useful they would be in the present – if there were any – since: "triunfan ahora, por pecados de las gentes, la pereza, la ociosidad, la gula y el regalo." (Nowadays, because of the sinfulness of the people, sloth, idleness, greed and luxury triumph.) This is another subtle, satirical observation which, though not directly aimed at Don Diego and his family, could nevertheless be said to apply to them and majority of their class, who mostly did not work, paid no taxes and lived mainly from land rents and the produce of the peasants on their estates. It is a preparation for the greater criticism of the higher aristocracy and great landowners, such as the Duke and Duchess, to whom we are introduced shortly afterwards.

Dukes, counts and other high aristocrats, did play their part in government and leading the Spanish armies in the reign of Philip II, but the movement was mainly towards creating a civil service of trained lawyers and accountants from the new universities, giving the state apparatus the appearance of a much more meritocratic service to the monarch. Philip III's personal idleness, and reliance upon *validos* (favourites) to head up the government for him, saw a succession of Dukes take the reins of state and fill their pockets while they enjoyed high office. The Dukes of Osuna, Lerma and Uceda in turn occupied the role of *valido* to the king, between 1598 and 1621, all being accused of corruption and personal vices which led to the fall from royal grace of all of them in turn. But by and large, neither the Spanish army nor the navy, nor the machinery of the state in the reign of Philip II could count on a leadership drawn from the aristocratic classes to the extent that Charles V was able to do in the first half of the sixteenth century. By the times of Philip III and IV, the position had deteriorated still further.

Cervantes' Duke and Duchess have a number of graces, talents and great wealth, but do not seem to concern themselves with affairs outside the jurisdiction of their own extensive estates, which are administered to serve the whim of the ducal couple and their courtiers. It is, of course, a major reflection upon them, that both can devote so much time and effort to organising, with the help of their household and servants, the elaborate and prolonged hoaxes that they play for their own amusement upon Don Quixote and Sancho. The reader, despite the terms in which Cervantes' narrator deals with them, is sooner or later obliged to ask him or herself just what kind of morality they display in engineering deceptions which can have damaging effects on others. Theirs would appear to be a self-centred and somewhat callous existence that is based on opulence and money, and guided by the preservation of power and status which, under a show of liberal generosity, nevertheless deals ruthlessly with individuals who incur their displeasure.

Literature, language, history and education were topics to which Cervantes devoted a good deal of thought. Not having been able to study at a university himself, he had become a committed auto-didact, an eclectic reader and self-taught writer and poet. His years in the Spanish army in Italy, followed by five more as a prisoner in Algiers, taught him more about the world, life and people than any university course could have done, yet it is likely that he regretted not having been able to study formally, and occasionally felt the lack of a thorough grounding in the classics. The kind of graduates emerging from Spain's new universities, and the nature of university teaching and learning in an era of censorship which directly affected many eminent scholars, were matters that he took seriously. Sansón Carrasco, newly graduated in Law from Salamanca, is therefore an interesting creation. Cervantes presents him as intelligent though somewhat over-confident in his own intellectual powers, with fixed ideas which can become obsessive, such as his determination to cure Don Quixote's madness by his own methods, with no thought of the possibility of an adverse outcome. Cervantes may have seen Sansón Carrasco as typical of the kind of young *letrado* of the time, who would either practise law or become a government functionary of some kind, and he clearly had reservations about the country's future in such hands.

Nevertheless, Cervantes seems to have taken – supposing, in this instance, that Don Quixote's views on the matter reflect those of his author – a liberal view of how higher study should be approached. Advising Don Diego about the university studies of his son who looks likely to want to become a poet, Don Quixote says:

> Que vuesa merced deje caminar a su hijo por donde su estrella le llame, que siendo él tan buen estudiante como debe ser, y habiendo ya subido felice-mente el primer escalón de las ciencias.[12]

> (Your honour should let your son go where his star leads him, since he is as good a student as could be expected, and has already happily surmounted the first step in the sciences.)

That sons should be allowed to study what they liked most and were best at, instead of following a course imposed by their parents, would probably have been contrary to most contemporary opinion, and chimes with Cervantes' view that men and women should be free to marry whom they choose (or not to marry at all).

But despite this liberal attitude, Cervantes had little patience with the relentless accumulation of "useless knowledge," as Don Quixote shows in a conversation with Basilio's unnamed cousin, who guides Don Quixote and Sancho to Montesino's Cave. When the cousin is asked about his occupation we are told:

> Él respondió que su profesión era ser humanista; sus ejercicios y estudios, componer libros para dar a la estampa, todos de gran provecho y no menos entendimiento para la república.[13]

> (He replied that he was a humanist by profession and that his work consisted of producing books for the publishing trade, all of great benefit and enlightenment to the populace.)

The humanist cousin is what the Augustans in eighteenth-century England would have been quick to call a "hack writer," who kept the printing presses grinding by churning out books on commission for mainstream consumption. His latest work is entitled *De las libreas* (On the Ceremonial Costume of Knights) which contains seven hundred and three examples, complete with colours and mottoes, of costumes for court knights to be worn at festivals and court occasions. Another book is entitled *Metamorfóseos, o Ovidio español* (Metamorphoses or the Spanish Ovid), which is a burlesque of Ovid's poems using places and characters in contemporary Spain. Yet another is called *Suplemento a Virgilio Polidoro, que trata de la invención de las cosas* (Supplement to Virgil Polydorus: About the Invention of Things)[14] which claims to include everything that Polidorus omitted. The cousin's enthusiastic detailing of these works, followed by a fatuous conversation with Sancho about who was the first man to scratch his head, prompts Don Quixote to exclaim:

> Hay algunos que se cansan en saber y averiguar cosas que después de sabidas y averiguadas no importan un ardite al entendimiento ni la memoria

> (There are those who wear themselves out learning and verifying things which, having once been ascertained and shown to be true, have not the least importance either for the mind or the memory.)

In keeping with the story of Don Quixote's adventures, and the type of character he is, Cervantes has shown him travelling the roads and exploring the wild places of La Mancha, and the Spanish countryside of Spain up to Barcelona and back. What he shows us is rural Spain in the early seventeenth century, with its bad roads, worse inns and the hardship of constant wandering. But the roads are the arteries of the country, and along them travel people of all kinds, from muleteers, peasants, shepherds and horse breeders, prostitutes, priests, merchants, aristocrats, ladies, lawyers and students, thieves and criminals; and, of course, the Santa Hermanidad, or rural constabulary of the time. Roads and inns served to bring Don Quixote and his squire into contact with all classes of people, combining them in a remarkable social kaleidoscope in a way that would not have been possible had the story been set in a village, town or any other individual place. The fact remains, however, that one of the most characteristic features of Golden Age Spain, the movement of impoverished labourers and peasants from the countryside to the rapidly expanding cities, is not something the reader is particularly conscious of. It was, furthermore, the cities which had begun to drive the life of Spain and its Empire. They were centres with large populations where the kind of social control that could be exercised by priests and landowners in country villages was impossible. The cities existed, in fact, in opposition to the countryside. They often contained sizeable criminal elements, which encouraged lawlessness, and were places where great riches and great poverty rubbed shoulders. They increasingly housed the great aristocratic families, whose tastes set the cultural tone of Spain, and who were attracted by the sophistication and entertainment the cities offered. It would be true to say, therefore, that despite the size and variety of the mirror Cervantes holds up to society, scarcely a trace of city life can be found reflected in it. Not even the knight's brief stay in Barcelona, which occupies a number of chapters at the end of the book, manages to create the presence and influence of a great city as a contrast to the rural world from which Don Quixote and Sancho have just come.

The picture we get of Barcelona, when Don Quixote and Sancho finally arrive there, is indeed a sketchy one. Apart from the harbour, and the naval operations going on within it, Cervantes does little to evoke the sights or atmosphere of the city.[15] Cervantes prefers to concentrate on people, as he has done all along. By means of a secret entrance to the City by boat at night time, Don Quixote and Sancho are given a highly stage-managed welcome by the companions of Don Antonio Moreno, a prosperous citizen of Barcelona and a friend of Roque Guinart. Don Antonio, like the Duke and Duchess and Don Diego, provides the knight and his squire with hospitality in return for which they derive amusement from his madness. Indeed, it is Don Antonio who, after Don Quixote's defeat at the hands of the Knight of the White Moon, upbraids Sansón Carrasco, putting to him the following question:

> ¡Dios os perdone el agravio que habéis hecho a todo el mundo en querer volver cuerdo al más gracioso loco que hay en él! ¿No veis, señor, que no podrá llegar el provecho que cause la cordura de don Quixote a lo que llega el gusto que da con sus desvaríos? Pero yo imagino que toda la industria del señor bachiller no ha de ser parte para volver cuerdo un hombre tan

rematadamente loco; y, si no fuese contra la caridad, diría que nunca don Quixote, porque con su salud no solamente perdemos sus gracias, sino las de Sancho Panza su escudero, que cualquiera de ellas puede volver a alegrar a la misma melancolía.[16]

(God forgive you the wrong you have done the whole world by seeking to return to sanity the funniest madman in it! Don't you see, my good sir, that the benefit that will result from Don Quixote's sanity can never surpass the pleasure caused by his follies? But I imagine that all your industry, master bachelor, will be insufficient to restore sanity to one so hopelessly mad. Indeed, if it were not uncharitable of me, I would say may Don Quixote never find a cure, because if his health is restored, we lose not only his comic doings, but also those of Sancho Panza his squire, for both of them can turn the same melancholy to joy.)

Sansón Carrasco receives Don Antonio's rebuke in silence and returns to his village to await the homecoming of Don Quixote and Sancho. Neither is there any comment or intervention from the narrator, so that the rightness or wrongness of Don Antonio's words is left entirely for the reader to judge. The bachelor has, from the moment of his introduction into the story, been determined to understand Don Quixote's madness and find a cure for it. He has conceived his strategy (we learn later) in consultation with the Priest and Barber, and pursued his aim with determination, effort and no small amount of pain, as a result of the defeat at Don Quixote's hands while posing as the Knight of the Mirrors (Chapter 14). However, Carrasco's motives for pursuing the knight and his squire the length of Spain in order to challenge him a second time are no longer, by his own admission, simply the desire to see him cured. He is now determined to even the score and not let the madman win. Don Antonio's condemnation of what Sansón had done may well have been better understood by the reader in Cervantes' day, when laughter was thought to have a therapeutic effect on some illnesses, particularly melancholy. Don Antonio was, in any case, convinced that Don Quixote's brain had been so badly turned that a cure would never be found; in which case, why prevent the mirth he generated from driving away the melancholy of others? But Cervantes' "lector discreto" would probably not have been fooled. Like the Duke, the Duchess and their plentiful entourage, Don Antonio Moreno is complaining for no other reason than because Sansón Carrasco's actions have robbed him of the personal amusement that he derived from exploiting Don Quixote's malady.

Cervantes makes Don Quixote's madness serve a number of purposes. The comic nature of his actions and beliefs are its most evident aspects, but probably the least significant. Madness of different kinds makes a frequent appearance in Cervantes' writing, as a phenomenon that is either observed or a topic for discussion and anecdote. Cervantes evidently had a well-informed interest in the topic, and despite the harsh nature of the way that the insane and mentally disturbed were often treated, Spain was the most enlightened country in Europe at the time in its efforts to understand and cure the condition. In imagining Don Quixote, then, Cervantes created a prototype for the kind of character familiar to nineteenth-century Russian literature as the holy (or wise) fool. His obsessive reading of novels of chivalry has resulted in Alonso Quijano's total immersion in the fantasy world of the genre, which makes it more real to him than the actuality of sixteenth- and seventeenth-century Spain in which he lives. He naturally faces frequent inconsistencies between these two worlds that are irreconcilable, but which he can dismiss by the simple expedient of the magic that pervades the novel of chivalry: his progress is being constantly opposed by evil enchanters who seek to stop him righting the wrongs of the world. Don Quixote is therefore at odds with his environment and those around him, to whom his "otherness" poses a direct moral and physical challenge.

The members of the society that Cervantes' novel shows us, notwithstanding their diversity, have one thing in common – they present the reader with their individual responses to the challenge the mad knight offers. They recognise him either as an unexplained but palpable physical threat, and react aggressively in self-defence, as do shepherds, horse wranglers and muleteers on different occasions. Others realise immediately that he is mad and to some extent accommodate their behaviour to his madness. The means by which they do the latter vary considerably and depend on their respective social position and learned behaviour. For example, inn-keepers are willing to tolerate Don Quixote and Sancho as paying guests, provided they do not cause trouble or damage the premises. Inn-keepers' daughters and servants are, however, prone to play tricks on the knight out of mischievousness and curiosity. Educated people – the Canon of Toledo, Don Diego Miranda, the friends of the dead Grisostomo – engage him in conversation and discussion to try to assess the degree of insanity he suffers from. Others, such as Basilio and Quiteria, are grateful for his help and happily demonstrate their gratitude, while the galley slaves he sets free do not understand his motives and simply take maximum advantage of his intervention. On the other hand, the ill-treated farm-boy, Andrés, and the brave Biscayan footman, both suffer directly as a result of his actions. The quartet of lovers, Don Fernando, Dorotea, Cardenio and Luscinda generously and altruistically agree to help the Priest and the Barber return Don Quixote to the safety of his village. On the other hand, Don Anonio Moreno and the Duke and Duchess, exploit his mental condition for their own amusement under the guise of generosity and friendship. The naïve and narrow-minded duenna, Doña Rodriguez, even takes him at face value and asks for Don Quixote's help in restoring her daughter's honour. In the background lurks the Holy Brotherhood, which occasionally brings Don Quixote into contact with the law and the state authorities.

Cervantes thus depicts the kind of society Spain has become by charting the imagined reactions of a wide cross-section of its population to the challenge Don Quixote sets them; that of imposing the social, moral and military codes governing a fictional genre, administered by heroic knights-errant on behalf of their ladies and the country's sovereign, upon the country as a whole. It is, of course an impossible vision, both utopian and dystopian at the same time, in which only the gullible and ignorant, like the incomparable Sancho Panza, could believe. Don Quixote is mad if for no other reason than he, like Winston Smith in *Nineteen Eighty-Four*, is in a minority of one. However, the rejection of Don Quixote's dream is shown to be the work of a society which chooses this path in part because of its own weaknesses and its inability to imagine a better future for its people. Cervantes, in a mood of characteristic irony and sadness shows us a country in which religious and political authority had increased racial and religious intolerance and curtailed scholarship and freedom of thought; in which social injustice was rife and good laws were often badly applied and administered; where the majority of people are mired in poverty and ignorance, and exploited by a rich minority with entrenched privileges, where women are discriminated against and repressed; where public standards and honesty are declining in a world where money calls most tunes; and where, lastly, military service to king and country which had made Spain great was being shunned by the landed and ruling classes, with a consequent decline in the country's fortunes.

where is it being shunned?

8

Authority and Subversion in *Don Quixote*
The Novel as Dialectic

So far, this study of *Don Quixote* has argued that, on balance, despite appearances that deceived the vast majority of Cervantes' contemporaries – including the censors – into reading the book as a comic entertainment (with all that that implies) the novel is far more concerned to probe critically beneath the surface of Counterreformation Spain's society than to uphold the conventional wisdom and attitudes of the times. Cervantes does not emerge as the bland, innately conservative humorist that many past scholars and commentators have claimed him to be, but as a writer whose experience, disappointments and scepticism lead him to test the appearances of early seventeenth-century Spain, and to interrogate and challenge many of the intellectual and moral positions of his age.

This is in no way denies that Cervantes also reveals a number of "traditional" Spanish values and attitudes: for example, the honourable and vital role he attributes to the army and navy in maintaining peace and order at home and abroad, particularly the altruism and self-sacrifice of the ordinary soldier in the service of king and country. The ideal of service to the monarch and the state, along with the spiritual and moral duty to God and the Church undoubtedly occupied a crucial position in Cervantes' thinking. But his experience as a commissioner for the armed forces and then as a tax collector, illustrated only too well the extent to which standards of honesty and probity among individuals could fall below what he expected. From the lowest echelons of public service to the highest levels of the aristocracy, corruption, self-interest and self-enrichment at public expense had become the norm rather than the exception. The reign of Philip III seemed to bring this to a head, with the King leaving the affairs of state in the hands of *validos* (favourites) like the Duke of Lerma, who amassed an immense private fortune from his position before his fall from royal favour.[1]

The preceding chapters have put forward a number of arguments about the book and why its author wrote it as he did. In particular the differences between Part I and Part II have been discussed and compared with the history of Spain and Cervantes' life in the ten years that separated them. In Part I of the story, the efforts of mankind to identify the truth are hindered by the desire of many to find the world as they wish it to be. In Part II, by an ironical twist, the quest for truth is made harder by the fact that reality is constantly being manipulated by those who have the power and means to do so in order to serve their own interests. But within this general context, Cervantes focuses upon a number of themes that are all part of the search. Those we have identified in different chapters are what History is, and what the role of historiographers should be; justice and the law; literature and how it should be written and read; love, marriage and the place of women in Spain and the nature of Spanish society in a moment of crisis under the control of the State and the Church.

Cervantes has generally been seen as a devout Catholic, who joined a religious lay order in later life. His depiction of religion in the novel was largely orthodox and certainly free from any dubious doctrinal ideas. But the Church had abrogated to itself a moral and cultural remit that went much further than matters of faith and theology, and it is in the wider moral, ethical, social and artistic fields that Cervantes showed himself to be less acquiescent. In the course of their adventures both Don Quixote and Sancho regularly commend themselves to God, who stands above even the moral and spiritual authority of the knight's lady, Dulcinea. However, in his portrait of Spanish society, which gathers force as the story enters Part II, Cervantes assiduously avoids any comment – direct or implied – about the Church as an institution, despite the prominence of its role. Monks and nuns are given only the most fleeting of background mentions, Don Quixote's travels never carry him to a monastery gate or the door of a wayside church, and priests are given only three speaking parts in the whole of the book's 1,200 pages. Don Quixote's friend the village priest, is the first, remembered mainly in Part I for his examination of the knight's library, his excursion into the wilds with the barber to bring the mad knight home again, and his reading of *El curioso impertinente* to the guests at the inn. He virtually disappears from Part II. The second prelate encountered is the Canon of Toledo, whose long discussion on literature and chivalresque novels occupies Chapters 49 and 50 0f Part I. The third one we meet is the intolerant and irascible cleric who, though a fellow guest in the palace of the Duke and Duchess, argues furiously with Don Quixote at the Duke's dinner table in Chapters 31 and 32 of Part II.

Cervantes' reasons for this very low-key portrayal of one of the country's two chief ruling institutions, is self-evident. It avoids any

censorship

doubts that might have arisen in the minds of the censors, and keeps the book anchored in the secular literary tradition while allowing the knight and his squire to express devout Christian sentiments. In similar fashion, Cervantes excludes from the story – with one fairly minor exception – any character who might be regarded as an influential political figure. Spain's greatest internal problem at the time, with which Cervantes was familiar at first hand, was the growing level of corruption in political decision-making and public administration. This had increased since the accession of Philip III, and the rule of his favourite the Duke of Lerma. But to devise a plot that revealed, either directly or indirectly, these failings in high places would have been as foolhardy as criticising the Church or Catholic theology. Save for the unnamed Viceroy of Catalonia, who puts in a brief appearance in Chapters 53 and 54 of Part II, we meet no high officials. The Viceroy is involved in the capture and questioning of the illegally returned *morisca* Ana Félix, and the crew of the Moorish brigantine intercepted off Barcelona. The Admiral of the Spanish Fleet, the Viceroy and his noble friend, Don Antonio Moreño, take a highly sympathetic view of Ana Félix's case, and her motives for returning to Spain. However, despite their willingness to plead on her behalf, and that of her father Ricote, Cervantes leaves her fate still unresolved, though with a heavy hint that an exception to the law of 1609 is unlikely to be made.

Deep-seated dialectical tensions therefore seem to run throughout this complex novel, many of them between what the author judged it was appropriate to say and on what he chose to remain silent. For the *lector discreto* however, who was seldom out of Cervantes' thoughts, the silences can also be eloquent. On one level, the opposites that Cervantes contrasts are mostly between the actual and the ideal. For example, on occasions his characters are placed in positions where their actions would receive a legal response that denies the natural justice of their case. Indeed, Don Quixote himself can only aspire to right wrongs and correct injustices by placing himself above the law. (The "Catch 22" of this situation is that while only a madman might have the vision to change the world, he would not be heeded because he is mad.) Don Quixote suffers from the tensions between what he is convinced he can achieve as a knight-errant, and what actually results from his interventions. The ideal and the real are therefore constantly at war with each other at every turn of the story. Furthermore these tensions are maintained because the knight – and increasingly his squire also – are able to "irrationalise" their failures, to impose their interpretations upon the world by attributing them to magic; the power of inimical wizards and enchanters to change the physical world in order to thwart their good intentions.

Cervantes thus makes the use of magic to create or resolve problems in the fantasy world of the chivalresque novels look so comic and ridiculous that it can almost be understood as a separate attack on the belief in witchcraft and sorcery that was still prevalent in early seventeenth-century Europe. It was a belief that the Catholic Church had tried to root out since its early days, asserting that it was a product of the pagan world, refusing to distinguish between "good" and "bad" magic and labelling it all the work of the Devil. Those who practised it were held to be in league with Satan, a sin punishable by death. But Cervantes' personal beliefs were almost certainly not those of the Church. Instead, he completely dismisses the existence of magic, refusing to believe that the natural laws of the universe can be altered by any power wielded by individual human beings, irrespective of its provenance. Only God and the Devil have the power to make or unmake the universe, and those who pretend otherwise by practising the dark arts are as deluded as his mad protagonist. Indeed, Don Quixote's delusions do not stop at the belief that others perform magic. He not only attributes truth to the superhuman (i.e. magical) powers with which writers have endowed the knights-errant who grace their pages, but of necessity transfers these also to himself. Indeed, Don Quixote's madness chiefly overcomes his reason in one key area – his belief in magic, which gives him entry into the fantasy world of the chival-resque romance.

The same kinds of dialectical tension are generated between the ideal and real in the other areas of life that the novel explores. The author's pretence that Don Quixote is a history, in which the two main characters are able to read, in Part II, the published record of their adventures in Part I, and are greeted wherever they go by people who have also read about them, is an imaginative masterstroke. Like the historian narrator who runs out of material in Part I, Chapter 8, it is a literary joke that has a very "postmodern" feel to it. It is also a sharp reminder of the gulf between the "truth" of human deeds and experiences and the inaccurate and fanciful accounts of them that are dignified with the name of "history." Despite all efforts to found history upon the truth, historians usually have direct access to very little of it. They are quite unlike the remarkable Cide Hamete Benengeli, who walks side by side with Don Quixote and Sancho, noting down every detail of their conversations, arguments and encounters with others. Instead they have to rely for the truth on second-hand accounts and third-hand documents. The average history book, however, supplements these "facts" (the nearest we can approach to historical truth) with supposition, probabilities, reinventions and even fiction. Even so, historians reject the fiction of the period they are studying as a credible witness to the truth they are seeking. Thus the line between history and imaginative literature, Cervantes asserts, is a blurred one, and historical truth can only be achieved by such doyens of historiography as Cide Hamete. (Which is to say that the kind of truth that historians are expected to produce is largely impossible.)

Indeed, Cervantes the humorist and sceptic presents his readers with a world in which most of what is taken for fact, truth, reality – call it what you will – is open to question, and Francisco Sanchez' "quod nihil scitur" reverberates as strongly as Descartes' "cogito ergo sum." The main reason for this state of mind is the fallibility of the human senses, which are skewed or coloured by imagination, faith, delusion, prejudice and inflexibility. Don Quixote's madness makes him an extreme example of how far personal faith – no matter how bizarre – can cause a completely delusional perception of both the outside world and of himself. Furthermore, as Cervantes has playfully demonstrated, an appeal to history is quite insufficient as a proof of truth. Indeed, the figurative truth of imaginative literature which imitates nature sufficiently well, is, in these circumstances, as good a reflection of actuality as the record written by historians.

Don Quixote's forays out along the highways and byways of Spain are made in search of adventures that will be witness to his courage, invincible might in battle and knightly reputation, but they also demand that, in the process, he defend the weak, correct wrongs, put right injustices, and protect widows and orphans. The numerous personal qualities that a fictional knight-errant is expected to demonstrate in pursuing these aims make him a paragon of virtue. He must be courteous, gentle, loyal, chaste, honest, long-suffering, fearless and able to withstand hardship, and above all he must be wise and just if he is to fulfil this most complex of superhero roles. In the world of medieval fantasy that was created around him, the knight-errant imposed order and administered justice by strength and the edge of the sword, as he roamed through territories where war and lawlessness threatened the stability of kingdoms which his prowess and wisdom saved by forcibly removing the forces that threatened them. In the popular imagination, knights-errant became arbiters in the constant power struggles they encountered, and in which they also aided the poor, oppressed and exploited in a scenario reminiscent of medieval Europe under despotic rulers and greedy aristocrats.

The elements of courtly love (given a suitably platonic twist), superhuman strength, supernatural opposition and intervention through magic and miracles, combined with descriptions of tempests, fantastic landscapes and thunderous battles in which knights slew enemies by the thousand, to supply elements of popular entertainment. But they were so grotesquely untrue to life that, despite their popularity, the chivalresque romances had, by the middle of the sixteenth century, begun to attract ridicule and moral objection, for being replete with lies and situations that might be morally damaging for their readers. Despite this opposition, the chivalresque romances in Spain were regular reading for enjoyment for over a hundred years, and virtually all ran to numerous reprintings. The question of why this should be so, is an interesting one. To what nascent or unsatisfied need among the people did these books respond? Is the position of this literature in sixteenth-century Spain any different from that of the innumerable books of fantasy which decorate twenty-first century station book stalls? One reason might have been pure escapism. People found in them a means to lift themselves above the everyday drudgeries of life.[2]

But precisely what kind of escape did the romance of chivalry offer? One possibility is that identification with the figure of the invincible but virtuous knight-errant provided readers in sixteenth-century Spain with an emotional refuge from a fog of growing doubt about what the country's future held for its people. The knight-errant of the romances was an imagined reversion to a vague and legendary past with codes of conduct and personal honour which, though equally fictitious, constituted a clear, recognisable alternative to the declining standards, social injustice and exploitation that often surrounded individuals and communities in renaissance Spain. How many times might ordinary Spaniards have dreamed that an Amadís, Belianis or Palmerín would burst upon the scene, and resolve with might and justice the internal problems of the country and the threats from without? Indeed, this is precisely the advice that Don Quixote offers to the King in the face of fresh threats of war with the Turks. In the first chapter of Part II, when the knight is recovering at home from the exertions of his second sally, he discusses the state of the nation and the Turkish danger with his friends the Priest and the Barber, and observes:

> Su majestad ha hecho como prudentísimo guerrero en proveer sus estados con tiempo, porque no le halle desapercibido el enemigo; pero si se toma mi consejo, aconsejárale yo que usara de una prevención de la cual Su Majestad, la hora de ahora, debe estar muy ajeno de pensar en ella . . .[3]

> (His Majesty has shown himself a very prudent war commander by buying time for his territories, so that the enemy will not find him unprepared, but if he were to take my counsel, I would advise him to make use of a resource which his Majesty has, up to this moment, been unwilling to think of . . .)

After some persuasion, Don Quixote discloses to his friends the measures that he regards as better than all the precautions the King has so far taken. This is none other than:

Hay más sino mandar Su Majestad por público pregón que se junten en la corte para un día señalado todos los caballeros andantes que vayan por España, que aunque no viniesen sino media docena, tal podría venir entre ellos, que sólo bastase a destruir toda la potestad del Turco.[4]

(His Majesty has only to summon by public proclamation all the knights-errant who are currently wandering about Spain to assemble on a certain date in the Royal Court, and even if only half a dozen turned up, between them they could achieve enough to destroy the power of the Turk on their own.)

The Priest and the Barber greet this pronouncement with incredulity and sorrow, seeing it as proof that the knight's madness has not abated in the slightest bit. But might not other, sane Spaniards have dreamed of just such an outcome?

The impossible powers that their authors gave the knights-errant of the romances of chivalry were infinitely distant from the truth, but precisely reflected the kind of escape the books offered their readers; namely, the avoidance of the limitations that truth placed upon the imagination, and the vicarious thrill of adventures that were unlikely to be equalled in the nation-state of Renaissance Europe. These heroic figures were also loyal admirers of great and noble ladies whose every whim they served, thus also opening up the romantic aspect of story-telling and the emotional sufferings and sensitivities it entailed. The chivalrous knight saw no contradiction between shedding tears at some slight – real or imagined – from his lady, and then rushing forth to slaughter a thousand enemies or to fight to the death in single combat with a rival knight, dragon or giant. But the criticism that this popular entertainment attracted had about it something more that the condemnation of bad writing (which many of the novels were) and the way in which it might distort the reader's judgement and taste. The fact that these novels were regarded, particularly by churchmen, as morally harmful, raises an interesting point. The fact of this harm was generally accepted, but its nature was rarely defined, other than to claim that the reader is beguiled into accepting a farrago of "lies" as the truth. But only an obsessive madman like Don Quixote was likely to be affected in this way and to act upon it. All other enthusiasts of the genre left its world of fantasy behind on the page when they closed the book's covers, though the more naïve and gullible may have believed that knights-errant, and their wondrous deeds, had really existed in the distant past. But the official campaign against the novels of chivalry, which Cervantes seemed to have joined wholeheartedly, was probably instigated for somewhat different reasons than those stated. The wide popularity and content of these works may have persuaded the authorities of a society which sought to channel thought and art along increasingly conventional and orthodox lines, that the alternative worlds they dangled before their readers encouraged a divergence of thought and ideas, and a release of the imagination, which might lead individuals to question the *status quo*; namely, rule by an absolute monarch guided by an increasingly authoritarian ecclesiastical establishment, and supported by a privileged aristocratic class. When large numbers of people prefer imagined fantasy to perceived reality, things are probably ripe for change, since it indicates a subconscious withdrawal from the material present.

This line of argument leads to the suggestion that, notwithstanding their authors' intentions, the novels of chivalry began to function as a kind of popular subversion, and acquired a role like that of the "folk" and carnival humour studied by Bakhtin, by providing an escape to a world of make-believe. Despite a certain amount of posturing, Cervantes did not condemn chivalresque literature out of hand. He inveighed against bad writing (which most of them were) and against superficial or literal reading of a fictional text. His pastiches of the overblown style often adopted by the authors of these novels confirm the first of these antipathies, and the invention of Don Quixote as the worst kind of literal reader corroborates the second. Indeed, Cervantes gave credit to a handful of these books for having literary merit, and probably adhered to the classical dictum he quotes that no book is so bad that some good things cannot be found in it.

By freeing people's imagination, in an age when the State and the Church made concerted efforts to restrict it, and to channel the arts into their service through patronage, the romance of chivalry was, whether by intention or chance, rowing against the moral and artistic tide. Cervantes took that current of subversion to a logical extreme in *Don Quixote* by making his protagonist a literal reflection of the knights-errant in the popular fiction, and setting him on a collision course with the social, economic and intellectual forces that comprised post-tridentine Spain. Cervantes' attack on the chivalresque novel was, therefore, certainly genuine in part. But it was also a convenient smokescreen – yet another source of dialectical tension in the book – masking the author's own critical and subversive intentions: namely, to use the philosophical tools of scepticism and humanism to challenge the "authority" of the conventional wisdom of his time. In his introductory essay (one in four) to the four hundredth anniversary edition of *Don Quixote* (2004) entitled "Una novela para el siglo XXI"[5] Mario Vargas Llosa makes a number of interesting points, the first of which is that:

El gran' tema de Don Quijote de la Mancha es la ficción, su razón de ser, y
la manera como ella, al infiltrarse en la vida, la va modelando, transfor-
mando. . . . Al final, . . . la ficción va contaminando lo vivido y la realidad se
va gradualmente plegando a las excentricidades y fantasías de Don Quijote.

(Don Quixote de la Mancha's great theme is fiction, its raison d'être, and
way in which, having infiltrated into real life, it proceeds to shape and transform it. . . . In the end, . . . fiction contaminates life and reality gradually
gives way to the eccentricities and fantasies of Don Quixote.)

Thus, he continues, the delusions which changed Alonso Quijano into
Don Quixote de la Mancha did not entail acting out the past, but something much more ambitions – the realisation of the myth, to make fiction
into lived history.

But, as Vargas Llosa also asserts, although it is a novel about literature,
Don Quixote is also a celebration of liberty. He quotes the mad knight's
conversation in Part II, Chapter 58, with his squire, in which he says:

La libertad, Sancho, es uno de los más preciosos dones que a los hombres
dieron los cielos; con ella no pueden igualarse los tesoros que encierra la
tierra ni el mar encubre; por la libertad así como por la honra se puede y
debe aventurar la vida, y por el contrario, el cautiverio es el mayor mal que
puede venir a los hombres.[6]

(Freedom, Sancho, is one of the most precious gifts that heaven gave to man;
neither the treasures buried in the earth nor those covered by the sea can
equal it, and for freedom, no less than for honour, one can and must take
risks in life. By contrast, captivity is the greatest evil that can be visited upon
men.)

The kind of liberty or freedom that Don Quixote has in mind here, Vargas
Llosa suggests, is exactly the same as that which characterised the end of
the eighteenth century in Europe. It was shared by those who regarded
themselves as liberals, through whom it passed to the Romantic movement. Vargas Llosa defines it as:

La libertad es la soberanía de un individuo para decidir su vida sin presiones
ni condicionamientos, en exclusiva función de su inteligencia y voluntad.[7]

(Freedom is the right an individual possesses to decide about his life,
without pressures and conditions, as part of the exclusive function of his
intelligence and will power.)

This type of freedom equates to the idea of "negative liberty" one of the two kinds discussed by Sir Isaiah Berlin,[8] who also argued that Political Theory was a branch of Moral Philosophy, since political relations and actions are based upon moral notions. The central questions of politics, and responsibility for political power, are things like "Why should anyone obey somebody else? If someone disobeys, should they be coerced? If so, by whom, to what degree and to what end?" Laws, of course, decide these questions for the most part. They also define the limits a society places on individual liberty by specifying which actions against individuals and their property will not be tolerated. But social justice for all also depends upon who makes the laws, who benefits from them and how they are administered.

The discussion on freedom between the knight and his squire takes place not long after they have left the Duke's palace, and Don Quixote confesses the unease he felt at being the recipient of so much lavish hospitality. He says:

> ¡Venturoso aquel a quien el cielo dió un pedazo de pan sin que le quede obligación de agradecerlo a otro que el mismo cielo![9]

> (Lucky is the man to whom Heaven gave a morsel of bread without leaving his obliged to thank anyone for it other than Heaven itself!)

The view Don Quixote puts forward here may also be one that reflects the belief of his author, and equates liberty with independence. To enjoy a feeling of genuine liberty, no man or woman should be beholden for their existence to the generosity or charity of others. By this reasoning, human beings should be able, through their own choices and actions, to obtain at least a minimum for their needs, the maintenance of their dignity and sense of themselves as rational individuals. The irony of this view is that, in his self-reinvention as Don Quixote de la Mancha, Alonso Quijano has abrogated to his *alter ego* a sense of freedom that figures high on the scale of "positive" liberty. That is to say that the knight-errant, secure in his beliefs, codes of conduct and his superhuman strength and fighting ability, imposes upon others his version of justice, and how wrongs should be righted, free of all restraints upon his liberty of action, save those imposed by his personal principles, his lady and the king or emperor in whose service he sometimes exercises his calling. While recognising some practical necessities, like carrying money and paying for things he needs, Don Quixote nevertheless places himself above the law, as his freeing of the galley slaves, his eagerness to kill "enemies" and to intervene in the lives of others in any way he feels to be necessary clearly demonstrates. As Vargas Llosa observes:

El Quijote no cree que la justicia, el orden social, el progreso, sean funciones de la autoridad, sino obra de quehacer de individuos que, como sus modelos, los caballeros andantes, y él mismo se hayan echado sobre los hombros la tarea de hacer menos injusto y más libre y próspero el mundo en viven.[10]

(Don Quixote does not believe that justice, social order and progress are the function of political authority, but the job of individuals who, like his models the knights-errant and he himself, have taken upon their own shoulders the task of making the world in which they live a less unjust, freer and more prosperous place.)

Don Quixote does not, it is true, respect any arm of the authority of the state, except possibly the king himself, because in the fantasy medieval world that the writers of the chivalresque novels created those aspects of the modern Renaissance nation-state were completely absent. Indeed, they would have been an impediment to the deeds of the knights-errant in those stories, just as they were to the "adventures" that Don Quixote encountered. Unlike the cities, the by-ways of rural Spain were still a law unto themselves in the early seventeenth century. Though policed by the Holy Brotherhood, thieves and bandits were still commonplace, but Don Quixote does not concern himself with bringing such felons to book. (By freeing the galley slaves, he probably added to their numbers!) It is easy to agree with Vargas Llosa that Don Quixote is concerned with literature and its effect on real life. His joint proposal that it is also about individual freedom in an increasingly authoritarian Spain is a bit more problematic however, unless one accepts it as a natural consequence of Cervantes' subversive and satirical intentions. To challenge key aspects of the moral and cultural edifice erected by the state, the Church and the universities, may inevitably lead to reflections on individual liberty in a rapidly urbanising society that was struggling to rule a vast, overseas empire. But it is difficult to argue that individual liberty in the early-modern monarchical state was, for Cervantes, anything more than a second-tier preoccupation that would arise from the questions we have considered earlier in this study. Indeed, Don Quixote's anarchic imposition upon the real world of the liberty of action permitted in the romances to the imagined knights-errant is condemned by being made to look ridiculous and achieving nothing.

Seen from a twenty-first century point of view, Don Quixote could be seen as a force for change that is "revolutionary," save that nowhere does any of Cervantes' characters advocate the overthrow of the state and its institutions by force in order to establish something different. Because, as a result of his madness, Don Quixote's direction for change is totally misguided, his vision remains a totally individual crusade which can gather no adherents. Cervantes thus cleverly avoids any accusation that he is, through his book, plotting the destruction of the *status quo*. Nevertheless, because he also shows discretion and good judgement in so many areas, often to the amazement of those listening to him, Don Quixote's insanity does not invalidate the social and moral criticisms implicit in his deluded adventures, or the social and economic changes that would result from them if they were acted upon as part of a policy of reform. Instead, the message seems to be that things can get better only from the common desire of individuals to make changes. The Don Quixote who tries to change the world from a position of complete isolation, however noble and altruistic his intentions, is doomed to failure – and probably to being certified insane! Instead, change starts from the incremental subversion of the conventionally accepted world about us.

Notes

Preface and Acknowledgements

1 In chronological order, these are the versions by Samuel Putnam (1949), J. M. Cohen (1950), Walter Starkie (1957), Burton Raffel (1996), John Rutherford (2000), Edith Grossman (2003) and Tom Lathhrop (2005).

2 Among these works are Williamson, Edwin (ed.), *Cervantes and the Modernists. The Question of Influence* (Tamesis, London, 1994); Cruz, Anne & Johnson, Carroll B. (eds), *Cervantes and his Post-Modern Constituencies* (Garland Publishing Inc., New York & London, 1999); Quint, David, *Cervantes' Novel of Modern Times: A New Reading of "Don Quixote,* (Princeton University Press, New Jersey, 2003), and Graf, E. C., *Cervantes and Modernity: Four Essays on "Don Quixote"* (Bucknell University Press, Lewisburg, 2007).

1 *Don Quixote*: The Author, Readers and Critics

1 Anthony J. Close, *The Romantic Approach to Don Quixote* (Cambridge University Press, Cambridge, 1977), pp. 2–3.

2 Quoted by Américo Castro in his book *El pensamiento de Cervantes,* (Editorial Noguer, S. A., Barcelona y Madrid, 1972), p. 21, first published in 1925. Fitzmarice-Kelly's *History of Spanish Literature* was reprinted in various editions in English, French and Spanish. Castro quotes from the 1921 Spanish edition (p. 211).

3 Anthony J. Close, *The Romantic Approach to "Don Quixote"* (Cambridge University Press, Cambridge, 1977).

4 Ibid., p. 2.

5 Peter E. Russell, "*Don Quixote* as a Funny Book," *MLR*, LXIV, No. 2 (April 1969), pp. 312–326.

6 Anthony J. Close, *Cervantes and the Comic Mind of his Age* (Oxford University Press, Oxford, 2000). Close bases his discussion of Cervantes's poetics of comedy on the notions of "propriedad" and "discreción," relating both to classical ideas on comedy set down by Aristotle and Horace, and to their restatement by Alonso López (El Pinciano) in his treatise *Philosophía antigua poética* (1596) which was one of Cervantes's chief theoretical influences. Close also examines the evolution of attitudes to comedy in Spain during the sixteenth century. Daniel Eisenberg devotes Chapter 6 of his book *A Study of "Don Quixote"* (Juan de la Cuesta, Newark, 1987) to the subject of humour in Cervantes's novel, and Ronald Paulson's book "*Don Quixote*" *in England: The Aesthetics of Laughter* (Johns Hopkins University Press, Baltimore, 1998) examines how Cervantes's style of humour influenced the

eighteenth-century English novel. John Jay Allen's "Smiles and Laughter in *Don Quixote*" *Comparative Literature Studies*, Vol. 43, No. 4 (2006), pp. 515–531, examines why Don Quixote is still found funny today.

7   James Iffland, "Do We Really Need to Read Avellaneda?" in *Cervantes: Bulletin of the Cervantes Society of America*, Vol. 21, No. 1 (2001), pp. 67–81. The short quotation given above comes from page 71.

8   See Edward C. Riley's, *Cervantes's Theory of the Novel* (Clarendon Press, Oxford, 1962) and *Don Quixote* (Allen & Unwin, London, 1968) and Stephen Gilman's *The Novel According to Cervantes* (University of California Press, Berkeley, Los Angeles and London, 1989).

9   Ruth El Saffar, *Beyond Fiction: The Recovery of the Feminine in the Novels of Cervantes* (University of California Press, Berkeley, 1984)

10 Salvador J. Fajardo, "Ruth El Saffar. *Beyond Fiction: The Recovery of the Feminine in the Novels of Cervantes*," *Renaissance Quarterly*, Vol. 39, No. 1 (Spring) 1986, pp. 126–128.

11 Ruth El Saffar and Diana de Armas Wilson (eds), *Quixotic Desire: Psychoanalytical Perspectives on Cervantes* (Cornell University Press, Ithaca & London, 1993)

12 Ibid., pp. 1–2.

13 Daniel Eisenberg, "Review of *Cervantes* by Jean Canavaggio (translated by J. R. Jones) (W. W. Norton, New York, 1991)" published in *Cervantes, Bulletin of the Cervantes Society of America*, 12.1 (1992), pp. 119–24. Canavaggio's book, first published in Paris in 1986 won the Prix Goncourt for Biography the following year. Despite Professor Eisenberg's reservations, Luis Astrana Marín's *Vida ejemplar y heroica de Miguel de Cervantes Saavedra* (Instituto Editorial Reus, Madrid, 1948–58), 7 vols., had introduced, for the first time in biographical research on Cervantes, large numbers of notarial and other official documents. The following biographies of Cervantes have all followed the documentary possibilities that, its deficiencies notwithstanding, Astrana Marín's work opened up: William Byron, *Cervantes: A Biography* (Doubleday, New York, 1978; Melveena McKendrick, *Cervantes* (Little, Brown & Co., Boston, Mass., 1980); Jean Canavaggio, *Cervantes* (Mazarine Paris, 1986)and Donald P. McCrory, *No Ordinary Man. The Life and Times of Miguel de Cervantes* (Peter Owen, London, 2002).

14 Michael McGaha, "Is there a Hidden Jewish Meaning in *Don Quixote?*" *Cervantes, Bulletin of the Cervantes Society of America*, 24.1 (2004), pp. 173–88.

15 Dominique Aubier, *Don Quichotte, prophète d'Israel* (R. Laffont, Paris, 1966). A Spanish translation, *Don Quijote, profeta y cabalista*, was published in Barcelona in 1981. A similar line of argument is taken by Ruth Reichelberg, *Don Quichotte ou le roman d'un Juif masqué* (Seuil, Paris,1999).

16 The *Zohar* is the foundational work in the literature of Jewish mystical thought known as the *Kabbala*. It is a group of books including a commentary on the mystical aspects of the Torah, and scriptural interpretations, as well as material on mysticism, mythical cosmogony and mystical psychology. The *Zohar* contains discussion on the nature of God, the origins and struc-

ture of the Universe, the nature of souls, redemption, the relationship of the Ego to Darkness, "true self" to "The Light of God," and the relationship between universal energy and man. The *Zohar*, was written mostly in the Aramaic that was the day-to-day language of Israel in the Second Temple period (539 BCE to 70 CE). The work first appeared in Castile in the thirteenth century, published by a Jewish writer named Moses de León. He ascribed the *Zohar* to Shimon bar Yochai ("Rashbi"), a rabbi of the second century during the Roman persecution.

17 Michael McGaha, op. cit., p. 186.

18 See for example Marina S. Brownlee and Hans Ulrich Gumbrecht (eds), *Cultural Authority in Golden Age Spain* (Johns Hopkins University Press, Baltimore and London, 1995).

19 See Henry Kamen, *Spain 1496–1714: A Society of Conflict* (Pearson Education, Harlow, 2005).

20 Donald P. McCrory, *No Ordinary Man. The Life and Times of Miguel de Cervantes* (Peter Owen, London, 2002), p. 149.

21 Ibid., p. 169.

22 Literary academies, of varying reputation and fame, existed in most Spanish cities by the end of the sixteenth century and showed a marked increase in number after 1625. They were usually presided over and patronised by local noble families, and were frequently headed by the educated wives or daughters of a notable aristocrat. Both daughters of Philip II, started academies in the Royal Court at Madrid. Generally speaking academies afforded a cultural and intellectual "space" in which a variety of participants, both women and men, could come together for the exchange of ideas, discussion and literary or philosophical debate. Some were established for women only, with the specific purpose of furthering women's education. Many of Spain's foremost men of letters and learning were regular attenders at meetings of academies, and the majority of Spain's few women writers benefited also from the experience they gained in debating with male academicians, and establishing a strong female voice within the academies they patronised. Famous and reputable academies with well-known members were founded in Madrid, Seville, Salamanca, Toledo and Valladolid. Cervantes and Lope de Vega attended the same academy in Madrid in the early seventeenth century, and despite their difficult relationship, Cervantes is once recorded as having borrowed Lope's spectacles in order to read a text that was under discussion at the time.

23 Cervantes' second oldest sister, Luisa de Cervantes (1546?–1625?), entered a Carmelite convent in Alcalá de Henares in 1565 of which she eventually became prioress.

24 Donald P. McCrory, op. cit., pp. 207–8.

25 Often performed in the intervals between the acts of the *comedias, entremeses* were often witty, comic or even farcical pieces at which Cervantes, with his ear for dialogue and instinct for characterisation, excelled. The *entremés* was usually a complete and much enjoyed contrast to the melodramatic action of the Lopesque *comedia*.

26   *Los trabajos de Persiles y Segismunda* is usually categorised as an early modern version of the classical fictional genre known as the Byzantine Novel, of which the best known example was Heliodorus' *Aethiopica*, a third-century narrative written in Greek. The work was well known throughout Europe, mainly through Jacques Amyot's translation into French, but three Spanish translations had also appeared in 1554, 1581 and 1587, an indication of the book's popularity with the growing reading public. Cervantes, always highly sensitive to the changes of taste and mood in his readership, no doubt saw this story as a source he could exploit in the spirit of *imitatio* (the imitation of classical models) and his imaginative borrowings from a number of diverse sources besides Heliodorus enabled him to create something that was recognisable yet new. A best-seller in its own day, and a work which also went through a number of translations in different languages, *Persiles y Segismunda* has, nevertheless, been largely overlooked subsequently. Donald P. McCrory (op. cit., p. 260) comments:

> "It is time for critics and commentators to turn their attention away from the knight-errant and the riches of the Exemplary Novels to focus on this encyclopaedic romance that is, in many respects, as sweeping and as vast in its episodic narrative as *Don Quixote*."

Certainly Cervantes is known to have stated that *Persiles y Segismunda* was his best work, and probably did so not just in the hope of selling a few more copies.

27   Often parodying Lope's popular style of *comedia nueva*, Cervantes' classically constructed plays often feature episodes, characters and settings that are taken from real life. His plays often have a multi-cultural tendency, featuring Christian and Moorish characters (some converted, some not) and demonstrate a sceptical attitude to the conventional Catholic world-view. Although his full length plays, and particularly his interludes, employ themes of popular comedy – honour, love and social rank – they are treated not so much as permanent institutions of social order, but as questionable and changeable social forces affecting characters who do not always conform to their conventional roles.

28   The term hegemonic discourse was probably first used in relation to the Hispanic world by Roberto González Echevarría notably in works like *The Voice of the Masters: Writing and Authority in Modern Latin American Literature* (1985) and *Myth and Archive: A Theory of Latin American Narrative* (1990). In these studies, Professor González Echevarría examines the influence of Spanish colonial practice and tradition in shaping the formal and thematic approaches to fictional narrative subsequently adopted by post-colonial Latin American writers.

29   Marina S. Brownlee & Hans Ulrich Gumbrecht (eds), *Cultural Authority in Golden Age Spain* (Johns Hopkins University Press, Baltimore & London, 1995), p. x.

30   The type of imitation – or *imitatio* – of which we speak here in relation to Renaissance culture has been defined, and redefined, on numerous occasions. It is generally accepted that imitation encompassed the re-creation of

specific verbal models of classical and Italian Renaissance provenance, and constituted a basic artistic practice in early modern Europe. The study of the literary and verbal sources and formulations of a given work was, at the beginning of the twentieth century, a stronghold of philological scholarship. This emphasis often resulted, however, in the analyst overlooking the text under scrutiny in favour of its "origins." Research into the sources of works now tends to be subsumed under the study of intertextuality as a mode of literary production.

2 Cervantes' Library of Literary Ideas

1   François Rabelais' comic and satirical masterpiece, now called *The Life and Adventures of Gargantua and Pantagruel*, was initially written in five parts between 1532 and 1564. The battle between humanism and scholasticism is joined in Book II, originally entitled *La vie très horrifique du grand Gargantua, père de Pantagruel* (The Very Horrific Life of the Great Gargantua, Father of Pantagruel) which appeared in 1534. The five books tell the story of the fantastic lives and adventures of the giant Pantagruel and his father Gargantua, along with their various companions, among them the rascally Panurge. Its humorous satire features much crudity, scatalogical comedy and violence, which the censors of the Sorbonne condemned as obscene. Now hailed by the literary theorist Mikhail Bakhtin as the high point of medieval carnivalesque humour, Rabelais' novel may well have influenced some of the wilder scenes of violent comedy in Part I of *Don Quixote*.

2   The sixteenth century saw numerous Spanish works published on the education, upbringing and conduct of princes and rulers. The most famous is Antonio de Guevara's *El reloj de príncipes* (1529), which, unlike the more illustrious book by Baldasare Castiglione, *Il Cortegiano* (1519), which was a behaviour manual for courtiers, analysed the roles, functions and behaviour of the secular members of a royal court which contributed to good government. The dialogues of Alfonso de Valdés (1490?–1532) included the satirical *Diálogo de Mercurio y Carón* (Dialogue between Mercury and Charon), and the *Diálogo de Lactancio y un arcidano* (Dialogue between Lactantius and an Archdeacon) also known as the *Diálogo de las cosas occuridas en Roma* (Dialogue of the Occurrences in Rome). The latter work appeared to justify Charles V's sack of Rome in 1527, but can also be read as a "satire of overstatement," which is in fact a criticism of the actions of the king. Other satirical works with broadly political implications, such as the anonymous *Lazarillo de Tormes* (1553–4), became very popular. But many others were not published in their day, but instead circulated, anonymously or under a pseudonym, in manuscript form to avoid suppression by the censors. These included humanist works like the Erasmian satire *El Crotalón*, now attributed to Cristóbal Villalón, and *Viaje de Turquía*, for which no author has been claimed so far. Both had their origins in the 1550s.

3   See Barry Ife, *Reading and Fiction in the Golden Age of Spain: A Platonistic*

Critique and some Picaresque Replies (Cambridge University Press, Cambridge, 1985), p. 15.

4 For an outline of the inseparability of law and history, see Susan Byrne, *Law and History in Cervantes' "Don Quixote"* (University of Toronto Press, Toronto and London, 2012), p. 16. This detailed and learned study describes how a debate in sixteenth-century Italy regarding the refutation by the philosopher Francesco Patrizi of Aristotelean and Ciceronian historical precepts, brought about the attempt of the great French jurist François Baudouin to "theorise the conjunction between law and history" as part of the *mos italicus* versus *mos gallicus* argument on the contemporary status and application of Roman law. Baudouin's works, which were well-known in Spain, include a gloss and commentary on various legal codes of the classical era, as well as the book *De institutione historiae universae et eius cum jurisprudentia coniunctione* (1561). Professor Byrne points out that in the opening to this work, Baudouin describes men as spectators, actors and judges in life's theatre, prefiguring the idea of "the world as a stage" found in the plays of Shakespeare and Calderón, and placing each person, very much as Cervantes was to do, in the role of judge.

5 Anthony J, Cascardi, *Cervantes, Literature and the Discourse of Politics* (University of Toronto Press, Toronto, Buffalo and London, 2012).

6 Ibid., p. 3.

7 E. C. Graf, *Cervantes and Modernity: Four Essays on "Don Quijote"* (Bucknell University Press, Lewisburg, 2007), p. 16.

8 E. C. Riley, *Cervantes's Theory of the Novel* (Clarendon Press, Oxford, 1962). This was followed by Stephen Gilman's similarly influential book *The Novel According to Cervantes* (University of California Press, Berkeley, Los Angeles and London, 1989), and a number of works on Cervantes's narrative strategies and technique, including his "distancing" and perspectivism.

9 Alonso López Pinciano (1547?–1627) was better known as "El Pinciano." His best known work, *Filosofía antigua poética* was published in Madrid in 1596, and took the form of a dialogue exchange of letters between the author and a friend, referred to as Don Gabriel, in the course of which they discuss and argue about aspects of classical and contemporary literary theory. Alonso López Pinciano was an eminent doctor, who was physician to María of Austria, King Philip II's sister, and to the Infanta Margarita. A follower of Aristotle and Horace, he is thought to have written *Filosofía antigua poética* as an attempt to impose a classically inspired brake on the ideas of the prolific playwright and poet Lope de Vega. This would have commended him to Cervantes who had already publicly fallen out with Lope on matters of literary politics.

10 E. C. Riley, op. cit., p. 13.

11 The dialogue format, with its roots in the philosphical writings of Plato, had become a common literary means of discussing matters of political, moral, religious and philosophical interest in sixteenth-century Spain. To the discussions attributed to the fictitious participants in these dialogues, El

Pinciano has added the fourth, "absent and independent voice" of Don Gabriel, broadening the debate still further.

12 Alonso López Pinciano, *Filosofía antigua poética* (Linkgua Ediciones, Barcelona, 2009), p. 95.

13 Susan Byrne, op. cit. Note 4 above, p. 13.

14 B. Ife, op. cit., p. 95.

15 The *Alumbrados* constituted a movement of religious mystics within the Catholic Church whose teachings and beliefs were still being combatted in the late seventeenth cenytury, despite frequent denunciations by the Inquisition. Some of their beliefs were only mildly heterodox, but others were regarded as heretical. They held that the soul is capable of reaching a degree of perfection while on earth, which allows the individual to contemplate and commune with God. All external religious practice – the sacraments, daily worship and the performance of good works, were considered superfluous for the achievement of the inner state of communition with God. Once in this blessed state, it was not possible for the individual to sin, irrespective of the acts committeed. There are similaries between the ideas of the *Alumbrado*s and the Calvinist doctrine of salvation through Grace.

16 Fr Juan Antonio Llorente worked within the Inquisition's commissary in Logroño, then as its Secretary General in Madrid at the time of the Napoleonic invasion of Spain. He sided with the Napoleonic forces and took refuge in France when King Ferdinand VII returned to the Spanish throne 1814. His *Histoire critique de l'inquisition espagnole* was published in Paris (1817–18), in which he made use of numerous documents to which he had had access. Henry Charles Lea became an expert in many areas of medieval and early modern Church history, and also wrote a study on the Inquisition in Spanish dependencies and a book entitled *The Moriscos of Spain: Their Conversion and Expulsion* (Lea Brothers, Pennsylvania, 1901). In the same year he became President of the American Historical Society. Lea saw the Inquisition, as had Llorens and William H. Prescott before him, as "an engine of immense power, constantly applied for the furtherance of obscurantism, the repression of thought, the exclusion of foreign ideas and the obstruction of progress," which was, at its worst "theocratic absolutism." He also sees it as an important contributing reason for Spain's decline from the late seventeenth century on. Lea was accused by some scholars of being anti-Spanish in his judgements and his monumental history was not available in a Spanish translation until 1983.

17 Marcelino Menéndez y Pelayo, *Historia de los heterodoxos españoles* (2nd edition, 6 vols, Ed. E. Sánchez Reyes (Madrid, 1947), Vol. 4, pp. 420–22, and *La ciencia española* (Madrid 1947), 2 vols, Vol. 1, pp. 379–83, and Vol .2, pp. 7–13. Both sources are quoted by Angel Alacalá in "Inquisitional control of Humanists and Writers" in Angel Alacalá (ed.) *The Spanish Inquisition and the Inquisitional Mind* (Social Science Monographs, Boulder, Colorado, Atlantic Research Publications Inc, New Jersey, 1987). First published as *Inquisición española y mentalidad inquisitorial* (Ariel, Barcelona, 1984).

18 Henry Kamen's book *The Spanish Inquisition* (Weidenfeld & Nicolson,

London 1965) was an influential work which preceded by ten years the explosion of new research into the Inquisition that followed the death of Franco and produced numerous results in the 1980s. Kamen revised and reissued his book, taking into account these new findings, under the title *The Inquisition and Society in Spain in the Sixteenth and Seventeenth Centuries* (Weidenfeld & Nicolson, London, 1985), and followed this up under the same publisher, with a second revised edition ten years later, *The Spanish Inquisition; A Historical Revision* (1997).

19 Angel Alcalá (ed.), *The Spanish Inquisition and the Inquisitorial Mind* (Social Science Monographs, Boulder, Colorado & Atlantic Research and Publications Inc, New Jersey 1987), p. 8. First published as *Inquisición española y mentalidad inquisitorial* (Ariel, Barcelona, 1984)

20 Diego Hurtado de Mendoza y Pacheco (1503–75) was a diplomat, scholar, poet and historian. Of noble family, and the great grandson of the Marquéz de Santillana. He is best known for his poetry and his *Guerra de Granada,* a history of the Morisco uprising in the Alpujarras (1568–70). There is also some documentary evidence that he was the author of *Lazarillo de Tormes,* but it has not yet been accepted as proven.

21 *El Crotalón* is a lucianic satire whose author, now identified as Cristobal de Villalón (1510?–1588?), wrote a number of published works such a his *Gramática castellana. El Crotalón* was written under the humorous pseudonym of Cristoforo Gnofoso and was circulated in manuscript form only. It was unknown in modern times until two copies were discovered in 1871 in the British Museum. Recognised by M. Serrano y Sanz as an important example of sixteenth-century Castilian prose writing, its authorship remained in doubt for some years. A similar situation grew up around the manuscript version of *Viaje de Turquía,* discovered at around the same time. The eminent French hispanist Marcel Bataillon attributed this anonymous humanist dialogue to the scholar, translator, physician and botanist Andrés de Laguna (1499–1559) whose output included a number of inportant medical teatises, including one on the treatment of the plague. Others, including Serrano y Sanz, rejected this attribution in favour of Villalón. The name of Juan de Ulloa Pereira, brother of the Marqués de la Mota, and a knight of the Order of St John of Jerusalem, who was condemned by the Inquisition for Protestant sympathies is also named. A high-ranking military officer who led many campaigns against the Turks, his position was later restored after an appeal to Rome. How many other semi-clandestine works of a similar kind were written, preserved only in manuscript form and are now lost is a matter for speculation. It can, however, be assumed that the Spanish authorities would have collected and destroyed all the copies they could find, and would also have punished their owners and readers.

22 Virgilio Pinto, "Censorship. A System of Control and Instrument of Action," in Angel Alcalá (ed.), op. cit., p. 303.

23 Ibid., pp. 304–6. Pinto points out that the authority for the Inquisition to proceed against those owning, reading or distributing prohibited books was granted by three different popes between 1539 and 1559. A succession of

papal edicts by Paul III (1539), Julius III (1550) and Paul IV (1559) gave the Holy Office the juridical power it needed to monopolise censorship in Spain. Edicts of fairth, furthermore, made the denunciation of suspects a public duty.

24 Quoted in English by Angel Alacalá, "Inquisitorial Control of Humanists and Writers" in Angel Alcalá (ed.), op. cit., p. 327.

25 Juan Huarte de San Juan was a leading physician and one of the first psychological theorists. Both Huarte de San Juan's *Examen de ingenios* and Mariana's *De mutatione monetiae* are thought to have made an impression of Cervantes, whose reference to Mariana's ideas can be found in *Don Quixote* Part I, Ch. 29.

26 Jeremy Robbins, *Arts of Perception. The Epistomological Mentality of the Spanish Baroque 1580–1720* (Routledge, London & New York, 20070 p. 1. Professor Robbins argues that the intellectual climate of Spain in the seventeenth century was largely formed by the "sustained, creative interaction" of scepticism and Stoicism, giving rise to a tradition of moral and political thought which eschewed abstract system building in favour of tackling practical issues in an accessible way. Though particular to Spanish thinkers, this strand of moral and political philosophy constituted a recognised contribution to the intellectual problems common throughout Europe at the time, and their works were avidly read abroad and translated into French, English, Italian, Dutch, Latin and German.

27 James Parr, *"Don Quixote": An Anatomy of Subversive Literature* (Juan de la Cuesta, Newark, Delaware, 1988), p. 37. Professor Parr maintains (p. xv) that, instead of a novel, *Don Quixote* should be regarded as a Menippean *satura* in the best tradition of Horace, its closest relation among Cervantes' other works being the exemplary novel *El coloquio de los perros*. Menippean satire is named after a style of indirect satire practiced by the Greek cynic Menippus (third century BC) whose works have been lost, but whose practices are preserved in the influence he exerted over writers such as Marcus Terentius Varro (115 BC–27 BC) and Lucian (125 AD–180 AD). Menippean satire is written mainly in prose with a length and narrative structure like that of a modern novel. It attacked general targets such as customs, patterns of conduct and mental attributes, and was originally characterised by parody and mythical burlesque. Later classical examples of this form are the *Apocolocyntosis* of Seneca the Younger – a parody of the deification of the Emperor Claudius – Petronuius Arbiter's *Satyricon* and *The Golden Ass* by Apuleius. The form has been used and adapted on many occasions since by early modern and modern writers.

28 See Julian Weiss's article "Between the Censor and the Critic: Reading the Vernacular Classic in Early Modern Spain" (dialnet.uniroja.es/descarga/articulo/3716464.pdf), p. 95.

29 Ibid., p. 98. Professor Weiss defines the "classic" - in this case the modern vernacular classic – as a category of literary text which, by the beginning of the sixteenth century in Spain, demanded a humanist concept of the literary subject, which encouraged the reader to "move across time, to set the past in

dialogue with the present, and to acquire a panoptic understanding of the text and the world of which it forms a part." He argues that works such as Juan de Mena's *Laberinto de Fortuna* (1444) and Jorge Manrique's *Coplas para la muerte de su padre* (1479) had, by the beginning of the sixteenth century been elevated to the status of vernacular classic.

30 *Don Quijote de la Mancha* (Edición de Francisco Rico) (Punto de Lectura, Madrid, 2008), p. 13. All quotations from the novel are taken from this edition.

31 James Parr, op. cit., p. 37.

32 See Ryan Prendergast, *Reading, Writing and Errant Subjects in Inquisitorial Spain* (Ashgate, Farnham and Burlington, 2011), Chapter 3, "Inscriptions of Transgression, Confession and Punishment."

33 Angel Alacalá, "Inquisitorial Control of Humanists and Writers" in Angel Alcalá (ed.), op. cit., pp. 333–350.

34 In the sixteenth and seventeenth centuries, what we now prefer to call biography, namely a detailed account of the life of person, was generally regarded as history. The "Histories" of Paulo Govio, which Susan Byrne suggest had an influence on Cervantes' views on what history was and how it should be written, were mainly of this biographical kind, and had their English equivalent in John Aubrey's *Brief Lives*, written in the last decades of the seventeenth century.

35 *Don Quixote*, Part I, Ch. 2, p. 35.

36 *Don Quixote*, Part II, Ch. 36, p. 830. Rico points out in a note that these lines were censored in the 1615 first edition, and included in the 1632 *Indice expurgatorio* of Cardinal Zapata. In terms of Catholic teaching, this proposition was debateable but not regarded as overtly heterodox.

37 Bartolomé Bennassar, *L'Inquisition espagnole, 1479–1834* (Hachette, Paris, 1979), pp. 392–393. Reprinted by Hachette 2009. English translation quoted by Alcalá, op. cit., p. 345.

38 Carlos Blanco Aguinaga, Julio Rodríguez Puertolas and Iris M. Zavala, *Historia social de la literatura Española* (Castalia, Madrid, 1978), 2 vols. Reprinted by Akal Ediciones, Madrid, 2000).

39 Antonio Pérez-Romero, *The Subversive Tradition in Spanish Renaissance Writing* (Bucknell University Press, Lewisburg, 2005).

40 Ibid., p. 131.

41 Ryan Prendergast, op. cit., pp. 5–6.

3 *Don Quixote*: A Book in Two Halves

1 In *No Ordinary Man* (Peter Owen, London, 2002), p. 236, Donald P. McCrory comments on Cervantes' reasons for writing *Viaje de Parnaso* in the light of the criticism and slurs that he had suffered from Lope and his followers:
   Bearing in mind Cervantes' socio-economic situation, age, his exclusion from the group around the Conde de Lemos, his stance vis-à-vis contemporary tastes in literature and his marginalised position in the academies, the fundamental question for Cervantes was how to frame his assault on a subject [literature] he held as dear as life itself. . . . By

1610 Cervantes had long known that Lope de Vega had been wrong in his view of *Don Quixote*. He also felt quite certain that Lope de Vega had been equally wrong in his earlier perverse criticism about his skill as a poet.

McCrory goes on to quote Ellen D. Lokos' study *The Solitary Journey* (Peter Lang, 1991) where she states that Cervantes' criticism of Lope was not based on an alleged lack of talent but that he "was a reprehensible artist because of the manner in which he chose to exert his influence." (p. 92). Lope was to blame, in Cervantes' opinion, for a lowering of taste which allowed many inferior poets and playwrights to flourish, and the failure of the literary academies, in which Lope and his followers were extremely influential, to maintain those higher standards.

2   *Viaje de Parnaso* (Journey to Parnassus) is the most neglected of Cervantes' works despite being by far his longest poem. This is in part due to recent scholars following the critical opinions of Cervantes' poetry put about by other Spanish writers of his time, who were either direct rivals or were seeking to win the good opinion of Lope de Vega, who had himself ridiculed Cervantes' poetry and also criticised *Don Quixote* Part I. Ellen D. Lokos (1991) provides a complete revaluation of *Viaje de Parnaso* however, which should promote further study of the poem. Rivalries were encouraged by the literary academies in seventeenth-century Spain, which organised poetry competitions (or "jousts"), giving rise to factionalism instead of offering an open forum in which literary ideas and theories could be discussed for the benefit of all. Cervantes saw the academies as failing in their duty to halt what he regarded as a dangerous decline in Spanish literature and culture, one which equalled in seriousness the country's economic and political condition. McCrory (2002) observes: "By and large, literary academies were no more than a poetic wilderness in which Cervantes belonged to the almost voiceless minority" (p. 241).

3   E. T. W. Aylward, *Cervantes*, 23.1, (2003), p. 253.

4   Luis Gómez Canseco (ed.), *Alonso Fernández Avellaneda, "El Ingenioso Hidalgo Don Quijote de la Mancha"* (Clásicos de Biblioteca Nueva, Madrid, 2000), pp. 12–13.

5   James Iffland, "Do We Really Need to Read Avellaneda?" *Cervantes* (2001) Vol. 21, No. 1, pp. 67–81.

6   Ibid., p. 74.

7   Replying with dignity and restraint to the personal insults that Avellaneda's prologue threw his way, Cervantes observes in his own prologue (Part II, Prologue, pp. 543–4:

> He sentido también que me llame envidioso y que, como a ignorante, me describa, qué cosa es la envidia; que en realidad de verdad, de dos que hay, yo conozco sino a la santa, a la noble y bien intencionada. Y siendo eso así, como lo es, no tengo yo de perseguir a ningún sacerdote, y más si tiene por añadidura ser familiar del Santo Oficio,
> (I notice also that he calls me "envious," and, as if I were an ignoramus, he describes for my benefit what envy is; of which, if the truth were

told, there are two kinds, of which I know only the good variety that is noble and well-intentioned. For, things being as they are, I have no wish to pursue a priest over the matter, particularly when he is a familiar of the Holy Office.)

This is a transparent reference to Lope de Vega, who, in a spirit of atonement for his early life, had been ordained a priest in 1614, and was reputedly a confidant (or *familiar*) of the Inquisition.

8   Part II, Ch. 59, p. 1,000. The editor Francisco Rico points out here (here see Note 26) that Avellaneda's book was licensed in July 1614 and produced in the workshop of Sebastián de Cormellas in Barcelona. By this date, Cervantes had reached Chapter 36 in his genuine second part. Rico therefore deduces that Cervantes was not aware of the book's existence until October of that year, when he had got as far as Chapter 59. Although this is very possibly true it is by no means certain as I will try to explain.

9   Ibid., p. 1001.This is probably said with Cervantes' tongue well in his cheek. As Francisco Rico points out (Note 30) either through carelessness or his at times ironical treatment of the chronicler Cide Hamete, Cervantes has given Sancho's wife various names so far, referring to her as Juana Gutiérrez and Mari Gutiérrez in Part I, and Teresa Sancha and Teresa Panza earlier in Part II. At least Avellaneda chooses a name and remains consistent to it throughout.

10   Jeremy Robbins, *Arts of Perception. The Epistemological Mentality of the Spanish Baroque 1580–1720* (Routledge, London & New York, 2007), p. 1.

11   Ibid., p. 3.

12   Jeremy Robbins, *The Challenges of Uncertainty. An Introduction to Seventeenth Century Spanish Literature* (Duckworth, London, 1998), p. 41.

13   Taking our lead yet again from Jeremy Robbins' summary of the distinction between scepticism and Pyrrhonism (*Arts of Perception*, Ch. 2) we find a line drawn between the "Academic sceptics" and the Pyrrhonists on the following grounds: sceptics, with an eye on the writings of Cicero, were happy to assert that "*nihil scitur*" (Nothing can be known). The Pyrrhonists however took a more radical view. Founded in the first century BC by Aenesidemus, and revised and recorded three hundred years later by Sextus Empiricus, Pyrrhonists held that to say categorically that we know nothing is to make a statement which implies that we do know *something*. Pyrrhonists, therefore, refused confirmation of all statements, even the *quod nihil scitur* of the Academic sceptics.

14   Mambrino and his helm are featured in both Bioardo's *Orlando inamorato* (1483–95) and Ariosto's *Orlando furioso* (1516, complete version 1532). Cervantes, who is thought to have spoken good Italian from his days as a soldier in Naples, was probably familiar with both of these epic romance poems in the original language. A fictional Moorish king, Mambrino was the owner of a helmet of pure gold which made the wearer invulnerable.

15   The Santa Hermanidad operated very much like a law enforcement agency in early modern Spain. Its main task was to police the roads and rural areas of Castile. Don Quixote's freeing of the galley slaves in Part I, Chapter 22, was

the first occasion on which his conduct reached the ears of the Santa Hermanidad, and his journey into the Sierra Morena was taken to avoid pursuit.

16 *Don Quixote*, op. cit., p. 620.

17 A. A. Parker, "Fielding and the Structure of Don Quixote," *BHS*, No. 33, (1956), pp. 1–16.

18 David Quint, *Cervantes' Novel of Modern Times: A New Reading of Don Quixote* (Princeton University Press, Princeton & Oxford, 2003), p. ix.

4 Truth and Lies in History and Fiction: *Don Quixote* as a Defence of Imaginative Literature

1 See Richard L. Kagan, *Clio and the Crown: The Politics of History in Medieval and Early Modern Spain* (Johns Hopkins University Press, Baltimore, 2009).

2 One exception to this tendency was the work of Antonio de Herrera y Tordesillas (1549–1625) Chief Chronicler of Castile and the Americas in the reigns of Philip II and III. His great work *Historia general de los hechos de los castellanos en las islas y Tierra Firme del mar Océano que llaman Indias Occidentales* which is usually known as *Las décadas*, is now reckoned to be the first general history of the New World which made use of all the known information by different chroniclers. His *Historia general del mundo* published in three parts in 1601, 1606 and 1612, covers the years from 1559 to the death of Philip II in 1598. Although it moves widely across contemporary Europe and the Americas, it nevertheless revolves primarily around Philip II. Its scope however, is much wider than the customary *historia de persona*.

3 Kagan, op. cit., p. 6.

4 Ibid., p. 7.

5 In some quarters, despite the virulent criticism his historical work received, Giovio's writings – particularly his *Elogia virorum litteris illustrum* – a series of pen-portraits of famous people, many of them generals – often remained popular. In 1568, the jurist Gaspar de Baeza, a close friend of Cervantes, translated this work into Spanish under the title *Elogios o vidas breves de los Cavalleros antiguos y modernos, Illustres en valor de Guerra que están al bivos pintados en el Museo de Paolo Iouia*. (Eulogies, or brief lives, of knights of ancient and modern times, who, illustrious in war, are painted from life in the Museum of Paolo Giovio). The book was one of the first to liken the characters of those portrayed to their portraits. Baeza dedicated his translation of the *Elogios* to Philip II, recommending them for their variety and readability. See Susan Byrne, *Law and History in Cervantes' "Don Quixote"* (University of Toronto Press, Toronto, Buffalo & London, 2012), pp. 24–26.

6 *Don Quixote*, op. cit., Part II, p. 88.

7 Ibid.

8 Parr, James A., *Don Quixote : An Anatomy of Subversive Discourse* (Juan de la Cueva, Newark, Delaware, 1988).

9 Menippean satire is named after Menippus, the third-century BC Greek cynic, parodist and polemicist. His works have now all been lost, but were

well enough known in the ancient world to influence writers such as Marcus Terentius Varro (116BC–27BC) and Lucian (120–192 AD). All of Varro's satirical works are lost, but quotations and fragments remain. The Menippean is a kind of prose satire, often of the length of a novel, which has a coherent narrative and attacks ideas, attitudes, customs, beliefs etc, rather than targeting individuals, which was the purpose of the older kind of satire that started with Aristophanes, and was carried on by Juvenal and others. The menippean model was continued in later works like Petronius' *Satyricon*, and Apuleius' *The Golden Ass*, and was revived by the humanists in the sixteenth century. Modern practitioners of it have been Rabelais, Diderot, Voltaire, Swift, E. T. A. Hoffman, Gogol, Thomas Peacock and Samuel Butler. Mikhail Bakhtin argues that its highest point of development is to be found in the novels of Dostoyevsky.

10　Parr, James A., op. cit., p. 29.
11　Ibid., p. 35.
12　Susan Byrne, *Law and History in Cervantes' "Don Quixote"* (University of Toronto Press, Toronto, Buffalo & London, 2012), p. 108.
13　Ibid., p. 110.
14　Anthony Cascardi. *Ideologies of History in the Spanish Golden Age* (Pennsylvania State University Trust, University Park, Penn, 1997), p. 215.
15　Ibid., p. 3.
16　L. A. Murillo, *The Golden Dial. Temporal Configurations in "Don Quixote"* (Dolphin Books, Oxford, 1975).
17　*Don Quixote*, Part I, Chapter 2, p. 35.
18　Ibid., Part II, Ch 2, p. 565.
19　Ibid., Part II, Ch 3, p. 566.
20　Ibid., Part II, Ch 3, p. 569.
21　Ibid.
22　Ibid.
23　Ibid., p. 572.

5　Justice, Law and Politics: *Don Quixote* as a Vehicle for Debate

1　Maureen Ihre, *Skepticism in Cervantes* (Tamesis Books, London, 1972), p. 30.
2　Francisco Sánchez, *Quod nihil scitur* (That Nothing Can be Known) (1581). Translated and edited by Marcelino Menéndez Pelayo as *Que nada se sabe* (Editorial Nova, Buenos Aires, 1944). Sánchez (or Sanches) was a Portuguese physician and philosopher, who studied medicine in France and Italy, where his family, which was of Sephardic Jewish origin converted to Catholicism, moved to avoid the attentions of the Portuguese Inquisition. Other major intellectual figures who embraced scepticism were Pedro de Valencia (1556–1620), a theologian, jurist and philosopher, and Royal Historian to Philip III, and Juan Huarte de San Juan (1529–1588). In his *Academia sive de judicio erga verum ex ipsis primis fontibus* (1596) Valencia states that "perfect knowledge" of anything is unobtainable. Juan Huarte de San Juan, a physician and one of the earliest psychologists, wrote a book which became famous across Europe entitled *Examen de los ingenious para las sciencias* (An Examination

of Men's Wits in Pursuit of Knowledge) in 1575. In this work he made a bold
and original attempt to link psychology with physiology and human talent
and capacity for different types of work. His views are frequently said to have
influenced the thinking of Cervantes, but his work was proscribed by the
Inquisition. His views on knowledge and its reliability show the influence of
scepticism.

3 Two well-known examples of dialogues of this kind are Juan de Valdés'
   Diálogo de Mercurio y Carón (The Discussion between Mercury and Charon)
   (1528) and the work of his twin brother Alfonso de Valdés, *Lactantius* (1529).
   Both were humanist scholars who held office under Charles V, and whose
   religious and political diatribes against Rome and Pope Clement VII were
   inspired by the sacking of Rome in 1527 by the Imperial Army. It has been
   suggested that a passage in Juan de Valdés' *Diálogo* may have inspired Don
   Quixote's advice to Sancho Panza on how he should rule when he becomes
   governor of the island of Baratrea (*Don Quixote*, Part II, Chs. LXII and
   LXIII).

4 The individual works to which this statement refers are as follows: Anthony
   J. Cascardi, *Ideologies of History in the Spanish Golden Age* (Pennsylvania
   State University Press, University Park, Penn, 1997) and *Cervantes, Literature
   and the Discourse of Politics* (University of Toronto Press, Toronto, Buffalo &
   London, 2012); Susan Byrne, *History and Law in Cervantes' 'Don Quixote'*
   (University of Toronto Press, Toronto, Buffalo & London, 2012); Henry
   Higuera, *Eros and Empire. Politics and Christianity in 'Don Quixote'*
   (Rowman & Littlefield, Lanham, 1995); Richard L. Kagan, *Clio and the
   Crown. The Politics of History in Medieval and Early Modern Spain* (Johns
   Hopkins University Press, Baltimore, 2009) and Roberto González
   Echevarría, *Love and the Law in Cervantes* (Yale University Press, New Haven,
   2012). While the studies by Kagan and Cascardi's *Ideologies of History* are
   general works, both have significant things to say about Cervantes and *Don
   Quixote*.

5 Susan Byrne, op. cit., p. 35.

6 King Alfonso X (The Wise) of Castile commissioned a group of jurists to
   undertake a fundamental legislative reform in the kingdom which was
   carried out between 1251 and 1265, with the King's personal involvement. It
   was intended to replace the corrupt text of the Forum Judicum which date
   from the Vizigothic kingdom, and to accommodate the mass of local, often
   unwritten *fueros* then in force in Castile, together with Alfonso's own *Fuero
   Leal*, and other legal texts. The resulting unifying synthesis, with a philosophical commentary, was called *Las Siete Partidas* (The Seven Registers) and
   was designed to serve as a guide for future monarchs, governors, administrators and jurists, laying down subjects, norms and legal dispositions for all
   occasions. The work was collected into seven volumes comprising:
   A canonical code defining the obligations of the clergy to the people,
   The prerogatives and rights of kings and rulers,
   Justice and its administration,
   Marital and family law

> Commercial law,
> Wills and inheritance,
> Criminal law and sentencing (including laws to apply to Jews and
> Moors in Spain)

Generally regarded as the most important and complete code of law written in the Middle Ages, the *Siete Partidas* attempted to determine the fairest and most moderate solutions to legal disputes and problems, and is centrally concerned with justice and rectitude in applying the law. It also displays an attitude towards tolerance which is believed to have been drawn from the Koran. Alfonso set great store by good relations between Christians, Jews and Muslims in what he termed the "Empire" of Castile, and styled himself Lord of the Three Kingdoms.

7   See Byrne, op. cit., pp. 3–5. At the end of her detailed and scrupulously researched study, Professor Byrne argues that the legal examples and questions about justice which form such a significant part of *Don Quixote*, comprise, while acknowledging the value of the *Fuero Juzgo* and the *Siete Partidas* collected under the direction of Alfonso X of Castile, a new, fictional *mos hispanicus* based on individual freedom, natural law and justice which looks to the future requirements of a modern nation state (p. 147).

8   The Holy Brotherhood (La Santa Hermanidad) was the forerunner of a federal police force in sixteenth-century Spain. It was nationally organised, but drew its recruits from local bands of vigilantes. The Brotherhood pursued criminals throughout the kingdom, irrespective of local fueros, privileges and immunities, behind which criminals often tried to hide, by seeking sanctuary in a place beyond the jurisdiction of the authorities in which a crime had been committed. The Brotherhood also policed rural areas (despoblados) in which gangs of outlaws and brigands often ruled unchallenged, and patrolled the roads.

9   Susan Byrne, op. cit., p. 6.

10   Roberto González Echevarría, *Love and the Law in Cervantes* (Yale University Press, New Haven & London, 2005). See Chapter 2, "Spanish Law and the Origins of the Novel."

11   Though only a handful of the political *guías* achieved widespread recognition at the time, their frequency indicates the strength and direction of political argument and debate throughout the sixteenth and early seventeenth centuries in Spain. These treatises all took a strongly critical view of Machiavelli's ideas, and the vast majority of them saw the ideal ruler as being a king or prince who governed according to Christian moral principles, dispensed justice to and minded the welfare of all classes of his subjects, and pursued a policy of peace and stability. (Erasmus took a particularly strong pacifist stance.) The second thing all have in common is their unquestioning support for a system of hereditary monarchy, which should not be permitted to degenerate into tyranny and oppression. The following list of works and authors give some indication of their number and the topics they singled out for debate and translation into practical political action by the ruler. Erasmus, *The Education of a Christian Prince* (1516); Antonio Guevara, *El*

reloj de príncipes (The Dial of Princes) (1529); Fadrique Furió Ceriol, *El consejo y el consejero del príncipe* (Advice and the Advisers of Princes) (1559); Cerdán de Tallada, *Verdadero govierno desta monarchía* (The True Government of the Monarchy) (1581); Felipe de la Torre, *Institución de un rey Christiano* (The Institutions of a Christian King) (1586); Bartolomé Felipe, *Tratado del consejo* (A Treatise on Royal Advice) (1589); Pedro de Ribadeneira, *Tratado de la religion y virtudes que debe tener el príncipe Cristiano,* (Treatise on Religion and the Virtues that a Christian Prince should have) (1597); Baltasar Álamos de Barrientos y Narbona, *Discurso politico al rey Felipe III al comienzo de su reino* (A Political Discussion directed to King Philip III at the start of his reign) (1598); Juan de Mariana, *De rege et regionis institutione* (On the King and Royal Institutions) (1599); Pedro de Rivadeneira, *El tratado del príncipe Christiano contra Machiavelo* (An Anti-Machiavelli Treatise on the Christian Prince) (1603); Francisco de Quevedo, *Política de Dios y gobierno de Cristo* (God's Policies and Christ's Rule) (1626); Diego Saavedra Fajardo, *Empresas políticas o idea de un príncipe Christiano,* (Political Undertakings or the Idea of a Christian Prince) (1640); Baltasar Gracián, *El político,* (The Politician) (1646).

12 Henry Higuera, *Eros and Empire. Politics and Christianity in "Don Quixote"* (Rowan and Littlefield, Lanham, Maryland, 1995) and Anthony J. Cascardi, *Cervantes, Literature and the Discourse of Politics* (University of Toronto Press, Toronto, Buffalo & London, 2012).

13 By the 1580s, this symbolic analogy had become the basis of Christian mysticism, particularly in the poetry of San Juan de la Cruz and the writings of Santa Teresa de Ávila.

14 *Don Quixote*, op. cit., pp. 30–1.

15 This may be an allusion to Christ's humble family background, despite which he is also the Son of God and divine.

16 Henry Higuera, op. cit., p. 185.

17 Anthony J. Cascardi, op. cit., p. 3.

18 Ibid., p. 7.

19 *Don Quixote*, op. cit., p. 96.

20 Ibid., p. 392.

21 Ibid., p. 393.

22 Ibid., p. 556.

23 Anthony J. Cascardi, op. cit., p. 26.

24 *Don Quixote*, op. cit., p. 35.

25 Ibid., pp. 490–1.

26 Cascadi, op. cit., p. 44.

27 *Don Quixote*, op. cit., pp. 196–7.

28 Ibid., p. 866.

29 Ibid., p. 870.

30 One of the first Renaissance moral and political guides for rulers, Desiderius Erasmus' *Institutio Principis Christiani* (1516) serves as a humanist directive for the tutors of monarchs, the king himself and his courtiers. Throughout the work, Erasmus invokes the rhetoric and wisdom of classical authors,

including Isocrates, Cicero, Seneca, Plutarch and Aristotle, which he reconciles with Christian thought and biblical references. The concept of
philosophia Christi, which inspires the author's ideas on politics, government
and education, was introduced by Erasmus himself some twelve years previously in his best-known book *Enchiridion Militis Cristiani* (1504) (The
Christian Soldier's Handbook), and entailed a life centred upon the example
of Christ, based upon inner faith rather than external observance.

Fr. Juan de Mariana, S. J., wrote *De Rege et Regis institutione* in 1599, at the
request of his friend Archbishop Loaysa of Toledo, a former tutor to Prince
Philip, by that time Philip III. Mariana was the most celebrated Spanish
historian of his time and a highly respected theologian, now regarded as the
last great scholastic academic of the age. Like Erasmus' work, Mariana's guide
on kingship, the source of royal power and the institutions that supported
it, was Christian-centred, drawing heavily upon classical example and
written in admirable Latin which draws upon the classical tradition of
rhetoric It was, however, unfortunate in that it aroused a furore abroad, for
justifying, in certain circumstances, the death of a tyrant at the hands of the
people he oppressed. The book was condemned and publicly burnt in Paris
in 1610, and removed from publication in Spain and Italy. It was not translated into Spanish until 1835.

31 *Don Quixote*, op. cit., p. 868.
32 Ibid., pp. 868–9.
33 Ibid., p. 869.
34 Ibid., p. 870.
35 Ibid. This and the other points listed above can be found on pages 871–873.
36 Ibid., p. 876.
37 Ibid., p. 877. Here, at the beginning of Chapter 44, the narrator begins with
    a discussion of Cide Hamete's original Arabic version and the erroneous way
    it has been translated. He states that the Moorish historian had originally
    included:

> Un modo de queja. . . . de sí mismo por haber tomado entre manos
> una historia tan seca y tan limitada como esta de don Quijote, por
> parecerle que siempre había de hablar de él y Sancho, sin osar de
> extenderse a otras digresiones y episodios más graves y más entrete-
> nidos. . . . y por huir de este inconveniente había usado en la primera
> parte del artificio de algunas novellas, como fueron la del *Curioso
> impertinente* y la del *Capitán cautivo* que están como separadas de la
> historia."

> (A kind of complaint . . . against himself for having taken up such a
> dry and limited story as that of Don Quixote, for it seemed to him
> that he had always to speak of the knight and Sancho, and could not
> risk broadening out into digressions and more serious and enter-
> taining subjects. . . . To avoid this inconvenience, he had had recourse
> in the first part of the story to the artifice of short fictions, like the
> *Curioso impertinente* and the *Capitán cautivo* which stand as if
> separate from the main story).

Cervantes is clearly responding to the criticisms of his use of the"interpo-lated episodes" in Part I, and here has his narrator state that in Part II, Cide Hamete had decided not to repeat this experiment, but to include instead matters that were related only to the events of the main narrative. The nature of Cide Hamete's complaint is very much that of a novelist rather than a historian, who, it has been established, should write nothing but the truth.

38 Ibid., p. 879.
39 Ibid., p. 888.
40 Ibid., p. 891.
41 Ibid., p. 892.
42 Ibid., pp. 901–2.
43 Ibid., p. 902. In notes 17 and 18 on this page, Francisco Rico informs us that this village is in the province of Ciudad Real, where "tirte (tírate) afuera" is a colloquialism for "go away" or "push off." Cervantes seems to enjoy satir-ical wordplay on place names, such as *Barataria* (Going Cheap), perhaps in imitation of Thomas More's *Utopia* (No-where). The University of Osuna was a relatively new and not particularly well-thought-of university, which did not, at that time, possess a medical faculty.
44 Ibid., p. 919.
45 Ibid.
46 Ibid., p. 940.
47 Ibid., p. 946.

6 Humour, Irony and Satire in *Don Quixote*: Public Merriment and Private Laughter

1 Peter E. Russell, "*Don Quixote* as a Funny Book," *MLR*, LXIV, 1969, pp. 312–326.
2 Anthony J. Close, *Cervantes and the Comic Mind of his Age* (Oxford University Press, 2000).
3 Ibid., pp. 20–21.
4 Ibid., p. 74.
5 *Don Quijote*, op. cit., pp. 13–14.
6 Anthony J. Close, op. cit., p. 75.
7 Gilbert Highet, *The Anatomy of Satire* (Princeton University Press, Princeton, New Jersey, 1962), pp. 14–15.
8 It is not until the end of the book (Part II, Ch. 64, pp. 1100–1101) that on his death bed Don Quixote recovers his sanity. He repudiates all the deeds he has done under the name of Don Quixote, anathematises Amadís de Gaula and all other knights-errant of his kind, and dies at peace with God and the Church under his real name Alonso Quijano, also known as El Bueno (The Good).
9 A Titan who, in ancient mythology, was the husband of Eos, goddess of dawn (*Don Quixote*, op. cit., Part I, Ch. 2, p. 35, note 17).
10 Antonio de Lofraso (1540–1600) was a Sardinian soldier and poet who is chiefly remembered for his pastoral novel *Los diez libros de fortuna de amor*,

published in Barcelona in 1573. The "novel" is written in verse (octavas reales). Though Cervantes appears to approve of *Los diez libros . . .* by having it saved from the flames, Lofraso is one of the many poets he subsequently satirises in *Viaje de Parnaso* (1614).

11   The *Sanbenito* (or *Sambenito*) was a penitential garment, like a long tunic, which penitents being punished by the Inquisition were forced to wear in processions of the condemned at an *auto de fe*. A tall, conical cap, called a *corroza*, was worn with it. The tunics were yellow in colour and of three kinds, distinguished by the designs they carried. The *samara* was worn by unrepentant heretics who were to be burnt alive at the stake; the *fuego revolto* was worn by last-minute penitents who were allowed the mercy of death by strangulation before the fire was lit; the *sambenito* was worn by heretics who had forsworn their errors, and were sentenced to undergo penitence only. These yellow robes should not be confused with the garments worn from the early sixteenth century by monks and priests who had voluntarily chosen to perform public penitence (like the priests in Chapter 8 of *Don Quixote*), which were of the same colour but carried different crosses to those which adorned the robes of the Inquisition. Both types were referred to as *Sanbenitos*, however.

12   The purpose of this lengthy piece of verse has rarely been investigated. If *Canción desesperada* was intended solely to record Grisóstomo's despair, in the tradition of disappointed pastoral lovers, it is hard to understand its somewhat tedious length and often heavy rhetorical flourishes. Grisóstomo's friends have hailed him as a gifted poet, but this is hardly an inspired piece of verse. Read in conjunction with Marcela's self-justifying speech which immediately follows it, it should, perhaps, be regarded as having a parodic purpose which ridiculed the conventional pastoral theme of the sufferings of unrequited "shepherds."

13   *Don Quixote,* op. cit., Part II, p. 571, where Sansón Carrasco observes:

> Una de las tachas que se ponen a la tal historia. . . . es que el autor puso en ella novela intitluda *El Curioso impertinente,* no por mala ni por mal razonada, sino por no ser de aquel lugar, ni tiene que ver con la historia de su merced.
>
> (One of the blemishes readers attribute to this history . . . . is that the author has placed in it a novella entitled The Man of Impertinent Curiosity, not because it is itself bad or poorly argued, but because it out of place and has nothing to do with the history of your honour.)

Don Quixote is adamant in his criticism of this as a way of writing, saying that it lacks order and would need a commentary to explain it.

7   The Novel as a Mirror to Society: Women, Class and Conflict in *Don Quixote*

1   The first translation of *Don Quixote* into English was carried out by John Shelton, who published his translation of Part I in 1612, and Part II in 1620. John Phillips' version was published in 1687, while John Stevens revised

Shelton's text in 1700. In the same year, Peter Motteux's well-known translation appeared. This was itself revised by John Ozell in 1719. Charles Jarvis' well-respected version followed in 1742, the same year that *Joseph Andrews* was published.

2 See Henry Fielding, *Joseph Andrews* (Penguin Classics, London 1999). Introduction and notes by Judith Hawley), Book III, Ch. 1, p. 203.

3 Ibid., p. 202.

4 Miguel de Cervantes y Saavedra, *The Ingenious Hidalgo Don Quixote de la Mancha*. (Translated with introduction and notes by John Rutherford) (Penguin Classics, London, 2000), p. xx.

5 Most scholars now accept the theory that Cervantes probably wrote the story of *El Cautivo y Zoraida* as an early experiment in short fiction, which might have had a place in the *Novelas ejemplares*. Instead he wove it into the longer narrative of *Don Quixote* almost certainly for a purpose, in that it illustrated a point he wishes to make in his fictional exploration of love, marriage and the roles of women in society.

6 *Don Quixote*, op. cit., Part I, p. 379.

7 Ibid., p. 951.

8 Ibid., Part I, Chapter 1, p. 27.

9 Ibid., Part II, Chapter XVI, p. 664. Don Diego's self-description is in reply to Don Quixote's announcement that he is wandering knight whose mission is to re-establish the order of knight errantry, and whose deeds are recorded in a famous history the has sold thirty thousand copies across most countries. Since a print run in those days was at most 1,500 volumes, it seems that the knight's imagination has again got the better of him.

10 Ibid., p. 672.

11 Ibid., p. 683.

12 Ibid., Chapter XVI, p. 668. The "first step" that Don Quixote refers to here, is the acquisition of a good knowledge of Latin and Greek, precisely what his own lack of a university education had denied him.

13 Ibid., Chapter XXII, p. 717. In footnote 18, Francisco Rico defines a humanist as a scholar of ancient history and languages, a somewhat limited use of the term. He goes on to observe, however, that: "En tiempos de Cervantes, la palabra *humanista* (que originariamente pertenecía a la jerga universitaria) y la imagen a que iba asociada, tenían resonancias más negativas que positivas." (In Cervantes' day, the Word "humanist" which originally belonged to university slang, had an image and associations that were negative rather than positive.) This would seem to imply that the virtual disappearance of humanist scholarship and its accompanying outlook by the end of the sixteenth century saw a semantic shift in the associations of the word. In Cervantes' day a humanist might have been understood as a pejorative term used to indicate scholars who spent their time in pursuit of detailed knowledge on matters of little importance.

14 Polydore Vergil Castellensis (1470–1556) was an Italian humanist and scholar, priest, historian and diplomat who spent most of his life in England.

Among his works was *De inventibus rerum* (1499), a history of discoveries and origins.

15 There is no clear evidence that Cervantes ever visited Barcelona, though it was within sight of the harbour that the passenger ship on which he was returning to Spain from Naples in 1575 was intercepted by pirates from Algiers, and he and his brother Rodrigo were taken prisoner. He imagines a similar but reversed situation in 1614, when he describes in *Don Quixote*, Part II, Chapter 62, the arrest by a Spanish galley of the pirate ship carrying the disguised Ana Felix to Algiers. If so, it might explain his sketchy portrayal of the city, which nevertheless makes considerable mention of the port and the ships anchored there, which the knight visits in the company of Don Antonio.

16 *Don Quixote*, op. cit., Part II, Chapter 65, pp. 1049–50.

8 Authority and Subversion in *Don Quixote*: The Novel as a Dialectic

1 Francisco Gómez de Sandoval, created first Duke of Lerma by Philip III, came from an ancient and powerful aristocratic family. A favourite of the young Prince Philip, he was made the King's *valido* in 1599, soon after Philip III's accession to the throne the year before. As such, he controlled the country's affairs of state and amassed an unprecedented amount of power and an immense fortune. He was, however, a competent ruler and administrator who guided Spain through a period of relative peace, despite severe economic problems. (The country declared itself bankrupt in 1606.) Enmity with England was finally ended in 1604, and the war in the Low Countries was discontinued in 1609. In expelling the *moriscos* from Spain in that same year, however, Lerma dealt the Spanish economy an additional body blow. After a lengthy period of intrigue, his rival Gaspar de Guzmán, Conde-Duque de Olivares and tutor to the young Prince Philip who would become Philip IV, in league with Lerma's son, Cristobál de Sandoval, Count of Uceda, forced him from power in 1618 by means of a palace coup.

   Lerma had persuaded Pope Paul V to make him a cardinal earlier in that same year, which effectively rendered him immune to prosecution after his fall from power. In 1624, however, at the instigation of Olivares, he was sentenced to return over a million ducats of his personal fortune to the Spanish Crown. He died the following year.

2 Popular literature in English from the second half of the twentieth century to the present day has been remarkable for the outpouring of epic fantasy novels that are set in imaginary worlds. By far the best known and critically respected is J. R. R. Tolkein's trilogy *Lord of the Rings* (1964), but George R. R. Martin's unfinished *A Song of Ice and Fire* (1996 - ?) may come to rival it. It is difficult to compare the modern epic fantasy tale with the romance of chivalry in Renaissance Spain. There are parallels in the levels of popularity that both achieved, also the reasons for their attraction may be very similar, inasmuch as both are the product of an age of turmoil and social and tech-

nical change, and both offered their respective readers, though 500 years apart, an escape from the present day which harked back to a legendary but chaotic past, governed by warriors and nobles who observed a heroic code of conduct and personal honour. The same kind of black and white "old fashioned" morality governed the literary and film genre of the American Western, which made a folk hero of the gunfighter. But the knights-errant of the sixteenth-century chivalresque romances also enjoyed a similar role and powers to the present-day super-heroes of film and comic book fame. In terms of epic fantasy, Amadís de Gaula has more in common with Superman than he has with Aragorn, Jon Snow or Wyatt Earp.

3 *Don Quixote*, op. cit., Part II, Chapter 1, p. 550.

4 Ibid., p. 552.

5 *Don Quijote de la Mancha* (Edición del IV centenario) (Real Academia Española y Asociación de Academias de la lengua Española, 2004), pp. xiii–xxviii. Apart from Vargas Llosa's "Una novela para el siglo XXI," this fine edition uses Francisco Rico's text and notes, and also contains essays by Francisco Ayala, "La invención del *Quijote*", Martín de Riquer, "Cervantes y el *Quijote*", and José Manuel Blecua "La lengua de Cervantes y el *Quijote*." This edition also possesses a full and very useful glossary.

6 *Don Quixote*, op. cit., pp. 984–5.

7 Mario Vargas Llosa, "Una novela para el siglo XXI," in *Don Quijote de la Mancha* (Edición del IV centenario), op. cit., p. xix.

8 Isaiah Berlin, *Four Essays on Liberty* (Oxford University Press, Oxford, 1969). In his discussions on Liberty, Sir Isaiah Berlin concentrates on two kinds, that which he calls "negative liberty" and what has become an opposing concept of "positive" liberty. Negative liberty is the amount of personal freedom needed by an individual person to determine their life choices without interference, influence or coercion from other people. It presupposes that there must be limits on personal liberty to prevent it from damaging the freedom of choice of other people. Positive liberty starts from the same point, but concerns the freedom an individual may then give himself to intervene in, or impose change on, the lives of others, primarily to improve their situations in some way.

9 *Don Quixote*, op. cit., p. 985.

10 *Don Quijote de la Mancha* (Edición del IV centenario), op. cit., p. xx.

Bibliography

The following works have been consulted in writing this book. All quotations in Spanish from *Don Quixote* are taken from the edition published by Punto de Lectura, Madrid, 2009, edited and with notes by Francisco Rico.

Editions of the text

Cervantes, Miguel de, *Don Quijote de la Mancha* (Edición y Notas por Francisco Rico)(Punto de lectura, Madrid, 2009). All quotations from the text are taken from this edition.

Cervantes, Miguel de, *Don Quijote de la Mancha* (Edición del IV Centenario, Edición y Notas por Francisco Rico) (Real Academia Española y Asociación de Academías de la Lengua Española, Madrid, 2004).

Translations of the text into English

Cervantes, Miguel de, *Don Quixote de la Mancha* (Penguin Classics, London, 2000). (Translated by John Rutherford).

Cervantes, Miguel de, *Don Quixote de la Mancha* (Ecco, HarperCollins, New York, 2003). (Translated by Edith Grossman).

Books

Alcalá, Angel (ed.), *The Spanish Inquisition and the Inquisitorial Mind* (Social Science Monographs, Boulder, Colorado & Atlantic Research and Publications Inc., New Jersey, 1987).

——, "Inquisitorial Control of Humanists and Writers" in Alcalá, Angel (ed.), *The Spanish Inquisition and the Inquisitorial Mind* (Social Science Monographs, Boulder, Colorado & Atlantic Research and Publications Inc., New Jersey, 1987).

Armas Wilson, Diana de & El Saffar, Ruth (eds), *Quixotic Desire: Psychoanalytical Perspectives on Cervantes* (Cornell University Press, Ithaca & London, 1993).

Armas Wilson, Diana de, *Cervantes, the Novel and the New World* (Oxford University Press, Oxford, 2005).

Avellaneda, Alonso Fernández de, *El Ingenioso Hidalgo Don Quixote de la Mancha* (Edited and with an Introduction by Luis Gómez Canseco) (Clásicos de Biblioteca Nueva, Madrid, 2000).

Aubier, Dominique, *Don Quichotte, prophète d'Israel* (R. Laffont, Paris. 1966).

Avalle-Arce, J. B. & Riley, E. C. (eds), *Suma Cervantina* (Tamesis, London, 1973).

Berlin, Isaiah, *Four Essays on Liberty* (Oxford University Press, Oxford, 1969).

Bjornson, Richard (ed.), *Approaches to Teaching Cervantes's "Don Quixote"* (Modern Language Association, New York, 1984).

Braun, Harald, *Juan de Mariana and Early Modern Spanish Political Thought* (Ashgate, London, 2007).

Brownlee, Marina S. & Gumbrecht, Hans Ulrich (eds), *Cultural Authority in Golden Age Spain,* Johns Hopkins University Press, Baltimore & London, 1995).

Byrne, Susan, *Law and History in Cervantes' "Don Quixote."* (University of Toronto Press, Toronto, Buffalo and London, 2012).

Cascardi, Anthony, *Cervantes, Literature and the Discourse of Politics* (University of Toronto Press, Toronto, 2012).

——, *Ideologies of History in the Spanish Golden Age* (Pennsylvania State University Press, University Park, Penn, 1997).

Castillo, David R., *(A)Wry Views: Anamorphosis, Cervantes and the Early Picaresque* (Purdue University Press, West Lafayette, Indiana, 2001).

Castro, Américo, *El pensamiento de Cervantes* (Editorial Noguer S.A., Barcelona & Madrid, 1972) Expanded edition with notes by the author and Julio Rodriguez Puertolas. First published 1925.

——, *Hacia Cervantes* (Taurus, Madrid, 1957).

Close, Anthony J., *The Romantic Approach to "Don Quixote"* (Cambridge University Press, Cambridge, 1979).

——, *Cervantes: "Don Quixote"* (Cambridge University Press, Cambridge, 1990)

——, *Cervantes and the Comic Mind of his Age* (Oxford University Press, Oxford, 2000).

Criado de Val (ed.), *Cervantes, su obra y su mundo* (Actas del 1 Congreso Internacional Sobre Cervantes, EDI-6, S.A., Madrid, 1981).

Cruz, Anne & Johnson, Carroll B. (eds), *Cervantes and his Post-Modern Constituencies* (Garland Publishing Inc., New York & London, 1999).

Eisenberg, Daniel, *A Study of "Don Quixote." In which Cervantes's Goals in "Don Quixote" are examined. With index and copious notes.* (Juan de Cuesta, Newark, 1987)).

——, *Romances of Chivalry in the Spanish Golden Age* (Juan de Cuesta, Newark, 1982).

El Saffar, Ruth, *Distance and Control in "Don Quixote:" A Study in Narrative Technique* (University of North Carolina Press, Chapel Hill, 1975).

——, *Beyond Fiction: Recovering the Feminine in the Novels of* Cervantes (University of California Press, Berkeley, 1984).

——, (ed.), *Critical Essays on Cervantes* (G. K. Hall, Boston, Mass., 1986).

Erasmus, Desiderius, *The Education of a Christian* Prince (1516) (Translated from the Latin and edited by Lisa Jardine) (Cambridge University Press, Cambridge, New York & Melbourne, 1997).

Evans, Peter William (ed.), *Conflicts of Discourse: Spanish Literature in the Golden Age* (Manchester University Press, Manchester, 1990).

Fielding, Henry, *The History of the Adventures of Joseph Andrews and his Friend Mr Abraham Adams* (1742). Reprinted as *"Joseph Andrews" and "Shamela"*

(Penguin Classics, London 1999) (Edited and with introduction and notes by Judith Hawley.)

Fuchs, Barbara, *Passing for Spain. Cervantes and the Fictions of Identity* (University of Illinois Press, Champaign Ill., 2003.)

Forster, David, Altamiranda, Daniel & Urioste, Carmén de, *Current Debates in Hispanicism* (Routledge, London, 2000).

Gilman, Stephen, *The Novel According to Cervantes* (University of California Press, Berkeley, Los Angeles and London, 1989)

González Echevarría, Roberto (ed.), *Cervantes's "Don Quixote:" A Casebook.* (Oxford University Press, Oxford, 2005).

——, *Love and the Law in Cervantes* (Yale University Press, New Haven & London, 2005).

Graf, E. C., *Cervantes and Modernity. Four Essays on "Don Quixote"* (Bucknell University Press, Lewisburg, 2007).

Hamilton, Bernice, *Political Thought in Sixteenth Century Spain. A Study of the Ideas of Vitoria, De Soto, Suárez and Molina* (Clarendon Press, Oxford, 1963).

Highet, Gilbert, *The Anatomy of Satire* (Princeton University Press, Princeton New Jersey, 1962.

Higuera, Henry, *Eros and Empire: Politics and Christianity in "Don Quixote"* (Rowman & Littlefield, Lanham, 1995).

Ife, Barry, *Reading and Fiction in the Golden Age* (Cambridge University Press, Cambridge, 1985).

Ihre, Maureen, *Skepticism in Cervantes* (Tamesis Books, London, 1972).

Kahn, Aaron M., *On Wolves and Sheep: Exploring the Expression of Political Thought in Golden Age Spain* (Cambridge Scholars Publishing, Newcastle-upon-Tyne, 2011).

Kagan, Richard L., *Clio and the Crown: The Politics of History in Medieval and Early Modern Spain* (Johns Hopkins University Press, Baltimore, 2009).

Kamen, Henry, *The Spanish Inquisition: An Historical Revision* (Weidenfeld & Nicolson, London 1997).

——, *Spain 1496–1714: A Society of Conflict* (Pearson Education, Harlow, 2005, 3rd edition). First edition published 1983, 2nd edition 1991.

Madariaga, Salvador de, *Guía del lector del Quijote: ensayo psicológico sobre el Quijote* (Ed. Sudamericana, Buenos Aires, 1967). First published 1926.

Mancing, Howard, *The Chivalric World of Don Quixote* (University of Missouri Press, Missouri, 1982).

McCrory, Donald P., *No Ordinary Man. The Life and Times of Miguel de Cervantes* (Peter Owen, London, 2005).

McKendrick, Melveena, *Cervantes* (Little Brown, Boston, 1980).

Menéndez y Pelayo, Marcelino, *Historia de los heterodoxos españoles* (2nd edition, 6 vols, Madrid, 1947) Edited by E. Sánchez Reyes.

Murillo, L. A., *The Golden Dial. Temporal Configuration in "Don Quixote,"* (Dolphin Books, Oxford, 1975).

Ortega y Gasset, José, *Meditaciones del Quijote e ideas sobre la novela* (1914) (Revista del Occidente, Colección El Arquero, Madrid, 1970).

Parr, James A., *"Don Quixote:" An Anatomy of Subversive Discourse* (Juan de la Cuesta, Newark, Delaware, 1988).

——, (ed.), *On Cervantes: Essays for L. A. Murillo* (Juan de Cuesta, Newark, 1991)

——, *"Don Quixote:" A Touchstone for Literary Criticism* (Reichenberger, Kassel, 2005).

Paulson, Ronald, *"Don Quixote" in England. The Aesthetics of Laughter* (Johns Hopkins University Press, Baltimore, 1998).

Peña, Aniano, *Américo Castro y su visión de España y de Cervantes* (Gredos, Madrid, 1975)

Pérez-Romero, Antonio, *The Subversive Tradition in Spanish Renaissance Writing* (Bucknell University Press, Lewisburg, 2005).

Pinciano, Alonso López (El Pinciano), *Filosofía antigua poética* (1596) (Lingkua Ediciones. Barcelona. 2009).

Prendergast, Ryan, *Reading, Writing and Errant Subjects in Inquisitorial Spain* (Ashgate, Farnham & London, 2013).

Quint, David, *Cervantes's Novel of Modern Times. A new reading of "Don Quixote"* (Princeton University Press, Princeton & Oxford, 2003).

Riley, Edward C., *Cervantes's Theory of the Novel* (Clarendon Press. Oxford, 1962).

——, *Don Quixote* (Allen & Unwin, London, 1968).

Robbins, Jeremy & Williamson, Edwin (eds), *Cervantes: Essays in Memory of E. C. Riley* (Routledge, London & New York, 2005).

Robbins, Jeremy, *Arts of Perception. The Epistemological Mentality of the Spanish Baroque, 1580–1720* (Routledge, London & New York, 2007).

——, *The Challenges of Uncertainty. An Introduction to Seventeenth Century Spanish Literature* (Duckworth, London, 1998).

Russell, Peter E., *Cervantes* (Oxford University Press, Oxford, 1985).

Sánchez, Francisco, *Que nada se sabe,* (Translated from the Latin by Carlos Mellizo) (Aguilar, Buenos Aires, 1977).

Sullivan, Henry, *Grotesque Purgatory: A Study of Cervantes's "Don Quixote" Part II* (Pennsylvania State University Press, University Park, Penn, 1996).

Taylor, Scott, *Honor and Violence in Golden Age Spain* (Yale University Press, Newhaven & London, 2008).

Unamuno, Miguel de, *La vida de Don Quijote y Sancho según Miguel de Cervantes* (Renacimiento, Buenos Aires & Madrid, 1914).

Valdés, Alfonso de, *Diálogo de Mercurio y Carón* (1528) (Translated from the Latin by Rafael Rodríguez Marín) (Castalia, Madrid, 1983).

Williamson, Edwin (ed.), *Cervantes and the Modernists; The Question of Influence,* (Tamesis, London, 1994).

——, *The Halfway House of Fiction: "Don Quixote" and Arthurian Romance* (Clarendon Press, Oxford, 1984).

Articles and Reviews

Allen, John Jay, "Smiles and Laughter in Don Quixote," *Comparative Literature Studies*, Vol. 43, No. 4, 2006, pp. 515–531.

Boyd, Stephen, "Parker and the Anti-Romantic Interpretation of *Don Quixote*," *BHS*, Vol. 85, 6 September 2008, pp. 3–16.

Deyermond, Alan D., "The Lost Genre of Medieval Spanish Literature," International Association of Hispanists, *Actas,* 1971, pp. 791–813.

Di Salvo, Angelo J., "Spanish Guides to Princes and Political Thought in Don Quijote" *Cervantes: Bulletin of the Cervantes Society of America,* Vol. 9, No. 2 (1989).

Eisenberg, Daniel, "Review of *Cervantes* by Jean Canavaggio (translated by J. R. Jones) (W. W. Norton, New York, 1991) in *Cervantes: Bulletin of the Cervantes Society of America,* Vol. 12, No. 1 (1992).

Fajardo, Salvador J., "Ruth El Saffar, *Beyond Fiction: The Recovery of the Feminine in the Novels of Cervantes,*" *Renaissance Quarterly,* Vol. 39, No. 1 (Spring) 1986.

Herrero, Javier S., "Dulcinea and her Critics" *BCSA,* Vol. 2, No. 1, (1982), pp. 23–42.

Iffland, James, "Do we really need to read Avellaneda?" in *Cervantes: Bulletin of the Cervantes Society of America,* Vol. 21, No. 1 (2001).

McGaha, Michael, "Is there a Hidden Jewish Meaning in Don Quixote?" *Cervantes: Bulletin of the Cervantes Society of America,* Vol. 24, No. 1 (2004).

Parker, Alan Austin, "*Don Quixote* and the Relativity of Truth" *Dublin Review,* Vol. 220, No. 441 (Autumn 19470 pp. 28–37.

——, "El concepto de la verdad en el Quijote" *RFE,* No. 32 (1948), pp. 287–305.

——, "Fielding and the Structure of *Don Quixote,*" *BHS,* No. 33 (1956), pp. 1–16.

Pinto, Virgilio, "Censorship. A System of Control and Instrument of Action" in Alcalá, Angel (ed.), *The Spanish Inquisition and the Inquisitorial Mind* (Social Science Monographs, Boulder, Colorado & Atlantic Research and Publications Inc., New Jersey, 1987).

Russell, Peter E., "*Don Quixote* as a Funny Book," *MLR,* LXIV, 1969, pp. 312–326.

Weber, Alison, "Don Quijote with Roque Guinart: The Case for an Ironic Reading," *Cervantes, Bulletin of the Cervantes Society of America,* Vol. VI, No. 2 (1986), pp. 123–140.

Weiss, Julian, "Between the Censor and the Critic: Reading the Vernacular Classic in Early Modern Spain" (dialnet.uniroja.es/descarga/artículo/3716464.pdf)

Williamson, Edwin, " 'Intención' and 'invención' in the Quixote," *Cervantes, Bulletin of the Cervantes Society of America,* Vol. 8, No. 1 (1988), pp. 7–22.

Index